MULTICAST
NETWORKING
AND
APPLICATIONS

MULTICAST NETWORKING AND APPLICATIONS

C. KENNETH MILLER

Addison-Wesley

An imprint of Addison Wesley Longman, Inc.

Reading, Massachusetts • Harlow, England • Menlo Park, California

Berkeley, California • Don Mills, Ontario • Sydney • Bonn

Amsterdam • Tokyo • Mexico City

Many of the designations used by manufacturers and sellers to distinguish their products are claimed as trademarks. Where those designations appear in this book, and Addison Wesley Longman, Inc., was aware of a trademark claim, the designations have been printed in initial caps or all caps.

The author and publisher have taken care in the preparation of this book, but make no expressed or implied warranty of any kind and assume no responsibility for errors or omissions. No liability is assumed for incidental or consequential damages in connection with or arising out of the use of the information or programs contained herein.

The publisher offers discounts on this book when ordered in quantity for special sales. For more information, please contact:

> AWL Direct Sales
> Addison Wesley Longman, Inc.
> One Jacob Way
> Reading, Massachusetts 01867
> (781) 944-3700

Visit AW on the Web: www.awl.com/cseng/

Library of Congress Cataloging-in-Publication Data

Miller, C. Kenneth.
   Multicast networking and applications / C. Kenneth Miller.
      p.   cm.
   Includes bibliographical references and index.
   ISBN 0-201-30979-3
      1. Multicasting (Computer networks)   I. Title.
TK5105.887.M56   1998
004.6'6 — dc21   98–29715
                                                                   CIP

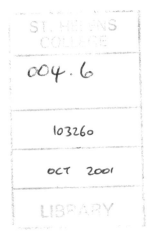

ISBN 0-201-30979-3

Text printed on recycled and acid-free paper

2 3 4 5 6 7   MA   02 01 00 99

2nd Printing   January 1999

CONTENTS

4 NETWORK INFRASTRUCTURES AND EASE OF IMPLEMENTATION OF MULTICAST IP

8   RELIABLE MULTICAST APPLICATIONS AND TECHNOLOGY

9

THE CREATION OF GROUPS

10

SECURITY SYSTEMS APPLIED TO MULTICAST APPLICATIONS

PREFACE

When I was approached in the summer of 1997 by Addison-Wesley to write a book on multicast networking and applications, I thought long and hard about whether to accept the offer. Although I had written a number of technical articles, I had never written a book before. Also, I was founder of a new company, StarBurst Communications, and had a high commitment to making it a success. This would mean I would need to write the book on personal time—nights, early mornings, and weekends.

As is obvious, I decided to take the plunge and make the commitment. The whole area of multicast networking and applications is an emerging market, and no books have been written on the subject by a non-academic or corporate researcher. I have been told that I am a clear writer on technology subjects, having spent some time as a columnist for *Data Communications* magazine in the early 1990s. I have targeted this book to IS staff members in commercial organizations who need to get a total view of this new technology, its pitfalls and promises, and its potential for helping the reader's specific organization.

The process of writing this book has been a gratifying learning experience. Although I had knowledge of all of the topics in the book, I needed to gain more detailed information on some of them. I cannot explain a subject clearly to a reader if I do not understand it thoroughly myself. This process has thus helped me have a complete understanding of all of the issues in this emerging area in much greater detail.

ACKNOWLEDGMENTS

Many people have given me help and encouragement in the writing of this book. My colleagues at StarBurst have been unstinting in their support. The reviewers have been helpful in giving critiques that prompted the addition of new subjects and changes in the organization of the book, which I think has greatly strengthened the final result. I wish to single out for thanks Ted Hanss from Internet2, who encouraged me to add case studies, and Don Brutzman of the Naval Postgraduate School and Matt Naugle of ZIPCOM, Inc., who provided useful suggestions for organization. Ray Patch from Microsoft and Bob Quinn, a consultant to the IP Multicast Initiative, provided suggestions on Chapters 7 to 9. Markus Hofmann from the University of Karlsruhe, Germany, gave me much encouragement and made many helpful suggestions relating to Chapter 8. Special thanks go to my brother, Don Miller, who is a former English teacher, English Department Chairman, and finally headmaster at a number of private high schools. He reviewed the book for grammar and content and proved to be a good test to see if the material is easily understood, given that he is not a "techie."

I also wish to acknowledge my editors at Addison-Wesley, Karen Gettman and Mary Hart, who provided me encouragement and guidance in the writing of this, my first book.

Finally, a special thanks to my wife Dorcas, who provided support and encouragement as I used our personal time to complete this project.

— KEN MILLER

August 1998

CONCORD, MASSACHUSETTS

1

INTRODUCTION

Multicast networking and its associated applications are poised to become important enablers of new applications over both private networks and the Internet. In the last few years, a number of start-up companies have been formed to exploit this new market. Industry giants are also throwing their support into multicast. In early 1997, for example, Microsoft, Intel, and Cisco formed the Networked Multimedia Connection (NMC) to promote multimedia and multicast networking. The IP Multicasting Initiative (IPMI) was formed in October 1996 to educate the user and networking communities about the benefits of multicast. The IPMI has attracted both large and small organizations and now encompasses more than eighty organizations.

What exactly is multicast? *Multicast is the sending of data from one to many recipients, or many to many recipients.* This approach contrasts with broadcast, where everyone is sent the content whether they want it or not, thereby flooding the network with redundant data. *Multicast networking* involves the provisions made to support multicast in the underlying network infrastructure. *Multicast applications* are the applications that use multicast network services as an underlying enabling service.

Multicast applications send data to multicast *groups,* which are the collection of hosts or sites that receive the common information sent to them. For example, in a conferencing application, the group members are the members of the conference. In a multicast "push" application, the group members are the recipients of the "push" information. Groups may be semi-permanent or they may be dynamically set up and torn down.

Multicast is becoming important because it enables desired applications to *scale* — that is, to service many users without overloading network and server resources. Widespread usage of these applications would be virtually impossible without the scaling provided by multicast services.

The first application of this sort to hit a scaling limitation was the "push" services of PointCast. PointCast offers a desktop "screen saver" that shows news headlines when the screen saver comes on or when the user calls up this feature. The news updates are "pulled" automatically in the background to ensure that the news shown on the user's desktop remains current. Thus PointCast's "push" technology is really "automated pull." Many large organizations have found that PointCast traffic clogs up their networks and have ordered employees to remove it from their desktop personal computers (PCs).

Large-scale events also have served to clog up the Internet. One prime example occurred when the latest version of Microsoft Explorer became available and caused a meltdown when too many users attempted to simultaneously download the new program from the Microsoft Web site. Such events will become even more commonplace in the future, as images become larger.

Similarly, the landing of Pathfinder on Mars ended up with "surfers" overwhelming NASA's Web site. Use of multicast technology could have largely eliminated those bottlenecks, had it been present.

Although IP multicast is usually considered within the context of multicast networking, two fundamental multicast networking technologies exist: Link-layer multicast and Network-layer multicast. The differences between the two technologies are discussed in Chapter 2; because Network-layer multicast using the TCP/IP protocol suite is overwhelmingly dominant, however, this book (with the exception of the discussion in Chapter 2) will exclusively describe multicast IP network and application technologies.

Before discussing the organization of this book, an introduction to applications follows. It is intended to give you, the reader, a feeling for the importance of multicast, as the applications actually confer the technology's power. These applications are based on multicast IP.

1.1 MULTICAST APPLICATIONS

TCP/IP has two Transport layers that applications may use: the Transport Control Protocol (TCP) and the User Datagram Protocol (UDP). Each Transport layer is responsible for end-to-end delivery of data—that is, from host to host. TCP provides a high level of service to the application above it, including packet ordering, port multiplexing, and, most of all, reliable, error-free delivery of data. UDP, in contrast, provides only minimal services, such as port multiplexing and error detection. If a packet is detected in error under UDP, it is simply discarded. Packets may be received out of order, and some may be missing.

Not surprisingly, then, most applications running above TCP/IP use TCP as the Transport layer for the rich services it provides. TCP, however, provides only point-to-point (unicast) services. Thus all multicast applications must run on top of UDP, as shown in Figure 1-1.* In addition, the specialized requirements put on the Transport layer by the application must be included in the application, in effect creating a special Transport layer for that application.

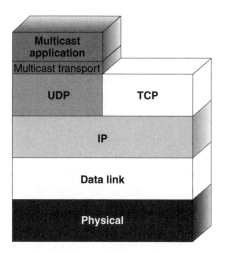

FIGURE 1-1

Multicast applications over UDP showing multicast transport

---

*A few multicast applications bypass UDP and operate over IP directly. See Chapter 8 for an example.

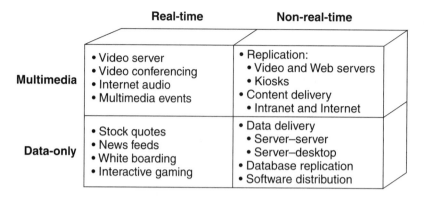

FIGURE 1-2

Multicast applications

Although most people think of multimedia streaming applications when multicast networking is mentioned, in fact a broad spectrum of multicast applications exists, as shown in Figure 1-2. These applications have widely varying requirements for transport. For example, the two quadrant application sets on the left require low latency and/or low jitter tolerance. Some of these applications do not have strict error-free requirements; others do not require a high level of scalability. The quadrant application sets on the right generally lack stringent latency requirements, but they usually have strict reliability requirements and generally call for a high level of scalability.

The natural tendency for a protocol designer is to attempt to create a generalized multicast Transport layer — in effect, a multicast version of TCP — that can handle all of the application sets shown in Figure 1-2. It is more efficient to tailor the transport to the application so as to meet the absolute requirements of the application by taking advantage of parameters that are not requirements.

This concept, called Application Layer Framing (ALF), was first expounded by some Internet researchers in a 1992 paper [1-1]. ALF also discusses taking advantage of the application to produce other benefits. For example, data recovery may be better served by operating on data blocks based on formatting on a disk (an application function) rather than data blocks arbitrarily created by a communication layer.

1.1.1   Real-Time Multimedia Applications

Real-time multimedia applications (the upper-left quadrant in Figure 1-2) come in two flavors — a conferencing many-to-many application set and a one-to-many "event" application set. In the conferencing application set, each member of the group is both a receiver and a transmitter. Scaling is not a major issue, as the members of the group typically number less than 100.

The second real-time multimedia application set is created as an event, similar to broadcast television. For example, some technical sessions of the Internet Engineering Task Force (IETF) are broadcast over the experimental Multicast Backbone (Mbone) of the Internet as scheduled events; someone not attending the session in person may tune in to view speakers from a desktop computer (the Mbone is discussed in Chapter 3). Similarly, Microsoft's Netshow product, which is built into Microsoft's Internet Explorer, provides a mechanism to create remote classrooms or broadcast special talks by corporate executives to their employees. Conceivably, President Clinton could talk to the nation and have his words transmitted over a multicast-enabled Internet, enabling people around the country to see him on their desktops. Such a one-to-many application would need to scale to hundreds of thousands, if not millions, of recipients.

Real-time multimedia applications do not require absolute reliability but rather tight limits on timing jitter. Data needs to be delivered in a smooth flow to ensure that motion is captured properly and looks natural, and that lip synchronization is correct. Some errors do not matter, especially if they are random, as they may appear as a flicker without much notice of degradation.

1.1.2 Real-Time (Streaming) Data Applications

Data-streaming applications (lower-left quadrant in Figure 1-2) similarly split into two basic types—conferencing/distributed games and event streams. Data conferences have characteristics similar to those of video conferences, with the exception that the conference members use a "whiteboard" on which attendees can draw, write, or place other written forms of communication that are shared by the other members of the conference. The underlying data must be sent error-free to ensure that the images and text are correct and latency requirements remain low, as extreme delay greatly reduces the utility of this service in this collaborative environment. The data streams sent by each member also have the characteristic of not being continuous, but rather being sent in bursts from each member at irregular intervals.

The second kind of collaborative data-streaming application involves network-based games. Network games using unicast transmissions can already be played on the Internet. Serious gaming scenarios are common in the military, and the reliable multicast protocol Reliable Adaptive Multicast Protocol (RAMP) was created by The Analytic Science Corporation (TASC) for this purpose. Network-based gaming applications place a similar burden on the transport protocol, as does data conferencing.

Both data conferencing and network-based gaming have modest scaling requirements, with group members typically numbering fewer than 100 and usually no more than ten to twenty.

A variety of one-to-many data-streaming applications has also emerged. The most prominent is the transmission of ticker-tape financial data. Ticker-tape streams list stock, bond, commodity, and other quotes for financial products. The requirements for the transport of ticker-tape streams can vary widely. For the casual user, the data need not be absolutely reliable; if a particular quote is lost, the next one will come soon. Latency is also not a strict requirement; if the data is a few seconds or minutes late, it does not matter much. In fact, the charge for the information feed is significantly lower if it is delayed, as the value of the information depends greatly on its currency. Scaling requirements can be high, possibly in the millions.

For the serious stockbroker in a financial institution, however, the requirements for reliability, latency, and concurrency for the transport of a ticker-tape stream are much more stringent. The company providing the service often sells the service to multiple financial organizations, hence the need for concurrency — that is, the requirement that one institution does not receive the information before another one, thus gaining a competitive advantage. Latency must be small — the more current the information, the more valuable it is. The information also must be reliable, as large financial decisions depend on it. Further, the scaling requirement can be high, at least in the tens of thousands. This combination of requirements is so stringent that, to meet it, financial institutions often create special networks that are guaranteed to have no congestion and have a high level of fault tolerance.

A second one-to-many data streaming application involves news feeds. Data is sent out as a stream, usually in text form. This stream has a reliability requirement but does not have the stringent latency and concurrency requirements of some ticker-tape feed applications. Scaling requirements can be high, potentially in the millions.

1.1.3   Non-Real-Time Multimedia Applications

Multimedia one-to-many streaming applications, such as remote classrooms and events, may wish to be transmitted in a non-real-time reliable manner for replay later. Two basic reasons underlie this approach:

1. The consumers of the information do not want to view the information when it is delivered; rather, they would like to view it at their leisure. This situation is analogous to capturing a television broadcast with a VCR for later viewing. It also provides an alternative to sending video tapes of an event out by mail for replaying; the content is sent as a file to a local server or some other data storage device that can be accessed by the consumer.

2. The network cannot support high-quality multimedia at the time of the event. Consumers are used to the quality of television, which requires a data rate of at least 1 megabit per second (Mbps) to provide comparable quality. Networks often cannot deliver this bandwidth for a particular event. The bandwidth may be too expensive, or the network may be too congested at the busy times of the day when events often happen. Consequently, the video quality seen on networks is usually poor. To avoid this problem, the network may transmit the multimedia content by non-real-time reliable multicast during off hours to a local server or storage device; the broadcast may then be replayed locally where no significant network bandwidth or congestion constraints exist.

Another trend is the use of distributed specialized kiosks to disseminate information. For example, kiosks may be set up to provide particular information to consumers. For example, informational kiosks were set up at the 1996 Olympic Games in Atlanta to help visitors to the event. These kiosks could have used non-real-time reliable multicast to deliver the information. Commercial outlets may use kiosks to show electronic catalogs and provide a mechanism to order goods. These catalogs are often based on Web technology.

Another large category of non-real-time applications includes the mirroring (replication) and caching of Web sites to bring content closer to the user. This category is not specific to multimedia, but it can be used to provide a higher-quality experience, as it potentially makes high-quality multimedia possible from a Web site without requiring huge network bandwidth in the network. Mirroring and caching are discussed in Chapter 5, as this technique is crucial to improving the performance of the Internet.

1.1.4 Non-Real-Time Data Applications

Virtually all of the many non-real-time data applications require absolute reliability. One of the most compelling is the distribution of software to remote sites from a central headquarters. Personnel located at the remote sites may not be very computer-literate, making the upgrade and maintenance of computer systems both difficult and expensive. Today, many organizations send software upgrades on CD-ROM to remote locations using the postal system. Often, these CD-ROMs end up gathering dust on a shelf somewhere, because no one is expressly given responsibility for this task. This case is especially common with members of a dealer network, as the dealer often may not even be a part of the parent company.

Electronic delivery of software is just not feasible in many instances without multicast delivery because of the number of receiving nodes, the size of the data to be sent, and the time available for transfer. Consider the following example.

A company has 1,000 branches. Software needs to be updated every three months, and a 56 kilobit per second (Kbps) multicast-ready TCP/IP network connects the home office to the branches. Today, it is not practical to send the software updates point to point because of the time required.

The software is 75 megabytes (Mbytes). At 56 Kbps, it takes more than 3 hours to send the image to each branch under ideal conditions; it actually takes longer because of congestion and errors. To send the updates to 1,000 sites point to point would take more than 3,000 hours or about 18 weeks (more than four months)! As a result, software is distributed by sending out CD-ROMs to each field office via Federal Express. The cost of support from the home office for helping to perform the installations and shipping the software is estimated at $500 per branch per occurrence, or $500,000 each time new software is distributed. At four times per year, this expense amounts to $2 million per year.

Using a reliable multicast protocol, however, the complete distribution of the software to all of the branch offices over the network would take a little more than three hours. Remote installation packages could install the software with little or no help from headquarters. All sites would be upgraded virtually simultaneously, eliminating any compatibility issues and accompanying extra cost.

A similar case can be made for the dissemination of business information to branch sites via multicast. Such business information can take the form of electronic catalogs, management reports, database updates, promotional material, and newsletters.

Another major application category being touted in the trade press involves "push" applications. Today's "push" applications are really "automated pull" and do not scale. They will be widely deployed only if they embrace reliable multicast technology for distribution. "Push" applications are discussed in depth in Chapter 6.

Another large application category includes the mirroring and caching of Web sites to bring content closer to users, as mentioned earlier in the discussion of non-real-time multimedia data distribution. This subject will be discussed in detail in Chapter 5.

As can be seen from the preceding discussion, a wealth of multicast applications exist that have widely varying requirements for their transport. Many of these applications are quite compelling and promise to change how organizations around the world communicate with their employees, their suppliers, their citizens, and their markets. Multicast technology is poised to help the Internet realize its promise of tying the citizens of the planet together.

1.2 ORGANIZATION AND TARGET AUDIENCE

The remainder of this book will focus on explaining multicast technology, its status, the barriers to its deployment, some promising areas of research and development, and ways in which today's organizations can realize some of its benefits. The explanations are designed to be easily understood by people knowledgeable in networking; you do not have to be a researcher to understand what follows. The goal has been to provide clear, concise explanations that can be understood by even "non-techies" who want to understand the "big picture" about multicast and its applications.

Chapters are relatively self-contained, so that the reader who has knowledge of some of the topics may read particular chapters out of order to gain an understanding of that aspect of multicast.

This book also focuses on commercial deployment and commercially available products. Many research books and articles have been written about the experimental Multicast Backbone of the Internet (Mbone) and its research protocols and applications. Multicast networking and applications have now matured sufficiently that a significant commercial deployment has occurred, and products have emerged to support that deployment. You can readily use knowledge from this book to understand how multicast technology can benefit your organization.

Chapter 2 deals with the difference between Link-layer multicast and Network-layer multicast. Chapter 3 discusses multicast IP technology and multicast routing protocols. Chapter 4 introduces the many differing network infrastructures that may be found in private networks and some emerging options; it also describes how well these infrastructures deal with implementation of multicast IP.

Chapters 5 and 6 introduce some generic multicast applications. Chapter 5 deals with replication and caching, and Chapter 6 focuses on "push" technology. Chapters 7 and 8 discuss the technology of the specialized transports used in the different applications and provide case studies of actual deployment and usage of multicast applications available today. Chapter 9 deals with the methods of group set-up and their appropriateness for the different applications.

Chapter 10 describes the special issues of security in a multicast environment. Chapter 11 presents some reasons explaining why multicast networking and applications have not yet become mainstream, given their obvious benefits. Finally, in Chapter 12, we go out on a limb and make some predictions about multicast's future.

REFERENCE

[1-1] Clark D, Tennenhouse D. Architectural Considerations for a New Generation of Protocols. Proceedings of ACM SIGCOMM '90, Sept. 1990: 201–208.

2

LINK-LAYER MULTICAST VERSUS NETWORK-LAYER MULTICAST

The Link layer, layer 2 of the seven-layer OSI model (see Figure 2-1), is responsible for transport of data over a particular *link*. For wide area networks (WANs), links are defined from a particular location to another. For local area networks (LANs), links are defined from one host to another.

Figure 2-2 depicts a network consisting of LANs and WANs. The WAN links are serviced by the WAN Link layer—for example, frame relay, Switched Multimegabit Data Service (SMDS), or the Point-to-Point Protocol (PPP)—and the LAN is serviced by a LAN Link layer—for example, 802.2 over an Ethernet/802.3

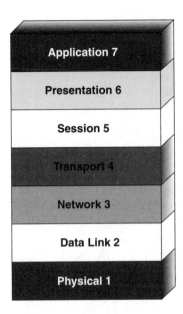

FIGURE 2-1

Seven-layer OSI model of communications

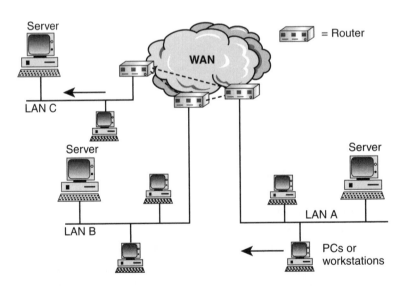

FIGURE 2-2

Network showing LAN and WAN links

Media Access Control (MAC), the Link layer used in Ethernet LANs. As can be seen from Figure 2-2, the WAN links tie together sites, whereas the LAN links tie together hosts.

The Network layer, layer 3 in Figure 2-1, figures out the optimal way to route packets through the various links to the end points. Network-layer functions are usually performed by routers, which use routing algorithms to determine optimal routes to the destination.

2.1   LINK-LAYER MULTICAST

Although IP multicast is usually considered within the context of multicast networking, a number of Link-layer multicast solutions exist. LANs have historically been shared media with connectionless service, meaning that all stations on the network listened to all transmissions. Nodes on a LAN have MAC addresses, sometimes called *physical* addresses because they designate a physical node on the network. MAC addresses are global—that is, each is unique in the universe.

MAC addresses come in three varieties: individual (unicast), multicast, and broadcast. Unicast addresses are used for normal point-to-point communications as a unique identifier of end points. One MAC broadcast address exists, composed of all 1's. MAC multicast addresses are primarily used to map to upper-layer multicast addresses. MAC broadcast frames are typically filtered by bridges and routers, confining them to the local LAN and preventing broadcast storms.

2.1.1   Frame Relay Multicast

Frame relay is a Layer 2 (Link layer) protocol designed for use over WANs. Frame relay is a connection-oriented protocol, meaning that it emulates actual physical links with permanent virtual circuits (PVCs) and switched virtual circuits (SVCs). PVCs and SVCs represent point-to-point connections with data link connection identifiers (DLCIs) and do not normally have the facility for one-to-many connections. In October 1994, however, the Frame Relay Forum released specifications for multicast services over frame relay. Three types of multicast service are accommodated: one-way multicast, two-way multicast, and N-way multicast.

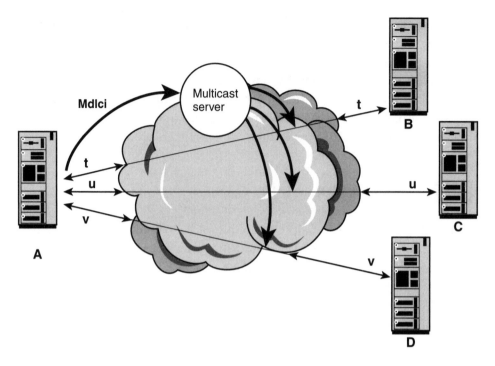

FIGURE 2-3

Frame relay one-way multicast

One-way multicast, illustrated in Figure 2-3, has a unidirectional multicast DLCI (frame relay address for a PVC). This PVC connects the source of information (A in Figure 2-3) of the multicast group to a "multicast server" in the network. The multicast server then distributes the data to the members of the multicast group (B, C, and D in Figure 2-3) over their own individual DLCIs (t, u, and v). This server is generally located at a convenient location by the network provider to minimize transmission of duplicate data in the network. Additionally, the source A has point-to-point (unicast) PVCs represented by the DLCIs t, u, and v between itself and the other members of the multicast group (B, C, and D). These PVCs are full duplex, meaning that data traffic can flow in both directions. In contrast, the multicast DLCI is unidirectional, flowing from source A only. Note that A, B, C, and D can be sites or subnets rather than hosts.

Two-way multicast frame relay was designed to enable migration of IBM SDLC multidrop configurations to a frame relay environment; it has no connection with multicast networking.

N-way multicast frame relay allows any node to be either a transmitter to the group or a receiver. This type of multicast is designed for teleconferencing applications. Only one-way multicast was ever offered as a service by a carrier.

2.1.2   Switched Multimegabit Data Service (SMDS)

SMDS was developed by Bellcore for local exchange carriers, primarily to enable them to provide high-speed connectivity between LANs in a metropolitan area. SMDS is based on, and is a subset of, the IEEE 802.6 Metropolitan Area Network (MAN) standard.

SMDS uses a connectionless network architecture within which all nodes inherently can communicate to all other nodes on the network, similar to shared LANs. All packets sent on the network are available for reception by all nodes, making multicast services easily accomplished. As a result, SMDS inherently supports multicast services as well as unicast and broadcast.

Some carriers offer SMDS services as an alternative to frame relay, but the services have not proved as popular as frame relay. SMDS is discussed in more detail in Chapter 4.

2.1.3   Asynchronous Transfer Mode (ATM)

ATM, like frame relay, is a connection-oriented service and offers PVCs and SVCs. It supports multicast in a similar way as frame relay, with a multicast server located judiciously in the network. Unlike with frame relay, however, standards are just being developed to allow an ATM sender to establish point-to-multipoint SVCs between itself and a set of known receivers. These standards are based on UNI 3.0/3.1 signaling mechanisms used in ATM.

This service appears destined to become a niche application, as ATM is today primarily used for high-speed backbones. ATM is discussed in more detail in Chapter 4.

2.1.4   Link-Layer Multicast Issues

A number of problems arise with wide area Link-layer multicast solutions. The most constraining (except possibly for ATM) is the fact that the multicast group is *provisioned*—that is, it is statically set up by the network provider and can be changed only by a reconfiguration of the network. Additionally, in frame relay, the multicast server should be placed in a desirable location in the network to gain the efficiencies that multicast can provide; this organizational task requires the services of a skilled network designer. Also, not all frame relay switch vendors support multicast frame relay, and those that do have scaling problems.

SMDS has a similar provisioning problem, but otherwise can more easily support multicast services. It has not received the same support as frame relay from carriers and service providers, however, and is not as widely available in the market. In addition, SMDS, unlike frame relay, is usually billed by the packet. Because the backbone acts similarly to a shared LAN, the SMDS switches in the network infrastructure will measure multicast traffic as broadcast for billing purposes, resulting in the user being billed for traffic not actually received.

The result has been a lack of Link-layer multicast solutions in the marketplace. MFS Communications (now part of WorldCom) was the only frame relay carrier that offered multicast frame relay services (to the author's knowledge), and it has now discontinued those services. SMDS carriers can inherently offer multicast services, and a few are actively promoting this option.

2.2 NETWORK-LAYER MULTICAST (IP MULTICAST)

Network-layer multicast provides multicast solutions at Layer 3. The specialized transports required for multicast applications, however, are essentially an extension of the Transport layer (Layer 4) but are implemented at the Application layer above UDP, as shown in Figure 2-4 for TCP/IP.* Note that the seven-layer OSI model in the case of TCP/IP shrinks to a five-layer model, with the Session and Presentation layers being bundled in the Application layer.

Besides TCP/IP, some other protocol stacks also support network-layer multicast—for example, Appletalk and DECNet. However, these protocols are rapidly going the way of the dinosaur, so they will not be discussed in this book.

Network-layer multicast IP solutions have a major advantage in that group set-up and tear-down is dynamic, requiring only seconds to set up a group or terminate one. Multicast IP group members are always hosts rather than sites or subnets, unlike the case with Link-layer multicast.

With IP networks supporting multicast, the routers in the network need to support *multicast routing* using a suitable protocol. Just as a variety of unicast or

---

* Some reliable multicast protocols actually bypass UDP and interface directly to IP using "raw sockets." See Chapter 8 for an example.

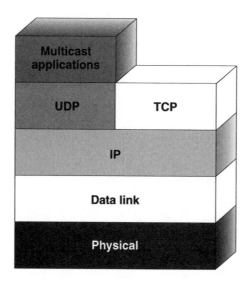

FIGURE 2-4

Multicast applications operate over UDP

point-to-point routing protocols exist, so do many multicast routing protocols populate the market.

A host needs to inform the nearest router supporting multicast IP of its membership in particular multicast groups. This task is accomplished by the use of the Internet Group Management Protocol (IGMP) as originally defined in Internet RFC 1112.

The details of multicast IP are discussed in Chapter 3.

3

MULTICAST IP

C hapter 3 and the remainder of this book discusses multicast networking and applications based on multicast IP.

Multicast networking and applications in TCP/IP environments are not new. The first major Internet Engineering Task Force (IETF) Request for Comment* (RFC) on multicast IP (RFC 966) [3-1] was authored by Steve Deering and Dave Cheriton in 1985, when Cheriton was Deering's professor at Stanford University. RFC 966 first suggested that Class D addresses be reserved for multicast. RFC 988 [3-2] first described the mechanism for routers to determine members of a group. It was superseded by RFC 1054 [3-3], which first described the Internet Group Management Protocol (IGMPv0), which hosts use to notify the nearest router that they have joined or left a group. RFC 1112 [3-4] superseded RFC 1054, was written in 1989, and remains the most common implementation of IGMP (IGMPv1).

---

* Requests for Comments (RFCs) are the documents within IETF used to describe Internet specifications and provide other documentation. Internet Drafts are IETF documents that represent work in progress.

RFC 1075 [3-5], which dates to 1988, describes the first multicast routing protocol, Distance Vector Multicast Routing Protocol (DVMRP).

Even though multicast IP was first described and specified in the Internet
community in the 1980s, it was not until the creation of the Mbone in 1992 that
activity and interest in multicast IP expanded significantly. The Mbone provides
a network test bed for these proposals and specifications as well as a vehicle to
try out new multicast applications. It continues to be used as a research tool by
university researchers and technical people in commercial organizations.

The Mbone comprises a set of multicast-enabled subnetworks tied together
by "tunnels," as shown in Figure 3-1. The tunnels encapsulate multicast datagrams within normal unicast datagrams and allow multicast traffic to traverse
parts of the network that do not support multicast natively. Tunneling is a common technique used to permit data to traverse networks that do not support
them; for example, IBM's System Network Architecture (SNA) protocol suite
can be tunneled into TCP/IP to traverse a network that does not support SNA.

Since 1992, the Mbone has grown substantially. In March 1997, it included
3,400 multicast-enabled subnets tied together. Often organizations may request
Mbone connections from their local Internet service providers (ISPs) that they

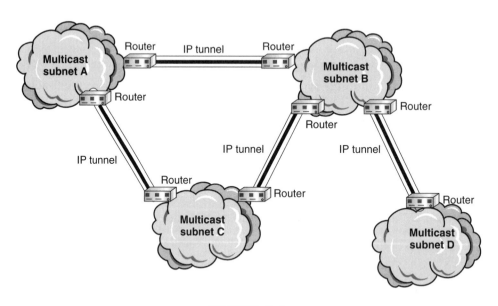

FIGURE 3-1

Architecture of Mbone

then use to watch an IETF meeting or share a whiteboard conference with members of another organization. Many multicast tools have been created by university researchers, and these options are generally available free of charge to the general public [3-6].

Lawrence Berkeley Laboratories (LBL), for example, has developed the "Visual Audio Tool" (vat) for use in multimedia video conferencing. A whiteboard application, "wb," allows users of a multicast group to write electronically on a whiteboard and have all members of the group be able to see the writings. Whiteboarding is essentially an electronic data conference where members of the group can collaborate visually on the shared whiteboard. Other video conferencing tools are also in use over the Mbone, although all are being run by universities and none has been commercialized as yet. Thus the Mbone should be viewed as a research network rather than a commercial network.

The routers in the Mbone have historically been software run on Unix workstations using a program called *mrouted*, a multicast routing daemon. Mrouted implements DVMRP, the first defined multicast routing protocol, in its software. The initial implementations of mrouted did not implement *pruning*, which means that multicast traffic in the Mbone was really broadcast throughout the backbone. This deficiency has recently been largely corrected, as the latest version of mrouted supports pruning. Additionally, a significant number of the routers in the Mbone have been upgraded to commercial router platforms rather than being dependent on software running in a Unix workstation.

Nevertheless, the elimination of nonpruning routers remains an issue within the Mbone. A July 1997 Internet Draft [3-7], "Multicast Pruning a Necessity," suggests that, as of an unspecified date, nonpruning implementations will become unacceptable on the Mbone. It has been almost two years (a millennium in Internet time), however, since attempts were made to remove nonpruning routers. This lag points out the research nature of the Mbone; if it were a commercial operation, the offending routers would be gone the next day. Without pruning, multicast is simply broadcast and the efficient use of the network using multicast routing is lost. The recent Internet Draft also lists the revisions of mrouted and various vendors' products that are needed to support pruning.

Additionally, the Mbone has limitations on speed. Historically, the highest speed supported by the Mbone was 512 Kbps. This speed constraint was caused by the limitations of the earlier versions of mrouted.

Usage of the Mbone is tightly controlled by the ISPs that provide the support for it.

3.1 MULTICAST IP ADDRESSING

Multicast IP uses different IP addresses than are used for point-to-point communications, as shown in Figure 3-2. Class A, B, and C IP addresses used for point-to-point communications have a host and network component; in contrast, Class D IP addresses used for multicast transmission to a group simply have one address space indicating the multicast group.

Class D addresses also differ in that often the address is used only on a session-by-session basis, as opposed to the semi-permanent nature of Class A, B, and C addresses.

Class A, B, and C addresses also support subnet and network broadcast. For example, a packet may be sent to the address 4.10.255.255, which is a broadcast to subnet 4.10.

The multicast address space occupies the range from 224.0.0.0 to 239.255.255.255. The Internet Assigned Numbers Authority (IANA) maintains lists of registered users and assigns new numbers for new uses. The range from 224.0.0.0 to 224.0.0.255 is reserved for permanent assignment for various applications, including use by routing protocols.

Some well-known addresses have been assigned to groups as follows:

All systems on this subnet	224.0.0.1
All routers on this subnet	224.0.0.2
All DVMRP routers	224.0.0.4
All OSPF routers	224.0.0.5
All OSPF designated routers	224.0.0.6
All RIP2 routers	224.0.0.9

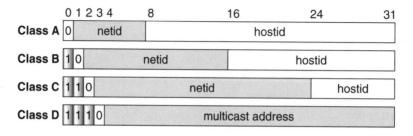

FIGURE 3-2

IP address types

| All PIM routers | 224.0.0.13 |
| All CBT routers | 224.0.0.15 |

DVMRP, OSPF, RIP2, PIM, and CBT are routing protocols used by routers to determine the optimal path along which to forward packets. The complete list appears in RFC 1700.

The remaining multicast addresses, 224.0.1.0 to 239.255.255.255, are either assigned to various multicast applications or currently unassigned. The set from 239.0.0.0 to 239.255.255.255 is reserved for various "administratively scoped" applications, which do not necessarily have an Internet-wide scope.

One unresolved issue in global multicast networking is the assignment of Class D addresses on a temporary, session-by-session basis in public networks and the Internet. Many multicast applications operate on precisely that basis; a group address is assigned on demand to an application for the duration of the session, after which it is surrendered for use by some other application. Recently, some proposals have been made that could resolve this issue, as discussed in Section 3.1.4.

This uncertainty does not mean, however, that an individual organization cannot implement some form of multicast address assignment that meets its need. Corporate networks that do not connect to the Internet can simply choose any set of addresses for their use.

3.1.1 Scoped Multicast Addresses

IP packets have a field called "Time to Live" (TTL). TTL is a mechanism that stops packets from potentially traveling around the network forever without reaching the destination address. It is based on hop count. A number is defined for the TTL of a specific application. Passage through a router decrements the TTL by one. When the number reaches zero, the packet is discarded. Thus the TTL number determines the scope of the network that the packet can traverse.

Historically, TTL has been the primary mechanism by which one sets the scope for multicast packets as well as unicast packets. Recently, however, it has been proposed that users implement administratively scoped multicast addresses — that is, certain addresses that are scoped to a local area or some other network boundary where they can be recognized by routers at a border and thereby blocked and confined to that area. Administratively scoped multicast addressing has recently become supported by Cisco routers.

Administratively scoped IP multicast addresses are described in a recent Internet Draft [3-8]. The administratively scoped IP address space is the range from 239.0.0.0 to 239.255.255.255.

Administratively scoped IP addresses provide two basic functions:

1. Packets addressed to administratively scoped multicast addresses do not cross configured administrative boundaries.

2. Administratively scoped IP addresses are assigned locally and thus need not be unique across administrative boundaries, permitting the reuse of address space.

Boundary routers (the routers located at the boundary of an administrative domain) need to support administrative scoping for each of their interfaces. These routers do not forward administratively scoped multicast datagrams outside their administrative domain, as shown in Figure 3-3. The boundary routers

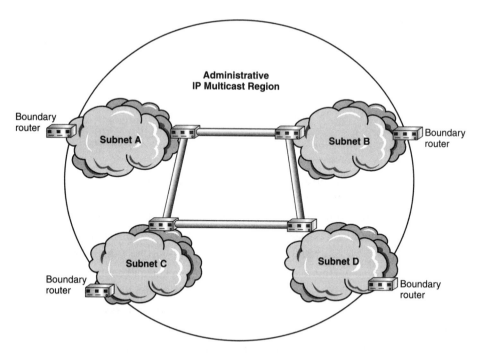

FIGURE 3-3

Administrative scoping

shown attached to subnets A–D serve as blocks to administratively scoped multicast datagrams.

239.255.0.0/16 is defined as IPv4 *Local Scope*. The Local Scope is the minimally defined scoping and cannot be divided further. Local Scopes may not overlap higher-level scope domains. The reserved address space for local scoping may be extended downward into the reserved ranges 239.254.0.0/16 and 239.253.0.0/16, should the preferred range prove insufficient.

The next highest scope is the *Organization Local Scope* with associated address space 239.192.0.0/14. An organization should allocate subranges from this space when defining scopes for its private use. These subranges are expandable to 239.0.0.0/10, 239.64.0.0/10, and 239.128.0.0/10 should the preferred range prove insufficient.

Administratively scoped addresses are considered more useful than TTL scoped addresses. Thus we can expect to see the use of administrative scoping grow and the use of TTL scoping decline in the future.

3.1.2   Binding to LAN MAC Addresses

Class D addresses are bound to Media Access Control (MAC) addresses* on a LAN differently than Class A, B, or C unicast addresses are. Unicast addresses become bound to particular MAC addresses by assigning an IP address explicitly to a host, which is then bound to its corresponding MAC address, or by dynamic IP assignment.

The Dynamic Host Control Protocol (DHCP) [3-9] provides a means for temporarily assigning an IP address to a host upon request, which is surrendered after the session ends. ISPs commonly use this approach to provide service to their customers at session start-up, usually by means of a dial call to the network.

In all of these unicast cases, an IP address is explicitly bound to a MAC address. In contrast, Class D addresses are automatically mapped to MAC multicast addresses by the simple procedure explained below.

MAC addresses are 48 bits (6 bytes) long. This constraint applies to all LANs that have become standards, such as Ethernet, token ring, and FDDI. In contrast, IP addresses are 32 bits (4 bytes) long. The low-order 23 bits of the

---

* MAC addresses are sometimes called physical addresses, as they identify the unique LAN interface card in a host device.

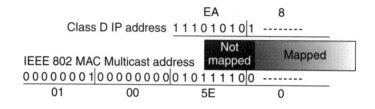

FIGURE 3-4

Mapping of Class D IP address to IEEE 802 MAC multicast address

Class D IP address are simply mapped to the low-order 23 bits of the IANA's reserved MAC layer multicast address block.

Figure 3-4 shows how this mapping occurs. In this example, the multicast group address 234.138.8.5 (E1-8A-08-05 in hex) is mapped to IEEE 802 MAC-layer multicast address (01-00-5E-0A-08-05).

Because 5 of the 28 bits of the Class D address that vary are not mapped, an ambiguity arises. Thus 2^5 or 32 valid Class D addresses exist for each valid MAC address, meaning that more than one Class D address could potentially share the same MAC multicast address. In practice, this issue is not a problem; the chance of an overlap is small and, even if one occurs, different applications should have different User Datagram Protocol (UDP) port numbers, so packets will be properly directed to the correct application even if they share the same MAC multicast address.

This mapping occurs automatically in network interface boards, requiring no protocol or other means for a binding.

3.1.3   Multicast IPv6

Our discussion so far has assumed that IPv4, the current version of IP, is operating in the Internet and in private networks. The IETF has recently created another version of IP, called IPv6 [3-10]. The primary motivation for this development was alarm about running out of address space in IPv4 because of the exponential growth of the Internet. IPv6 has 128 bits of address space, compared with 32 bits in IPv4.

Multicast addresses in IPv6 are identified by all ones in the first eight bits of the address, as shown in Figure 3-5. Two other fields, "flgs" and "scop," indicate the type of multicast address being described. For multicast purposes, the three

FIGURE 3-5

IPv6 multicast address organization

higher-order bits of flgs are set to zero. The lower-order bit, if set to one, indicates that the multicast address is transient.

The "scop" 4-bit field is used to limit the scope of the multicast group—that is, the scope of the network that the group traverses in a manner similar to that used in IPv4. The values for scop are as follows:

0	Reserved
1	Node-local scope
2	Link-local scope
3	(Unassigned)
4	(Unassigned)
5	Site-local scope
6	(Unassigned)
7	(Unassigned)
8	Organization-local scope
9	(Unassigned)
A	(Unassigned)
B	(Unassigned)
C	(Unassigned)
D	(Unassigned)
E	Global scope
F	Reserved

This set-up leaves 112 bits of group address identity in the IPv6 multicast address field.

3.1.4 Multicast Address Allocation

The specifications for allocating multicast addresses within a global Internet are just now being formulated [3-11]. The underlying philosophy is that Class D addresses are allocated by administrative scope for a finite time, where almost all applications would be assigned temporary addresses with a high level of reuse. Only a few broadly recognized applications would be assigned permanent, "well-known" addresses — for example, 224.0.1.1 for the Network Time Protocol and 224.2.127.255 for global-scope multicast session announcements. In general, static multicast addresses should not be used unless they provide basic infrastructure and therefore cannot use a dynamic address.

Thus almost all applications should use dynamic addresses. Each address will have a finite lifetime and a particular scope. The architecture assumes that the scope will be administrative, and that the use of TTL scoping will eventually cease.

The global Internet multicast address allocation architecture is hierarchical and includes three parts. In the lowest level of the hierarchy, applications obtain addresses by using multicast extensions to the DHCP called Multicast Dynamic Host Control Protocol (MDHCP) [3-12]. These addresses are obtained from a Multicast Address Allocation Server (MAAS).

MAASs "claim" addresses that they have allocated using the Address Allocation Protocol (AAP) [3-13] and, if necessary, defend these addresses if another MAAS attempts to allocate the same address. A MAAS keeps track of other multicast addresses in use within the same *allocation domain* and, when allocating an address, ensures that the address is not already being used in that domain. AAP uses multicast, and AAP advertisements are sent periodically in time scales ranging from milliseconds to seconds.

Certain nodes, which are usually routers, in an allocation domain use the Multicast Address Set Claim (MASC) protocol [3-14] to claim address sets that satisfy the needs of MAASs within their allocation domain. MASC nodes are also hierarchical, so MASC nodes below the top level in the hierarchy see address set advertisements by higher-level MASC nodes and must choose address sets from those advertised.

Figure 3-6 shows this hierarchy. Allocation domains are administratively scoped, multicast-capable regions of the network. Allocation domains will normally coincide with unicast Autonomous Systems (ASs). Section 3.5 discusses interdomain multicast routing between ASs.

No final central authority exists for multicast address allocation. Likewise, no enforcement mechanism is available to ensure that addresses are not duplicated across the global Internet. In fact, administrative scoping permits considerable duplication of multicast address space by design in different domains, without actual collision of addresses due to the scope limitation.

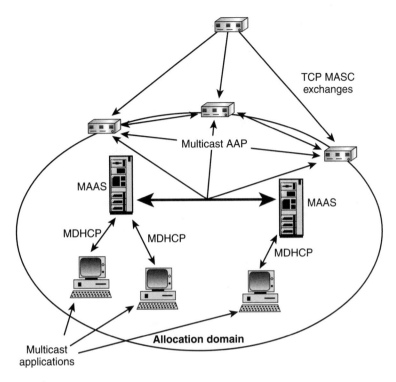

FIGURE 3-6

Proposed multicast address allocation architecture

The MASC nodes are typically multicast routers that claim a set of multicast addresses that is tied to a particular domain. This set will be used for interdomain multicast routing, as will be discussed in Section 3.4.

The Internet Multicast Address Allocation architecture and protocols are very new, with first Internet Drafts dating from late 1997 and the first presentation to the IETF made in the December 1997 meeting. Thus, it remains in an early stage of development, and the ISPs need to buy in to the concept before any deployment occurs.

Intranets that are multicast-enabled, however, will be able to utilize the lower part of the hierarchy and realize its benefits soon. Consensus exists that MDHCP will be used by servers to allocate multicast addresses to applications. In this case, only one allocation domain will likely match one AS. Multiple MAAS servers within the network will therefore communicate with each other

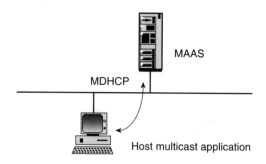

FIGURE 3-7

Multicast application obtains multicast address using MDHCP

using AAP, as shown in Figure 3-7. Of course, if there is just one server, no AAP communications are needed.

The operators of the private network would initially allocate any set of multicast addresses that is administratively scoped to be confined to the Intranet by the border routers. This exercise is trivial if only one MAAS exists; if two or more are present, they would communicate using AAP to ensure that the addresses of each MAAS do not overlap. This architecture will likely be quite common within Intranets in the future. No products actually support this architecture today—stay tuned.

3.2   IGMP AND JOINING MULTICAST GROUPS

Joining particular multicast groups is receiver initiated using the Internet Group Management Protocol (IGMP). IGMPv1 (the version most commonly implemented) is specified in RFC 1112 [3-4], and defines a dialog that occurs between routers supporting multicast routing and hosts on a subnet attached to that router. IGMP has been upgraded twice, but neither of these upgrades has achieved official standard status as yet. The version specified in RFC 1112 is referred to as IGMPv1; the updates are called IGMPv2 and IGMPv3.

3.2.1   IGMPv1

RFC 1112 defines the IGMPv1 protocol and the dialog that occurs between a host in a multicast group and the nearest router supporting multicast as shown in Figure 3-8. Multicast routers periodically transmit Host Membership Query messages to determine which host groups have members on their directly attached networks. These messages are sent to the "all hosts group" (224.0.0.1) and have an IP TTL of 1. Thus they are confined to the directly attached subnetwork and are not forwarded by any other multicast routers.

When a host receives an IGMP Query message, it responds with a Host Membership Report for each group to which it belongs. These messages are sent to the group address to which the host belongs. If a host belongs to multiple groups simultaneously, it must therefore send multiple Host Membership Reports to each group. Host Membership Reports likewise have an IP TTL of 1 and are confined to the local subnetwork.

Host Membership Reports suppress redundant messages by means of random back-off timers. Each host generates a random back-off time, after which it sends any necessary Host Membership Reports. If, during the timeout period, a host receives a Host Membership Report identical to one it was preparing, it suppresses its response. A multicast router does not need to know the exact host in the group in that subnetwork; it needs to know only that at least one host belongs to that group on the specified subnetwork. This feature reduces the traffic required on that subnetwork.

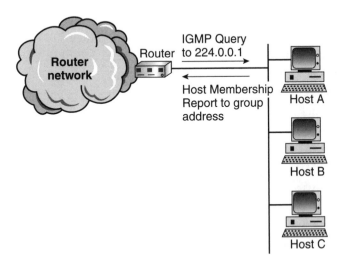

FIGURE 3-8
IGMP dialog

Even though the nearest multicast router is not in the host group being reported, all multicast addresses must be received promiscuously by all of the relevant interfaces. The sending of the Host Membership Report on its group address also enables other hosts in that group on that subnetwork to listen and suppress identical Host Membership Reports from hosts coexisting on the subnetwork.

Multicast routers periodically transmit IGMP Queries to the subgroups to which they are attached. In contrast, hosts do not send Host Membership Reports unless they are queried by a router, with one exception—when a host first joins a group. At that time, a host sends a Host Membership Report without waiting for an IGMP Query. Thus, members joining a group are immediately reported to the nearest multicast router, whereas those leaving a group are determined only by a timeout—that is, a lack of a response to an IGMP Query. Polling intervals for IGMP Queries and timeout to declare a leave are both configurable parameters.

The total latency in setting up a group depends on the sum of the time to notify the nearest router of the joining member, plus the time to set up the multicast routing by the routers in the network. Typically, this latency is measured in seconds. The latency to leave a group is longer, as the timeout needs to expire based on the absence of a response to an IGMP Query before a leaving member is recognized. That leaf of the multicast tree needs to be torn down by the routers. This total time lasts approximately a minute for typical configurations.

3.2.2   IGMPv2

IGMPv2 was first added as an enhancement to mrouted DVMRP source code version 3.3 to 3.8. Initially, it was not documented except in this source code, though it has since been written up in an Internet Draft, which has now been upgraded to RFC 2236 [3-15]. IGMPv2 added a number of enhancements, while maintaining backward compatibility with IGMPv1.

In the case of multiple multicast routers on the same subnet, IGMPv1 requires that the multicast routing protocol determine which of the routers is designated to send the IGMP Queries. In the case of IGMPv2, the multicast router with the lowest IP address on the subnet is automatically elected to be the multicast querier, simplifying the requirements placed on the multicast routing protocol.

IGMPv2 defines a new type of Query message—the Group-Specific Query message. It allows a router to transmit a Query message to a specific multicast group on a particular subnet rather than to all multicast groups.

The most notable new feature of IGMPv2, however, is the creation of an explicit Leave Group message that can greatly reduce the latency for leaving a group in IGMPv1. In IGMPv1, the notice of leaving a group is implicit—that is, it is determined by an expired timeout to an IGMP Query. Thus there is latency associated with leaving a group that is not present upon joining a group. The Leave Group message of IGMPv2 was created expressly to make these join and leave latencies more comparable.

When a host in a group wishes to leave, it sends a Leave Group message to the all routers group address (224.0.0.2), with the group field being set to the group being left. The designated multicast router responds with a Group-Specific Query message to the subnet from which it received the Leave Group message. If no Host List Reports are generated in response to the Group-Specific Query messages, this subnet is removed from the delivery tree by the multicast routing protocol, just as occurs in IGMPv1 when a leave group is determined. The extra step of sending a Group-Specific Query ensures that all members of a specific group have exited from that subnetwork. This situation is shown in Figure 3-9.

It could be the case, however, that the multicast routing protocol determines that this particular subnetwork is needed to reach additional members of that group downstream from the subnet. If so, group packets are still forwarded to that subnetwork even though all members on that subnetwork have left. This case applies with IGMPv1 as well.

IGMPv2 implementations have just begun to become commercially available, with the first versions present in some UNIX operating systems.

IGMPv2 is stable as a specification and is on standards track in IETF.

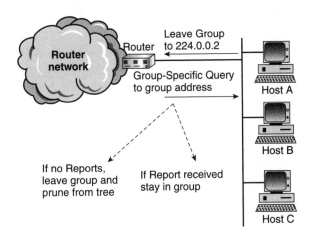

FIGURE 3-9

IGMPv2 Leave Group dialog

3.2.3 IGMPv3

IGMPv3 is in preliminary draft status [3-16]. The primary feature added in IGMPv3 is the capability for hosts to select only specific sources of multicast traffic to receive. This feature gives receivers more control over which sources they allow to deliver information to them.

This control is accomplished in two ways. An Inclusion Group-Source Report message allows a host to specify the IP addresses of the sources it wants to receive. An Exclusion Group-Source Report message allows a host to explicitly exclude sources it does not want to receive from. In IGMPv1 and IGMPv2, all traffic from all sources to a particular group is forwarded to the host's subnetwork if any host on that subnetwork is a member of that group. Note that source traffic to a particular group need not derive from just one source.

Through providing selection by source, IGMPv3 will help conserve bandwidth further by not even setting up unwanted branches of the multicast tree.

Additionally, the Leave Group messages in IGMPv2 have been enhanced in IGMPv3. The Group-Source Leave message has been introduced to allow a host to specify the IP addresses of any source-group pairs it wishes to leave. At this time, not all of the multicast routing protocols can take advantage of this information. Further work on IGMPv3 will address this issue as work continues. Thus IGMPv3 should be viewed as work in progress.

3.3 MULTICAST ROUTING PROTOCOLS

Routers in a network or internetwork use multicast routing protocols to optimally route multicast packets through the network or internetwork from the source to multiple destinations that consist of the members of the multicast group. This approach is similar in concept to the unicast (point-to-point) routing protocols that serve as the backbone of operation in all TCP/IP networks, including the Internet.

Unicast routing protocols use one of two basic techniques: *distance vector* or *link state*. Earlier routing protocols were all based on distance vector, such as the Routing Information Protocol (RIP) and Interior Gateway Routing Protocol (IGRP, Cisco's proprietary protocol). Open Shortest Path First (OSPF) became the dominant link-state routing protocol. Link-state routing protocols converge more quickly, an important consideration for networks that may change dynamically, at the expense of requiring more computing and memory resources.

Some multicast routing protocols are derived from distance-vector or link-state unicast routing protocols. A new category of *shared-tree* protocols has also been introduced for multicast. Thus multicast routing protocols now come in three basic flavors: distance vector, link state, and shared trees. Distance Vector Multicast Routing Protocol (DVMRP) and Protocol Independent Multicast—Dense Mode (PIM-DM) are based on distance vector, Multicast Open Shortest Path First (MOSPF) is based on link state, and Protocol Independent Multicast—Sparse Mode (PIM-SM) and Core-Based Trees (CBT) are based on shared trees.

DVMRP, PIM-DM, and MOSPF have been called *dense-mode* multicast routing protocols, as they require some form of flooding of datagrams to the network to find multicast routes. This tactic is most suitable for areas with dense concentrations of group members, such as campus networks. In contrast, the shared-tree protocols — PIM-SM and CBT — have been called *sparse-mode* multicast routing protocols, as they are best suited for widely dispersed group members in a wide area network. Figure 3-10 shows the family tree of multicast routing protocols.

All multicast routing protocols must set up *distribution trees* to route datagrams to the members of the group in an optimal way. Figure 3-11 shows a typical distribution tree that might be established on the Mbone. This tree is quite large and complex. The challenge is to create multicast routing protocols that can set up these distribution trees quickly, efficiently, and without excessive

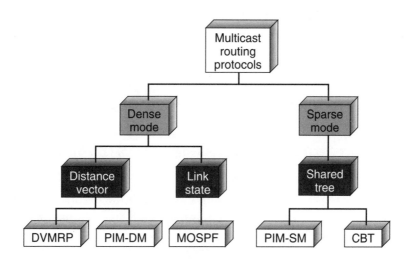

FIGURE 3-10

Multicast routing protocol family tree

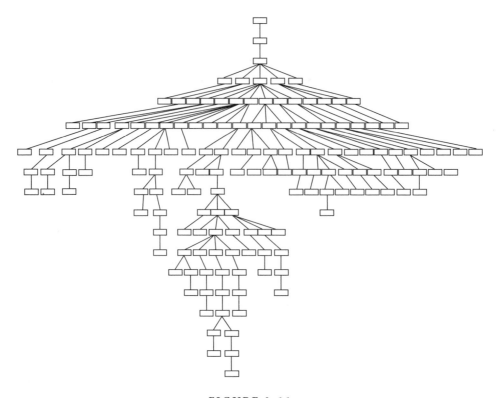

FIGURE 3-11

Example of an Mbone distribution tree. NASA Shuttle video,
May 21, 1996. *(Courtesy of Mark Handley.)*

network traffic. The different multicast routing protocols each have their strengths and weaknesses, as discussed in the rest of this section.

3.3.1   Distance Vector Multicast Routing Protocol (DVMRP)

DVMRP, the oldest multicast routing protocol, was first defined in RFC 1075 and then updated in a recent Internet Draft [3-17]. It is the routing protocol first used to implement the Mbone, and remains the dominant multicast routing protocol used there. DVMRP built on the principles of the RIP distance-vector unicast routing protocol and extended the ideas to multicast.

   In its most recent version, DVMRP uses a technique known as Reverse Path Multicasting (RPM) to generate IP multicast delivery trees. When a router receives a datagram at an interface, the reverse path to the source is checked to see whether it is the shortest path to that source by using a unicast routing table of known source networks. If the datagram came from the shortest path from the source, the router floods the datagram to all paths except one—the path that leads back to the datagram's source. Otherwise, the datagram is discarded because it has come from a redundant, nonoptimal path.

Figure 3-12 shows how this process works. The source is the host on subnet A. Datagrams sent to router B1 on subnet B arrive via two interfaces: directly from subnet A (the shortest path) and through router C1 of subnet C. The latter datagram is discarded in router B1 on subnet B, as it did not come from the shortest path to the source.

DVMRP includes a unicast routing protocol that is used to determine shortest path source routes. This routing information is exchanged between the DVMRP routers in the network.

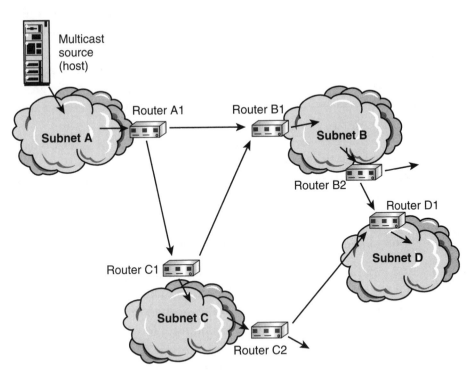

FIGURE 3-12

DVMRP flooding

This technique allows multicast data to reach all subnetworks, possibly multiple times. If a router is attached to a subnetwork that does not want to receive data for a particular multicast group, it sends "prune" messages back up the distribution tree; this action prevents subsequent datagrams from being forwarded in the network to hosts that are not valid group members. Similarly, "graft" messages are used to dynamically add new members to the group by grafting new sections to the tree. DVMRP implements its own unicast routing protocol, which closely resembles RIP, one of the earliest unicast routing protocols, to determine routes back to the source.

Prunes have a limited lifetime. When they expire, DVMRP periodically refloods, refreshing the routes to a group. Every (source-group) pair and pruned interface requires a stored entry in the router's memory to enable it to remember that the interface was pruned. To avoid storing this information for an infinite time, the prune eventually expires and the tree is rebuilt by reflooding and repruning (if the source is still sending traffic to the relevant group).

DVMRP includes an extensive capability for tunneling as a part of its routing protocol, as this feature is required in the Mbone where DVMRP was first implemented. Interfaces are defined to be either physical or tunneled in a DVMRP multicast router.

DVMRP is a dense-mode multicast routing protocol. Such protocols are best suited to network infrastructures in which a number of members of the group are densely distributed and the bandwidth inefficiency of flooding is not a large detriment.

Upgrades to DVMRP are under development in the IETF Inter-Domain Multicast Routing (IDMR) working group.

DVMRP is supported in mrouted software on Sun workstations and by most router vendors.

3.3.2   Protocol Independent Multicast—Dense Mode (PIM-DM)

PIM comes in two flavors: PIM-DM and PIM-SM (sparse mode). It was created primarily for the sparse-mode version, which aims to improve the efficiency of multicast routing protocols over WANs. In the creation process, PIM-DM was developed as a companion protocol that has protocol formats like PIM-SM yet operates well in dense-mode network infrastructures. The creators of PIM intend to develop a multicast routing set that can become the complete standard for all situations.

PIM-DM operates very much like DVMRP. It floods initially (as shown in Figure 3-12 for DVMRP) and then prunes back leafs where no members of the group exist. One big difference is that PIM-DM depends on the existing unicast routing protocol to determine routes back to the source, rather than including its own protocol as DVMRP does. Other minor differences separate PIM-DM and DVMRP as well. For example, DVMRP routers know their "children" (downstream routers) in the multicast tree for each group rooted at the source and can determine whether these children are on leaf nodes with respect to the tree. By using this information together with a technique known as "split horizon with poison reverse," duplicate messages on links can be avoided, even before pruning occurs. In contrast, PIM-DM routers do not store children and leaf node information for all their links, saving router resources; they pay a price for this approach in that multicast packets may be sent twice on the same link before pruning takes place.

PIM-DM is described in an Internet Draft [3-18], "Protocol Independent Multicast Version 2, Dense Mode Specification." Even though the protocol is still in draft stage, it has already been implemented as a routing protocol by Cisco Systems in its routers. (Cisco Systems has been the primary commercial force supporting the PIM multicast routing protocols.)

3.3.3   Multicast Open Shortest Path First (MOSPF)

MOSPF provides multicast extensions to the popular unicast routing protocol, OSPF. OSPF is an Interior Gateway Protocol (IGP) — that is, it is used to route packets within a single autonomous domain. OSPF uses link-state algorithms that permit rapid route calculation with minimum routing protocol traffic on the network. MOSPF is described in RFC 1584 [3-19].

Each OSPF router in the network has complete understanding of all links in the network, and it uses this information to calculate routes from itself to all other destinations within that network. MOSPF works by including multicast information in OSPF (version 2) Link State Announcements (LSAs). As a consequence, multicast routing capability can be incrementally introduced into an OSPF routing domain.

LSAs are the mechanism that OSPF uses to communicate link-state information to other OSPF routers. In the case of MOSPF, special multicast LSAs called Group-Membership LSAs are used to calculate optimum routes to the group from the source. Designated routers on a subnetwork (the router that sends IGMP Queries) communicate group membership information to all other routers in the OSPF area by flooding Group-Membership LSAs within the network.

When an initial multicast datagram arrives, the source subnetwork is located in the MOSPF link-state database, which is simply the standard OSPF link-state database plus the Group-Membership LSAs. Calculations made from information in this database enable the construction of a source-based, shortest-path tree. Group-Membership LSA data is used to prune the tree, ensuring that the remaining branches lead only to those subnetworks containing group members. The final result is a pruned, source-based tree rooted at the packet's source subnetwork.

Because this process uses data available in each router's database, MOSPF does not need to flood the first datagram of a group transmission, unlike with DVMRP and PIM-DM. Group-Membership LSAs, however, are communicated to other MOSPF routers via flooding.

A forwarding cache is maintained after the creation of the source-based tree. This cache is not aged or periodically refreshed. If the topology of the underlying OSPF domain changes, then the underlying shortest-path trees must be recalculated — normally a rare event. More frequently, changes occur with group membership variation, as new Group-Membership LSAs then need to be flooded to the routers in the network to change the tree by adding or deleting members of the group.

MOSPF also provides for inter-area routing between multiple OSPF domains (areas), which may be set up within an Autonomous System. This strategy is often implemented so as to reduce the computing requirements at any individual router and thereby improve performance, as illustrated in Figure 3-13.

OSPF describes area border routers (ABRs) that serve as gateways between areas. A subset of these routers serve as inter-area multicast forwarders, responsible for forwarding group membership information and multicast datagrams between areas. A "wildcard multicast receiver" receives all multicast traffic generated in an area. Inter-area multicast forwarders are usually wildcard multicast receivers.

MOSPF/OSPF areas can reduce the load on router resources, as link-state routing represents a more resource-intensive routing algorithm than distance vector.

MOSPF is a good multicast routing solution when the routers in the network use OSPF as the unicast routing protocol, as MOSPF is simply an extension of OSPF. Additionally, MOSPF-capable routers can be intermixed with OSPF routers without multicast capability, permitting the incremental deploy-

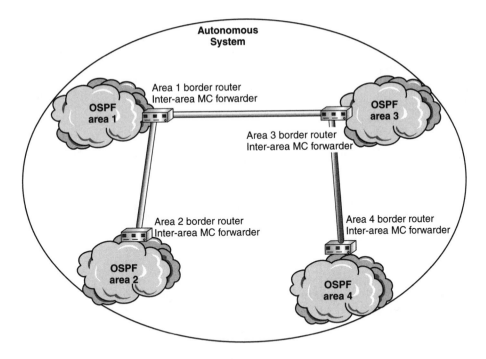

FIGURE 3-13

MOSPF in OSPF areas

ment of multicast capability in a network. If a different unicast routing protocol is being used, however, MOSPF will not work.

Some questions have arisen regarding performance when the system includes many groups that have dynamic membership, which may require significant recalculation of routes and a reflooding of Group-Membership LSAs. As described earlier, this problem can be mitigated somewhat by segmenting the network into OSPF areas.

MOSPF is supported by a number of major router vendors, particularly those that have embraced OSPF as a unicast routing protocol.

3.3.4   Shared-Tree (Sparse-Mode) Multicast Routing Protocols

Shared-tree (sparse-mode) routing protocols use new techniques for multicast routing; they are not extensions of current unicast routing protocols. Two such protocols have emerged:

TABLE 3-1

COMPARISON OF DVMRP AND CBT ROUTER STATE

Number of groups	10			100			1,000		
Group size (number of members)	20			40			60		
Number of sources per group	10%	50%	100%	10%	50%	100%	10%	50%	100%
Number of DVMRP router entries	20	100	200	400	2,000	4,000	6,000	30,000	60,000
Number of CBT router entries	10			100			1,000		

- Protocol Independent Multicast—Sparse Mode (PIM-SM)
- Core-Based Trees (CBT)

These protocols have been designed to operate efficiently over a WAN infrastructure where bandwidth is scarce and group members may be widely scattered. The term "sparse" in "sparse mode" is meant to indicate that group membership is widely dispersed. Rather than use flooding techniques, which are used by the dense-mode protocols and can waste bandwidth in WAN environments, they essentially set up routes in advance.

Shared-tree protocols require far fewer router resources. A recent Internet Draft [3-20] provided rough estimates on the differences in router state required between DVMRP as a representative dense-mode protocol and CBT as a representative shared-tree protocol. Table 3-1 shows this comparison.

As can be seen, if numerous sources of traffic exist for a group, as would be the case for conferencing applications, DVMRP requires typically greater than an order of magnitude more state than CBT.

3.3.4.1 Protocol Independent Multicast—Sparse Mode (PIM-SM)

PIM-SM, which was derived from CBT, was designed (with PIM-DM) to provide a routing protocol set with common packet formats to provide both sparse and dense modes. It is described in a recent RFC [3-21].

The term "shared" in "shared tree" indicates that the tree is the same for all members of a group, regardless of which member is the source. In contrast, the dense-mode protocols create a new tree for each source of traffic, even if it exists within the same group. This choice has important consequences, especially for many-to-many multicast traffic, such as that seen in conferences.

In PIM-SM, members of a group join a *rendezvous point* (RP). Routers with adjacent or downstream members are explicitly required to join a sparse-mode delivery tree by transmitting Join messages to the RP assigned to that group, as shown in Figure 3-14.

The PIM-SM router with the highest IP address is selected as the designated router (DR) for that subnet and is responsible for sending Join and Prune messages to the RP. When a receiver joins a particular multicast group, it notifies the DR through IGMP. The DR router then determines the RP to which that group is assigned and transmits a unicast PIM-Join message toward the RP for the group. Intermediate routers forward the unicast PIM-Join message and create a forwarding entry if one does not exist. In Figure 3-14, new members of the

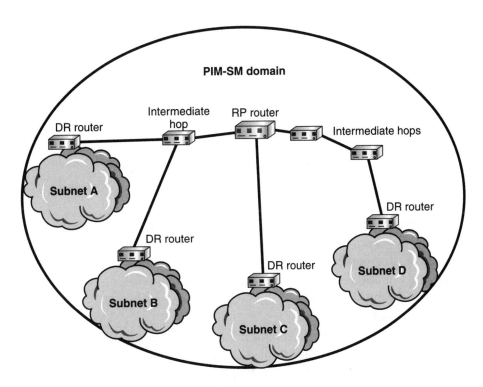

FIGURE 3-14
PIM-SM domain and RP

group from subnets A and B have PIM-Join messages forwarded from subnet C directly through the same intermediate router, and from subnet D through two different intermediate routers.

The developers of shared-tree protocols have debated how to map a particular multicast group to a particular RP. With PIM-SM, RP information is first obtained by the PIM-SM routers in a PIM domain by collecting *Bootstrap* messages. A bootstrap router (BSR) is elected for the domain and originates Bootstrap messages, which carry out a dynamic election of a BSR from among the candidates in a PIM domain and distribute RP information in steady state.

Selected PIM routers in the PIM domain are configured as candidate RPs. Each candidate RP unicasts a Candidate-RP-Advertisement message to the BSR in the domain. This message also includes group address prefix(es) for which that RP is advertising. The set of RPs for the domain is then included in the Bootstrap messages, which are distributed hop-by-hop throughout the domain.

Routers in the domain receive and store the Bootstrap messages upon their receipt. When a host joins a particular group, the DR uses the Bootstrap information stored to select the RP for that group by using a deterministic hash function to select one whose prefix matches that group. BSR messages are also used to indicate availability of RPs; RPs that are not available are removed from the list.

When a source first transmits a multicast datagram to the group, its DR forwards the datagram to the selected RP for that group for distribution. The DR encapsulates the multicast packets inside a PIM-SM-Register packet and unicasts them to the group RP. This action triggers the RP to send a PIM-Join message back to the source's DR and allows future forwarding from the source to the RP natively without encapsulation inside a unicast packet.

When group members leave the group, the DR sends PIM-SM Prune messages to the RP. Part of the tree can then be pruned back.

The same tree that is built through the RP accommodates all traffic in the group. For example, in a many-to-many multicast conference application, all members of the group may be active senders as well as receivers. In such a case, the same distribution tree is used to send information to the group. In contrast, in the case of dense-mode routing protocols, a separate source distribution tree is created for each traffic source.

The tree that is built by PIM-SM is not necessarily optimal in terms of providing the shortest path. Although many RPs exist within a particular PIM-SM domain, the RP for the group is typically designated without regard to its location. Thus an RP could be located in New York while all group members are in California, requiring traffic to traverse the continent twice to reach group members. Additionally, all group traffic goes through the RP, which represents a potential bottleneck and single point of failure.

PIM-SM addresses some of these issues, and ongoing work seeks to resolve the other problems. For example, RPs send keep-alive messages periodically to the DRs on subnets with active members. If a DR determines that an RP is no longer there, it switches to a preconfigured backup RP. Work is also ongoing to enable the RP for a group to be chosen more intelligently.

PIM-SM also offers the optional ability to switch to a shortest-path tree once it begins receiving packets from the source. This feature could be used to alleviate the cross-continental traffic problem described earlier. This switch can be triggered if the data rate from the source exceeds a predefined threshold or by some other criteria.

The two PIM protocols are likely to become standards in the future. PIM-SM implementations are available in Cisco routers.

3.3.4.2   Core Based Trees (CBT)

CBT, a multicast routing protocol that closely resembles PIM-SM, actually preceded the latter's development. What is called an RP in PIM-SM is called a *core* in CBT. The core acts much like an RP; group joins and leaves are made to the core, and all traffic for a single group traverses a single core assigned to that group.

CBT offers two ways of mapping a particular group to a particular core. The first uses the same Bootstrap mechanism as previously described for PIM-SM. The second method involves a manual placement of cores to create more optimal distribution trees; this technique, however, creates a significant administrative burden.

The developers of CBT decided not to provide the option of switching to a shortest-path tree from the shared tree, unlike with PIM-SM. Their belief is that router state maintenance in the network is an important scaling benefit that should not be compromised.

The DR for a subnetwork is selected by using CBT's "Hello" protocol. When a host joins a group, the DR for the member's subnetwork sends a JOIN_REQUEST unicast message to the core router. This Join message must be explicitly acknowledged with a JOIN_ACK either by the core router or by an intermediate router on the unicast path to the core that has already successfully joined the tree. This process is similar to the one employed under PIM-SM.

If a nonmember of the group sends data to the group and its DR is already on the shared tree, the DR simply forwards the data packet over all outgoing interfaces corresponding to that group's forwarding entry. In contrast, PIM-SM must encapsulate data from a nonmember sender regardless of whether the DR for that subnetwork has joined the shared tree. If the sender's subnetwork is not attached to the shared tree, the local DR must encapsulate the data packet and unicast it to the group's core router. The core router de-encapsulates the data and disseminates it over all shared-tree interfaces, according to the forwarding entries for that group.

Routers between a nonmember sender and the group's core do not need to know anything about the group or even be multicast-enabled.

CBT is described in RFCs 2189 [3-22] and 2201 [3-23] and an Internet Draft [3-24] describing a later revision.

3.4 INTERDOMAIN MULTICAST ROUTING

The previously discussed multicast routing protocols all applied within a domain, making each an *interior gateway protocol* (IGP). One major shortcoming for multicast routing protocols is the lack of an *exterior gateway protocol* (EGP) for multicast routing. The IDMR group of the IETF continues its work on developing a multicast exterior gateway routing protocol.

Interdomain routing protocols adapted for multicast are crucial for implementing a fully multicast-enabled Internet. Without it, group members cannot reside in different ISP locations. For example, group members in general can be from multiple companies using different ISPs. Thus members can be in the domain of UUNet, MCI, or any other ISP. Each of these is a different domain, or *Autonomous System* (AS). An AS is defined as a network administered by one entity and operating with one IGP routing protocol. An AS can be a *stub* AS, a *multihomed* AS, or a *transit* AS, as shown in Figure 3-15. ASs are connected by routers using exterior gateway routing protocols that enforce policies.

An AS can be controlled by an ISP, such as UUNet or MCI, or it can be an organization that is a customer of an ISP. Customer ASs are generally stub or multihomed ASs, but virtually never transit ASs. The ISPs that serve today's Internet have generally worked out *peering* relationships — that is, policy agreements to carry one another's traffic. A policy outlining ISPs' responsibilities for multicast traffic has not been established.

A recent Internet Draft [3-20] discusses some of the issues involved in interdomain multicast routing. Scaling is a major issue for this type of multicast, and,

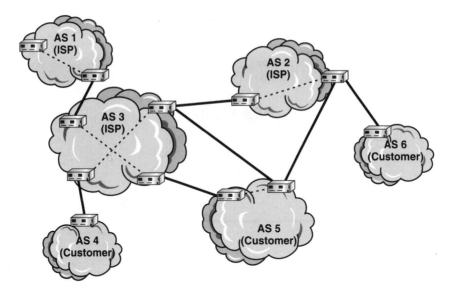

FIGURE 3-15

Interconnection of autonomous systems

for this reason, a sparse-mode protocol should be used as it requires much less state than a dense-mode protocol.

Recently, developers have proposed a sparse-mode (shared-tree) interdomain multicast routing protocol called Border Gateway Multicast Protocol (BGMP). BGMP was first documented in an Internet Draft in November 1997. It was first publicly described at the December 1997 IETF meeting held in Washington, D.C., and updated in March 1998 [3-25].

BGMP builds on the concepts of the two intradomain shared-tree multicast routing protocols, CBT and PIM-SM. BGMP uses the knowledge of MASC multicast address allocations per allocation domain discussed in Section 3.1.4 to set up *roots* (equivalent to CBT's cores or PIM-SM's RPs) corresponding to the multicast addresses allocated to the domain. Good practice would dictate that traffic sources for groups select multicast addresses allocated to their domains, ensuring that at least one group member resides in the same domain as the root. This set-up is shown in Figure 3-16.

As our discussion of PIM-SM and CBT has revealed, the mapping of an RP or core to a multicast address is relatively arbitrary within a domain, and

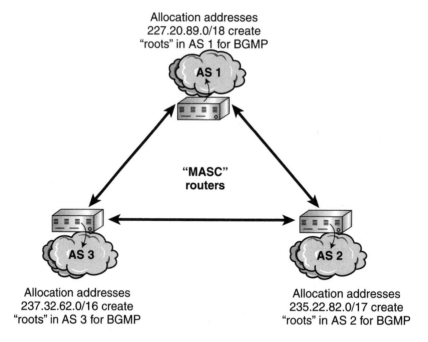

FIGURE 3-16

Multicast addresses allocated to ASs determine the location of BGMP roots

PIM-SM has the facility to switch to a source tree based on certain criteria to construct a more efficient tree. For interdomain routing, the root should be placed within the domain where most group members are likely to reside; hence the root is tied to the allocated multicast addresses for that domain to keep third-party dependencies at a minimum.

BGMP also constructs bidirectional trees, in contrast to the unidirectional trees created by intradomain shared-tree multicast routing protocols. Once again, this strategy minimizes third-party dependencies.

BGMP and Internet-wide multicast address allocation, which is used by BGMP, are both very new and still in the research and development stage. It remains to be seen whether BGMP and the multicast address allocation architecture on which it partially depends will continue to evolve and be tested. Much work remains to be done and ISPs need to be persuaded to accept these concepts and approaches.

Until these issues are resolved, native multicast network services are likely to be offered only by individual ISPs or in a private domain. For example, today's Mbone is administered as one AS.

REFERENCES

[3-1] Deering S, Cheriton DR. Host Groups: A Multicast Extension to the Internet Protocol. RFC 966, December 1985.

[3-2] Deering S. Host Extensions for IP Multicasting. RFC 988, July 1986.

[3-3] Deering S. Host Extensions for IP Multicasting. RFC 1054, May 1988.

[3-4] Deering S. Host Extensions for IP Multicasting. RFC 1112, August 1989.

[3-5] Waitzman D, Partridge C, Deering S. Distance Vector Multicast Routing Protocol. RFC 1075, November 1988.

[3-6] Information on Mbone tools can be found at http://pipkin.lut.ac.uk/~ben/video/.

[3-7] Hawkinson J. Multicast Pruning a Necessity. Internet Draft, Work in Progress, draft-ietf-mboned-pruning-02.txt, July 30, 1997.

[3-8] Meyer D. Administratively Scoped IP Multicast. Internet Draft, Work in Progress, draft-ietf-mboned-admin-ip-space-04.txt, November 1997.

[3-9] Droms R. Dynamic Host Configuration Protocol. RFC 1531, October 1993.

[3-10] Bradner S, Mankin A. IPng: Internet Protocol Next Generation. Reading, MA: Addison Wesley Longman Publishing Company, 1996.

[3-11] Handley M, Thaler D, Estrin D. The Internet Multicast Address Allocation Architecture. Internet Draft, Work in Progress, draft-handley-malloc-arch-00.txt, December 15, 1997.

[3-12] Patel BV, Shah M. Multicast Address Allocation Extensions to the Dynamic Host Configuration Protocol. Internet Draft, Work in Progress, draft-ietf-dhc-mdhcp-03.txt, November 1997.

[3-13] Handley M. Multicast Address Allocation Protocol (AAP). Internet Draft, Work in Progress, draft-handley-aap-00.txt, December 15, 1997.

[3-14] Estrin D, Handley M, Kumar S, Thaler D. The Multicast Address Set Claim (MASC) Protocol. Internet Draft, Work in Progress, draft-ietf-idmr-masc-00.txt, November 1997.

[3-15] Fenner W. Internet Group Management Protocol, Version 2. RFC 2236, November 1997.

[3-16] Cain B, Deering S, Thyagarajan A. Internet Group Management Protocol, Version 3. Internet Draft, Work in Progress, draft-ietf-idmr-igmp-v3-00.txt, November 21, 1997.

[3-17] Pusateri T. Distance Vector Multicast Routing Protocol Specification. Internet Draft, Work in Progress, draft-ietf-idmr-dvmrp-v3-06.txt, March 1998.

[3-18] Deering S, Estrin D, Farinacci D, Jacobson V, Helmy A, Wei L. Protocol Independent Multicast Version 2, Dense Mode Specification, Internet Draft, Work in Progress, draft-ietf-idmr-pim-dm-05.txt, May 21, 1997.

[3-19] Moy J. Multicast Extensions to OSPF. RFC 1584, March 1994.

[3-20] Ballardie A. Core Based Trees (CBT) Multicast Routing Architecture. Internet Draft, Work in Progress, draft-ietf-idmr-cbt-arch-06.txt, May 1997.

[3-21] Estrin D, Farinacci D, Helmy A, Thaler D, Deering S, Handley M, Jacobson V, Liu C, Sharma P, Wei L. Protocol Independent Multicast—Sparse Mode (PIM-SM): Protocol Specification. RFC 2117, June 1997.

[3-22] Ballardie A. Core Based Trees (CBT version 2) Multicast Routing: Protocol Specification. RFC 2189, September 1997.

[3-23] Ballardie A. Core Based Trees (CBT) Multicast Routing Architecture. RFC 2201, September 1997.

[3-24] Ballardie A, Cain B, Zhang Z. Core Based Trees (CBT version 3) Multicast Routing: Protocol Specification. Internet Draft, Work in Progress, draft-ietf-idmr-cbt-spec-v3-00.txt, March 1998.

[3-25] Thaler D, Estrin D, Meyer D, eds. Border Gateway Multicast Protocol (BGMP): Protocol Specification. Internet Draft, Work in Progress, draft-ietf-idmr-gum-02.txt, March 12, 1998.

4

NETWORK INFRASTRUCTURES AND EASE OF IMPLEMENTATION OF MULTICAST IP

The discussion of multicast IP routing protocols in Chapter 3 assumed a network architecture similar to today's Internet—that is, a highly meshed, land-line routed series of networks, each of which is autonomous and tied to the others using exterior gateway routers.

Large numbers of private networks are also used by organizations in the conduct of their business. In the past, many of these private networks ran IBM's System Network Architecture (SNA) protocols and were mainframe-centric. Other smaller organizations historically operated networks that focused on a local campus or area and used Novell's Internetwork Packet Exchange/Sequenced Packet Exchange (IPX/SPX) protocol suite. With the explosive growth of the Internet, however, these networks are quickly migrating to TCP/IP and can also benefit from multicast IP services. Private networks using TCP/IP and Web technology are now being called *Intranets*.

Similarly, organizations are creating networks to tie themselves with other organizations that may be their suppliers or customers; these networks are based on TCP/IP and Web technology. These types of networks are being called *Extranets*.

The infrastructures that these organizations use as the underpinnings for their networks are quite varied. In many cases, they are not the same structure as is typically present for the Internet. These infrastructures vary in their ability to support multicast services. Organizations are pioneering the use of multicast applications in real operational environments via these networks rather than the experimental operations being performed by researchers on the Mbone.

Thus it is important to understand the issues regarding multicast support in these different network infrastructures. This chapter examines these issues.

4.1   LANS AND CAMPUS NETWORKS

LANs have evolved considerably since the 1980s. The first LANs were *shared* LANs—that is, all hosts on the LAN shared the bandwidth available on the LAN. As traffic grew on these shared LANs, they became segmented via bridges that isolated traffic to logical entities where most of the traffic between hosts occurred and that blocked traffic from other logical segments. This approach was later taken to the ultimate with switched LANs, where each host is an independent segment and thus has access to the full LAN bandwidth. Routers are also used to connect different LANs into a campus network.

4.1.1   Shared LANs

All common LAN technologies were originally conceived as shared LANs, including Ethernet, token ring, token bus, and Fiber Distributed Data Interface

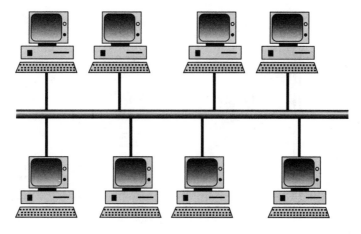

FIGURE 4-1
Shared Ethernet LAN

(FDDI). Although they use somewhat different access protocols, they share the same characteristic that all traffic is potentially available for all hosts on the network, as shown in Figure 4-1 for an Ethernet LAN. The network interface card (NIC) in the host filters the traffic based on MAC address and passes on only frames destined to that host. Broadcast frames are also passed to the host, as are frames with destination multicast addresses to which that particular host is bound.

Thus, shared LANs inherently support multicast traffic, and the multicast IP Class D address is mapped to MAC multicast addresses as described in Section 3.1.2.

4.1.2 LANs Segmented by Bridges

As shared LANs became saturated with traffic, they were segmented by local bridges, where each segment was chosen such that most of its traffic moved between hosts in that segment, as shown in Figure 4-2. Thus traffic was localized, reducing traffic on a particular segment, even though all of the segments collectively acted as one logical network. Multicast and broadcast traffic was propagated through the bridges (unless bridge filters were instituted to block them) to all segments except the segment from which the traffic originated. Consequently, all segmented LANs with bridges could inherently support multicast traffic.

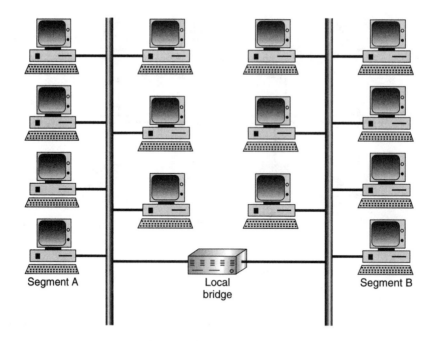

FIGURE 4-2

Shared Ethernet LAN segmented with a local bridge

4.1.3   Switched LANs

Today, switched LANs are rapidly displacing shared LANs as a way of supporting more network traffic with minimal changes in network infrastructure. The only change involves the hub, which now supports LAN switching rather than simply being a wiring concentrator for a shared LAN. The network wiring and NICs in the host do not need to change from those found in a shared LAN.

In switched LANs, the hub acts as a switch so that each LAN segment is one node, greatly increasing the effective bandwidth of the network. This easy upgrade has fueled explosive growth in the market for LAN switching equipment.

Early versions of LAN switches treated multicast packets as a broadcast, transmitting them to all nodes, thereby negating the benefits of both switching and multicasting. Newer versions of LAN switching equipment, however, monitor IGMP packets and direct IP multicast packets only to group members, alleviating possible traffic congestion. Additionally, some vendors are moving in the direction of Layer 3 switching, where the switching is performed at the IP layer rather than the Link layer. This equipment inherently supports IP multicast.

Thus all switched LANs support multicast, with the more modern networks doing it more efficiently by switching multicast packets only to the hosts in the particular multicast group to which the multicast packet is addressed.

4.1.4 Campus Networks

Campus networks often consist of multiple LANs connected together by local routers, as shown in Figure 4-3. The local routers segment the network, just as networks over a WAN are connected via routers.

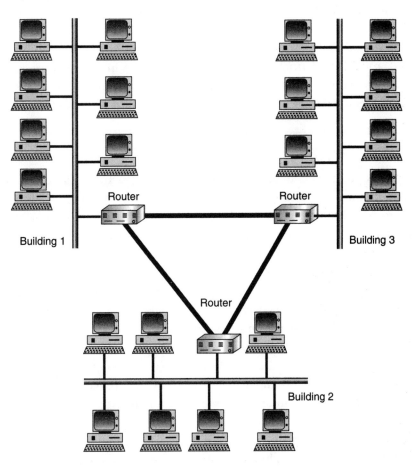

FIGURE 4-3

Campus Network

Because the underlying subnetworks (the LANs) support multicast, the campus network infrastructure inherently supports multicast. Routers in this environment simply need to have multicast turned on. These routers should use dense-mode routing protocols, such as DVMRP or PIM-DM, which are most suitable for these environments.

4.2 WIDE AREA NETWORKS (WANs)

The real winner with multicast is the WAN. WAN bandwidth is not "free" as is the case for a LAN, increasing the incentive to use the network efficiently. WAN infrastructures also vary widely and differ greatly in their ability to support multicast.

The discussion of routing protocols in Chapter 3 assumed a land-line, meshed, routed infrastructure similar to that present in the Internet. Routing protocols were devised with this infrastructure as the assumed norm; this infrastructure is not necessarily the case for private networks, however.

4.2.1   Frame Relay

The most popular private Link-layer network infrastructure relies on frame relay [4-1]. Frame relay carrier service offerings have boomed in the 1990s for several reasons: The technology is inexpensive, flat-rate-priced, distance price-insensitive, and connection-oriented, so that carriers can offer logical circuits similar to their historical private-line offerings. The last characteristic ensures that carrier salespeople can sell frame relay easily and service personnel can manage it, as frame relay offerings are similar to selling leased lines. The result has been a ubiquitous, inexpensive service available from many carriers, whose market in the 1990s has experienced double-digit annual growth rates.

Frame relay is a relatively simple Link-layer protocol that takes advantage of the low error rates present on modern fiber land-line networks. Frame relay simply discards bad frames and lets the Transport layer (Layer 4) provide the recovery mechanism. The Link layer can therefore remain simple and have short delays.

Addresses in frame relay are called data link connection identifiers (DLCIs). Each DLCI identifies a data link and is 10 bits long, so there are 1,024 possible DLCIs in a frame relay network.

DLCIs are used to form permanent virtual circuits (PVCs) and switched virtual circuits (SVCs). A PVC provides a "virtual" logical circuit, as opposed to an actual physical circuit. Multiple PVCs (and/or SVCs) may occupy one physical link, as shown in Figure 4-4, multiplexing multiple kinds of data streams together. In the figure, three PVC connections (DLCIs) between Los Angeles and New York use one physical link.

Frame relay includes a feature called the Committed Information Rate (CIR) that is designed to accommodate bursts in an efficient manner. The CIR is the rate that is "guaranteed" to a particular subscriber on a particular DLCI. The physical port to the subscriber is usually set at a rate higher than the CIR. If the data source tries to send data at a rate exceeding the CIR, the network attempts to send the excess burst on a best-effort basis. One physical link can include multiple DLCIs, each one boasting its own CIR.

IP multicast can be deployed by setting up appropriate PVCs between a sender and its receivers. Because the flat-rate pricing scheme for frame relay is usually not distance-sensitive, it does not matter whether a PVC remains local or spans the country. As a result, the easy way to arrange multicast PVCs is a "star" configuration, with the sender at the center of the star and all receivers located exactly one hop away from the sender, as shown in Figure 4-5. This configuration does not provide bandwidth savings, however, as the multicast replication occurs at the source, reducing the rate at which the multicast traffic can be sent by a factor of $1/N$, where N is the number of remote locations. It does provide a benefit in significantly offloading the processing and input/output (I/O) resources of the sending server.

To provide efficient IP multicast support in frame relay networks, the underlying frame relay PVCs should be a "hub and spoke" design with a router overlay, as shown in Figure 4-6. In this configuration, particular remotes act as "hubs" that then "spoke" out to other remotes in the nearby area. This design

FIGURE 4-4
Multiple PVCs on one physical link

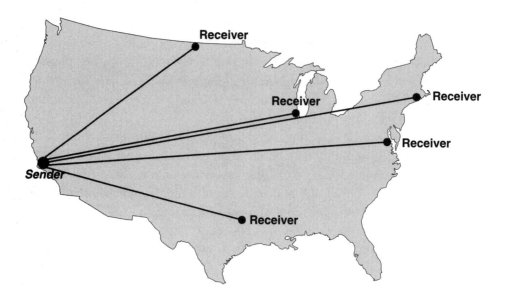

FIGURE 4-5

Frame relay star configuration

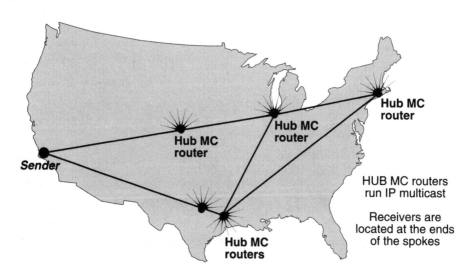

FIGURE 4-6

Frame relay hub and spoke with router overlay for IP multicast

requires more hops to reach a particular location, but it distributes the replication in the network to the multiple hubs rather than keeping it all at the central site. This architecture greatly reduces the bandwidth constriction at the central site and takes full advantage of IP multicast over the frame relay network. In essence, the network becomes more mesh-like and begins to resemble the characteristics of the Internet, albeit on a much smaller scale.

Thus the design of the frame relay network greatly affects how much benefit a multicast IP router overlay can provide for multicast services. Frame relay provides logical links; if it is set up as a meshed network, it can support multicast very effectively. For example, suppose it is desired to send a multicast stream of 56 Kbps from the sender to receivers located off the hub multicast routers in Figure 4-6. Two PVCs of 56 Kbps need to be supported at the sender to the hub multicast routers. The routers replicate the stream to multiple 56 Kbps links to the subnets where the receivers are located. In this example, twice the bandwidth of the transmission is needed, independent of the number of receivers.

If the architecture takes the form of the simple star network shown in Figure 4-5, network efficiency suffers. For N receivers, the bandwidth at the sender needs to be $N \times 56$ Kbps. The only efficiency gain occurs with the load on the sending host, which needs to send the transmission only once instead of N times.

4.2.2   X.25

WAN Link-layer protocols developed in the 1970s had to cope with links having bit error rates of 10^{-6}, or 1 in 1 million. In this environment, the best strategy was for the Link layer to correct errors. A good example of such error correction is Link Access Protocol B (LAP B), the Link layer associated with X.25. LAP B uses an Automatic Repeat reQuest (ARQ) error correction scheme, where all frames are acknowledged as good or bad and bad ones are retransmitted. The result is a complex Link layer with significant delay. X.25 networks are rapidly being phased out in favor of frame relay or other, more modern WAN Link layer technologies. Nevertheless, a number of X.25 networks remain in operation.

X.25 has PVCs and SVCs similar to those in frame relay. Networks can be structured in the same way as frame relay networks are, and the same issues apply. If the network is constructed in a "hub and spoke" type of meshed network, a multicast IP overlay can provide significant multicast services and savings in bandwidth. If the network is constructed as a star, bandwidth is constricted at the sender, just as it is with frame relay.

4.2.3   Switched Multimegabit Data Service (SMDS)

SMDS is a public data-link service that is provided by regional and long-distance carriers [4-2]. This connectionless, high-speed terrestrial service was originally developed by Bellcore to enable local exchange carriers to provide high-speed connectivity between LANs in a metropolitan area — for example, LANs at branch offices and factories within a single company. It later evolved to offer lower-speed service and was extended to cover the entire country. SMDS service is offered for data at rates between 1.544 Mbps and 44.736 Mbps over T1 and T3 circuits. An SMDS network acts like a high-speed LAN backbone, allowing packets from one LAN to flow to any other LAN. The LANs are located in the customers' offices; the SMDS cloud resides in the telephone company's offices.

SMDS network addresses are basically telephone numbers. They consist of a 4-bit code followed by the standard components of a telephone number: country code, area code, and subscriber number. The customer may be assigned a special number that represents a list of SMDS telephone numbers; any packet sent to that number is delivered to all members of that list.

In the United States, only MCI offers nationwide SMDS services; in Germany, Deutsche Telekom offers a nationwide SMDS service called Datex-M. SMDS is designed to accommodate bursty traffic; as long as the average data rate remains below an agreed-upon value, SMDS will make a best-effort attempt to deliver traffic to the correct destination.

As noted earlier, SMDS is a connectionless service, meaning that a physical or logical connection need not be established before sending data. All packets sent on the network are available for reception by all nodes; that is, SMDS appears as a wide-area shared LAN. As a result, this service supports multicast natively, and IP multicast as an overlay is easily accomplished.

SMDS carriers usually charge for the service based on SMDS traffic as measured by an SMDS switch inside the network. For IP multicast traffic, groups will be set up at the IP layer so that not all nodes receive all IP multicast traffic. The user will then be charged for traffic inside the SMDS network cloud that is not received, however—a situation that is unacceptable to most customers.

One possible solution is to create a number of multicast groups at the SMDS level and then map particular IP multicast groups to them. The resulting groups are therefore relatively static, as SMDS groups are provisioned like frame relay.

SMDS is less popular than frame relay in both U.S. and international markets, and its market share is declining.

4.2.4   Asynchronous Transfer Mode (ATM)

ATM is a cell-switching technology that was originally devised by telephone carriers to support multiple sources of traffic (that is, digitized voice, video, and data) at very high speeds [4-3]. Traffic is broken into constant-size, 53-byte cells, and different adaptation layers are used with those cells to handle different traffic types.

There were two primary motivations for developing cell switching technology:

1. Cell multiplexing means that the basic fabric can support multiplexing of data sources that have timeliness requirements, such as voice and video.

2. With fixed-length cells, the switching fabric is easily implemented in hardware, allowing very-high-speed switching engines to be built.

Switches take the place of routers in ATM networks. Today, ATM is often used as a very-high-speed backbone by carriers—that is, for T3 and greater—and frame relay often runs on top of it. The most common speed for an ATM network is 155 Mbps, but some networks operate at speeds of 622 Mbps (four 155 Mbps channels). The technology is scalable and can support gigabit speeds via the use of multiple channels.

Like frame relay and X.25 networks, ATM networks are connection-oriented; a connection must be set up before messages can be sent. Connections are established by using either PVCs or SVCs. When a PVC or SVC is established, a specific physical route is selected from the source to the destination, and all the switches along that pathway create table entries so that they can route packets accordingly. After a PVC or SVC connection is set up, all messages for that connection follow the same path to the destination.

Like frame relay, ATM supports one-to-many multicast at the Link layer. Where frame relay multicast is strictly a PVC, however, standards efforts in ATM are being directed at enabling a sender of a multicast group to establish a point-to-multipoint SVC between itself and a set of known receivers, via UNI 3.0/3.1 signaling mechanisms. If the SVC sender-based, Link-layer multicast service in ATM can be effectively mapped to receiver-based, Network-layer IP multicast, then IP multicast should be able to use an ATM infrastructure.

A number of architectural issues must be overcome before this goal can be achieved. In ATM, the sender sets up and tears down the multicast PVC; in IP multicast, groups are set up, changed, and torn down at the initiation of receivers, and the sender need not know the identities of the receivers. Additionally, the

ATM multicast model is only one-to-many, whereas many-to-many applications (for conferencing, for example) are a part of the IP multicast model.

ATM incorporates the concept of a Multicast Address Resolution Server (MARS) [4-4], which acts as a registry to associate IP multicast group addresses with the ATM interfaces representing the group's members. Essentially, MARS resolves the architectural differences in the approaches to multicast taken by ATM and IP.

Two different approaches for supporting multicast IP with ATM-level multicasting are provided: meshes of point-to-multipoint PVCs or use of ATM-level multicast servers (MCS). The latter architecture is very similar to the configuration of multicast frame relay.

Each MARS manages a "cluster" of ATM-attached end points. Each IP subnet must be supported by a different MARS, which then defines the end points in the "cluster" as the end points in the subnet to which that MARS belongs.

Support for multicast IP over ATM and MARS is described in detail in RFC 2022 [4-5]. This protocol is on standards track within the IETF.

In today's practice, however, ATM is primarily used as a backbone protocol by carriers at OC3 speeds (155 Mbps) and greater. Most usually, frame relay — another Link-layer protocol — serves as the interface to ATM so that the Network layer of IP rarely connects to ATM directly. Thus, except for some specialized high-speed networks, support for multicast IP over ATM directly is a configuration that remains relatively rare, although its use is likely to grow in the future as network speeds increase.

4.2.5 Virtual Private Networking (VPN)

"Virtual private networks" is a term created by service providers to describe offerings where they carve out a part of the Internet to create a private network for an organization. The carved-out private network is "firewalled" from the rest of the Internet via access control and tunneling of the private traffic.

VPNs are considered an emerging market for ISPs, and many companies now offer VPN services. These networks represent a convenient way for an organization to gain wide geographical coverage without building its own private network. The organization's "road warrior" employees may connect to the private network by simply making a local telephone call in any location throughout the world.

Because VPNs are based on the network infrastructure of an ISP's part of the Internet or a separate IP network that excludes general Internet traffic, the network is likely to be a highly meshed, routed type (like the Internet itself). Thus the ISP simply turns on multicast services in the routers. ISPs that offer multicast are therefore likely to offer this feature with their VPN service as well.

The VPN is the Internet vehicle where multicast services are likely to emerge first.

4.2.6   Two-Way Satellite (VSAT)

VSAT stands for very-small-aperture terminals. VSAT antennas are typically 0.9 to 1.8 meters in diameter. VSAT services represent a significant source of data network services around the world. These offerings are available as either one-way or two-way service. This section discusses two-way service, illustrated in Figure 4-7.

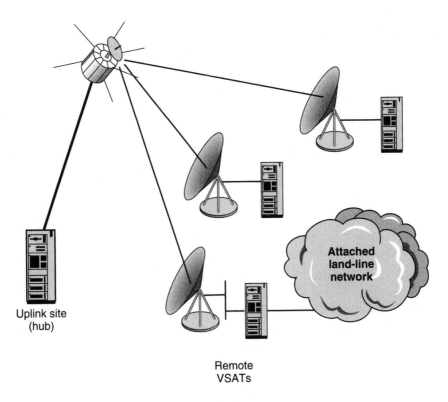

FIGURE 4-7

VSAT network

A VSAT network consists of a central hub ("uplink site") and many remote VSATs that can link directly to a host or connect to a LAN that may, in turn, connect to a land-line network. Many VSAT network services provide native TCP/IP service, including support for multicast IP, eliminating the need for external routers. The multicast routing function in a VSAT is quite simple, as the satellite network is by nature a broadcast network. If a group member is present at a site, the VSAT forwards packets destined for that group; if not, it blocks those packets.

VSAT networks are most often deployed in organizations which must support a central headquarters and many remote sites—for example, field offices or retail stores. Many VSAT carriers, in fact, claim that VSAT is more cost-effective than a land-line alternative when the number of remotes exceeds 100.

The uplink site (hub) is most often set up near the data center of the central headquarters, although it could also be accessed via a land-line link from a faraway site. Similarly, VSATs do not have to be physically at the same place as the remote facility, although that set-up is the normal case.

Some VSAT carriers offer a service in which multiple organizations that are located at the same facility—such as retail stores in a mall—share the network, reducing the cost to any one of them.

The back channel from the remote to the uplink (hub) almost always operates at a lower data rate than the forward (multicast) direction from the uplink to the VSATs. In many instances, the back channels may not be permanently assigned but rather can be switched on demand. This configuration is often called Demand Assignment Multiple Access (DAMA). DAMA channels are accessed by contention; the first VSAT with data receives access to the channel, which is then released when data demand ceases. This configuration makes sense when the flow of data sent to the remotes greatly exceeds data flow in the opposite direction.

VSAT services use geostationary satellites—that is, satellites in fixed positions above the Earth. Geostationary satellites reside approximately 22,600 miles (36,000 kilometers) above the Earth, resulting in a significant round-trip network delay of more than 0.5 second simply because of the speed of light. Some multicast applications that require low latency may not be able to handle this delay. Additionally, VSAT is most naturally suited for one-to-many multicast applications, with the source of transmission at the uplink site. Many-to-many applications, such as conferencing and network games, would need to transmit from the uplink; although this transmission is possible, it is not a natural fit for VSAT services.

VSAT networks are the infrastructure through which most multicast applications have been implemented in real-world production environments. For example, the "Big Three" automobile companies (General Motors, Ford, and Chrysler) have all implemented VSAT dealer networks and are using reliable multicast applications to distribute software and business data to their thousands of dealers.

VSAT networks will continue to be a natural network infrastructure to support multicast services.

4.2.7 Hybrid One-Way Satellite Overlay to Land-Line Routed Networks

One-way VSAT systems are commonly used today for broadcast TV distribution, providing service to more than nine million homes in the United States as of May 1998. Digital television broadcasting by satellite has even greater penetration in Europe, where its growth is driven by the relatively recent adoption of Digital Video Broadcast (DVB) [4-6] standards. The equipment and antennas are inexpensive (on the order of a few hundred dollars), and one-way VSAT antennas are smaller than their two-way counterparts.

The acceptance of this technology opens up the prospect of using this infrastructure to send data as well. This service is already being offered by some satellite carriers, such as Hughes Network Systems with its DirecPC.

By working with land-line networks, it could potentially lead to a hybrid satellite–land-line solution that uses the one-way satellite strictly for multicast delivery of data and the land-line network for unicast traffic. As shown in Figure 4-8, the land-line network can be the Internet or any other network, private or public, as long as it supports the TCP/IP suite.

This hybrid approach shows much promise for implementation of multicast services quickly and without risk in today's Internet, as well as in private networks. It also holds promise for being cost-effective and it can reach rural areas effectively. The satellite data channel used for multicast delivery can operate at high speeds as well, offering high performance to the user.

Note that the land-line connection could be a dial-up connection to the Internet. The dial channel can handle the administrative traffic needed by any multicast application sent over the satellite channel as well as for any requests from the user (for example, a Web browser on a host).

This configuration can also accommodate certain many-to-many applications, as shown in Figure 4-9. The satellite delay is now only in one direction, making it less onerous to applications. Figure 4-9 shows two sending sites and two receiving sites for clarity, but sending and receiving sites could easily be

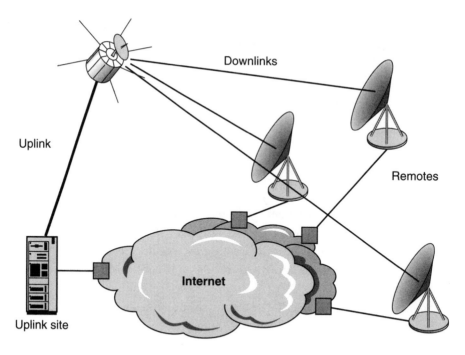

FIGURE 4-8

One-way satellite overlay to land-line internet

combined to permit collaborative multicast applications. Multicast packets are sent via tunneling through a non-multicast-enabled Internet to the satellite up-link site, where a multicast router exposes the multicast packet and forwards it to the satellite for multicast distribution. At recipient sites, the local multicast router forwards the multicast packets to the local subnetwork if any multicast group members are present. Unicast packets destined to return to the source may be sent normally over the land-line Internet.

A working group in the IETF, UniDirectional Link Routing (UDLR) [4-7], has recently been formed to make sure that the routing protocols can automatically cope with one-way satellite overlays. Routing protocols assume the link is bidirectional, whereas this configuration is viewed by routing protocols as unidirectional. The current UDLR proposals would create tunnels back to the source, thereby allowing the routing protocols to operate without change. The UDLR working group, however, views this strategy as a temporary approach to

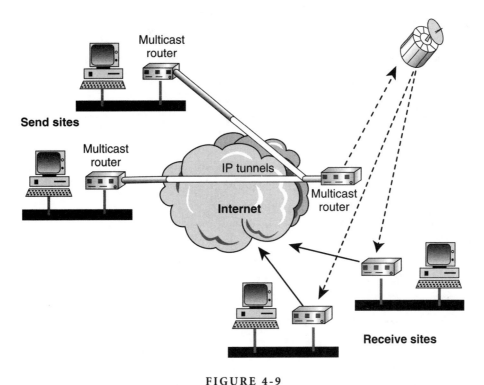

FIGURE 4-9

One-way satellite overlay — many-to-many multicast

the upgrade of the routing protocols. Cisco Systems recently developed some experimental software to change the multicast routing protocols to deal with this environment and offered it to interested operators of one-way satellite overlay networks in April 1998 for testing. A recent paper [4-8] also suggests that the CBT multicast routing protocol might be adapted to handle this network infrastructure.

In the meantime, this network infrastructure needs to implement static multicast routes in its routers to be operational.

Table 4-1 shows how inexpensive this approach can be on a recurring basis. The costs shown are per-month recurring expenses, which are independent of the number of remote sites. The cost per site drops as the number of remote sites increases.

TABLE 4-1

ONE-WAY SATELLITE RECURRING COSTS

Data Rate	Price/Month	Price/Receiver (100)	Price/Receiver (1,000)
38.4 Kbps	$8,746	$87.46	$8.75
56 Kbps	$9,546	$95.46	$9.55
64 Kbps	$9,746	$97.46	$9.75
128 Kbps	$10,746	$107.46	$10.75
256 Kbps	$13,746	$137.46	$13.75
512 Kbps	$16,746	$167.46	$16.75
1.0 Mbps	$22,246	$222.46	$22.25
1.5 Mbps	$33,846	$338.46	$33.85
2 Mbps	$42,846	$428.46	$42.85

SOURCE: Microspace Corporation.

4.2.8   Future High-Speed Satellite Data Infrastructures

Although the systems will not come online until after the year 2000, we would be remiss if we did not discuss the new low-orbit Earth satellite data systems being planned for deployment early in the next century. A number of projects have been proposed, though many will not obtain financing and probably will not happen. Before late May 1998, there were three prominent systems that appeared well financed and likely to be deployed: Teledesic and Celestri from the United States, and SkyBridge from Europe. As of late May 1998, however, Celestri has joined forces with Teledesic, and Motorola, the prime backer of Celestri, will become a minority owner in Teledesic and will supply much of the equipment needed for the system.

Teledesic is backed by Craig McCaw, the cellular multimillionaire who serves as the company's chairman, and Bill Gates, the Microsoft billionaire. Teledesic also has the support of Boeing Corporation. With the May announcement, Teledesic now has the backing of Motorola.

Teledesic [4-9] is planning to spend $9 billion (yes, billion!) to launch 288 low-Earth-orbit (LEO) satellites and is scheduled to be in service by 2002. LEO satellites—unlike conventional geostationary (GEO) satellites, which maintain a constant position relative to the Earth—rotate around the Earth in orbit and require hand-offs to other satellites to provide constant coverage to a particular area of the Earth, as shown in Figure 4-10. Essentially, a data network operates in the sky, continually passing off data to other satellites to assure coverage is distributed throughout the area as needed. One major advantage of LEO satellite systems is their lack of delay, as the satellites remain close to the Earth. They also require smaller Earth stations, as less signal attenuation occurs. This advantage is balanced by the considerable added complexity of running a network in orbit. Additionally, the satellites will need to be replaced more often because of the friction caused by the atmosphere at lower altitudes.

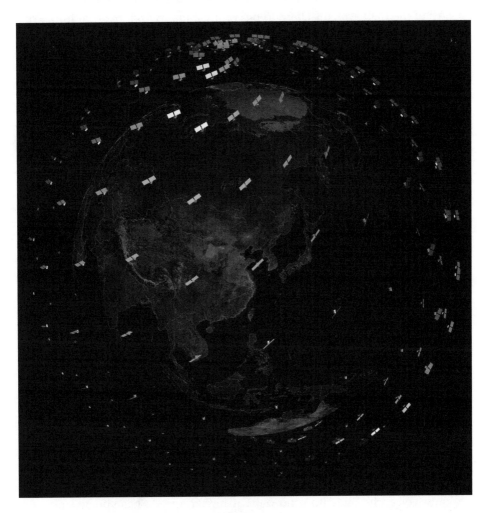

FIGURE 4-10

Teledesic system: 288 polar orbit LEO satellites. *(Courtesy of Teledesic Corporation.)*

Data rates can reach 64 Mbps on the downlink (to the user) and 2 Mbps on the uplink (from the user). It is too early to determine exactly what this service will look like and who the target customers will be. Like GEO satellites, however, this service is in a perfect position to offer multicast services, as it is broadcast in nature.

The SkyBridge project is being led by France's Alcatel, with support and investment from Loral, Toshiba, Mitsubishi, Sharp, and the French space agency. The system consists of 64 LEO satellites. Like the other candidates, SkyBridge is targeting high-speed broad-band services using IP and Internet access and can easily support multicast. Service introduction is planned for 2001.

All of the LEO systems claim to be complementary to terrestrial infrastructure, providing broad-band access to areas with low and medium population density and emerging countries where land-line infrastructures are skimpy or largely nonexistent.

A less expensive, nonsatellite approach involves High-Altitude, Long-Endurance (HALE) platforms [4-10]. This type of project is exemplified by the plans of Sky Station International, a U.K. company. Its system consists of solar-powered blimps that reside in the lower stratosphere and hover over high-density population areas (that is, cities) and provide high-speed, broad-band data services to the city. The zeppelins gain power from solar panels and use a propulsion system to remain in fixed positions relative to the Earth.

The HALE platform has the advantage of being much less expensive than a LEO system, while keeping many of its advantages, such as low latency. The Sky Station system is scheduled for service availability early next century, with data service transmission rates ranging from 64 Kbps to 2 Mbps. Like satellite systems, this system is ideally poised to offer multicast services.

4.3 COPING WITH THE "LAST MILE"

The "last mile" has historically been a constriction point for data distribution. The "last mile" refers to local distribution from the closest carrier point of presence (POP) to the actual facility using the service—that is, a business, home, or other organization. Typically, these local connections are made with twisted-pair telephone wires that are strung from the telephone company's central office to buildings. Because these twisted-pair wires were originally designed to handle only voice, the quest to send data at higher speeds has spurred research intended to enable the twisted-pair wires to handle higher-speed data cost-effectively to provide alternative last-mile solutions.

This issue has relevance to multicast infrastructure as well. Often the multicast application requires a minimum bandwidth to be effective. Other multicast applications would like to include "road warriors" in groups (that is, people with laptop computers who travel and connect to the network via dial-up lines). Even small offices may use some kind of switched connection if their traffic patterns indicate relatively small traffic flows concentrated at particular times.

4.3.1 High-Speed Permanent Links

Two widely touted technologies have been developed to speed up the last-mile connection without incurring huge infrastructure upgrade costs. One uses the cable plant for data as well as broadcast television; the other, Digital Subscriber Line (DSL) technology, enables high-speed data transmission over normal twisted-pair telephone lines on an inexpensive basis.

Data over the cable infrastructure uses cable modems to send data over a broadcast cable television channel (6 Mhz) at speeds of a few megabits per second, although the modems are often set to have asymmetric rates. The cable plant is then connected to the Internet at an upstream point. The cable plant also often needs to be upgraded to be bidirectional, as its normal mode is unidirectional only.

An example of this use of cable is the @Home network [4-11], where a new backbone independent of the Internet was put in place with strategic connections to the main Internet. In effect, @Home has become a new ISP, using the cable plant for the last mile to deliver high-speed data services at a low price to subscribers. @Home has implemented multicast services in its network from the start.

The telephone carriers have responded with xDSL technology, which supports high-speed transmission over twisted-pair wires. Many flavors of this technology exist, all of which are modem techniques, with much history. The first is simply DSL, a modem standard for basic-rate ISDN, tansmitting data at 160 Kbps in both directions. The next in the family is HDSL, which delivers T1 or E1 (1.544 Mbps or 2.048 Mbps, respectively) over two twisted-pairs. For connection to the Internet, ADSL is touted as the premier offering. ADSL is asymmetrical and is capable of achieving speeds of 1.5 Mbps to 9 Mbps downstream and 15 Kbps to 640 Kbps upstream over two twisted-pair wires. ADSL trials are now under way, and HDSL and DSL are in common use today.

Both cable and xDSL promise to deliver high-speed data services to business and home consumers at low cost—a positive feature given that many streaming multicast applications require a minimum bandwidth. Keep in mind, however, that both of these techniques deliver data at asymmetric rates.

In contrast, the architecture of today's Internet assumes symmetric rate channels everywhere.

4.3.2   Switched Links

Two other last-mile technologies are switched services: basic-rate ISDN and dial modem via a dial call. To receive multicast service, any switched service must have a connection in place. There is another potential complication as well — many ISPs arrange to supply the host with an IP address at the time of connection using the Dynamic Host Control Protocol (DHCP). Thus a particular host may not have a semi-permanent IP address with which it can be identified. This issue can pose a challenge for some multicast applications that exert centralized control over groups, as hosts cannot be identified by IP address.

Basic-rate ISDN includes three channels, "2B + D." Each "B" channel is one DSO in telephony nomenclature, capable of supporting data transmission rates of 56 Kbps or 64 Kbps. Inverse multiplexers may be used to combine the two "B" channels with two ISDN calls to provide a total speed reaching 128 Kbps. The "D" channel is an ever-present 16 Kbps signaling channel that is used for call set-up and other signaling traffic. Because the "D" channel is always available, it can transfer information not related to telephony at any time.

Figure 4-11 shows this configuration. Low-speed traffic can also be sent over the "D" channel to advantage. For example, a low-speed multicast channel can be used to announce availability of content; when something of interest is found, "B"-channel calls are made to receive it.

This capability was recently touted by U.S. carriers that offered a new ISDN service called "Always On." "Always On" was announced by U.S. ISDN carriers

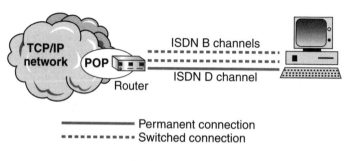

FIGURE 4-11

Basic-rate ISDN connection to host

in June 1997, with launch in the fourth quarter of 1997. It offers benefits to basic-rate ISDN users by providing a low-speed, permanent connection using the ISDN "D" channel.

"Always On" uses the packet data capability that is an integral part of the ISDN international standard. Over the "D" (signaling) channel of the ISDN line, the user establishes a packet connection to a remote LAN or an ISP. The user creates this bidirectional connection by logging on to a work-at-home computer and e-mail package. Once the connection is established, the user is online and can exchange packets with the remote network as required — to send and receive e-mail, for example.

When more information than can be handled by the 16 Kbps packet connection must be transferred, a circuit-switched connection (telephone call) is placed using one or both of the ISDN "B" channels. This connection can be made automatically and without user intervention and permits data to move at speeds ranging as high as 128 Kbps. Once the data transfer is complete, the circuit-switched connection is dropped and the user remains online via the "D" channel.

Dial modem connection to networks is one of the most common techniques for establishing a remote host connection to a network, whether private or public. This technology's speed capability has increased so that 56 Kbps modems are now available (although these modems are limited to connecting at the highest speed that the line can support, which is seldom as high as 56 Kbps). These speeds would definitely support many multicast applications. As mentioned previously, however, to receive them the host needs to be connected; if it is not connected, no mechanism exists for notification of multicast events.

In the United States, local calls are often charged at a flat rate, meaning that no cost penalty is imposed for long connections. Consequently, many users simply leave their dial call connected for long periods of time, but this approach is not a general solution to the multicast notification problem. Another approach would rely on scheduled multicast events at the time the dial call is initiated from the remote host, ensuring that the host is connected when the session starts.

4.4 SUMMARY AND CONCLUSIONS

As this chapter revealed, various network infrastructures often used in private networks can accommodate multicast services with different levels of ease.

Many of these infrastructures, however, are not the same as those found in today's Internet, on which researchers have focused their multicast research efforts. In particular, satellite offers a very simple approach to providing multicast services thanks to its inherent broadcast nature.

Multiple billions of dollars are planned to be spent on some revolutionary wireless systems in the sky, with scheduled service availability in the period 2000–2005. These new projects promise high-speed data services with global coverage directly to the facility, bypassing the last-mile bottleneck. These systems inherently can support multicast just as GEO satellite systems do, but they do not have the latency issues of the latter systems.

Other new technologies besides satellite are offering asymmetric services, including cable and ADSL, a new model that differs from the present-day Internet. Last-mile links, especially when switched, also add some complications. All of these issues, however, are being addressed and solved.

Now that we have discussed networking issues in Chapters 3 and 4, we now consider multicast applications and their importance to network-based applications.

REFERENCES

[4-1] Information on frame relay can be found at the Frame Relay Forum Web site at http://www.frforum.com.

[4-2] Klessig RW, Tesink K. SMDS Wide-Area Data Networking with Switched Multimegabit Data Service. Englewood Cliffs, NJ: Prentice Hall, 1995.

[4-3] General information on ATM can be found at the ATM Forum Web site at http://www.atmforum.com.

[4-4] Talpade R, Ammar M. Multicast Server Architectures for MARS-based ATM Multicasting. RFC 2149, May 1997.

[4-5] Armitage G. Support for Multicast over UNI 3.0/3.1 based ATM Networks. RFC 2022, November 1996.

[4-6] A background document about DVB can be found at http://www.m4.com/about/dvb.html.

[4-7] Information on the UDLR working group in IETF can be found at http://www.ietf.org/html.charters/udlr-charter.html.

[4-8] Baras JS, Secka I. High Performance IP Multicasting over Wireless Satellite–Terrestrial Networks. Center for Satellite and Hybrid Communication Networks, Institute for Systems Research, University of Maryland, 1998.

[4-9] Information on Teledesic's LEO system can be found on the company's Web site at http://www.teledesic.com.

[4-10] Pelton J. Telecommunications for the 21st Century. *Scientific American*, April 1998: 81–85.

[4-11] Information about the @Home network can be found on the company's Web site at http://www.home.com.

5

REPLICATION, MIRRORING, AND CACHING

The Internet has experienced exponential growth since the late 1980s, with its expansion initially being fueled by e-mail and then by the World Wide Web, which started becoming significant in 1992. IDC estimated that 28 million people used the Internet worldwide in 1996, and that number continues to grow exponentially, with 175 million users predicted by 2001. New applications are emerging to exploit the Internet infrastructure, such as Internet telephony and Internet facsimile (fax), further fueling its growth. Telephony and facsimile are two services traditionally handled by the world's telephone systems that are being considered for the worldwide Internet because of the dramatically lower cost of using the Internet infrastructure rather than the world's telephone infrastructure.

Growth is also occurring in private networks (Intranets) and networks of multiple organizations (Extranets), largely based on the ease of use associated with Web technology. In fact, as pointed out in Chapter 4, virtual private networks, where an Internet service provider (ISP) carves a private network out of a piece of the Internet, are considered a huge potential emerging market by ISPs.

Any network with the explosive growth of the Internet and its derivatives can be expected to experience growing pains. Many articles have appeared in the trade press extolling problems with the Internet. "Cybercrawl," the "World Wide Wait," and other terms are less-than-complimentary names for the problems associated with clogged-up networks struggling to cope with the exponential growth of the Internet.

Today, the Internet and all other TCP/IP networks are structured as a classless network, so that all traffic has equal priority, and the network is designed so that all users of the network get their "fair" share of resources. Thus, it is not structured to offer differing levels of service, thereby allowing a higher-level service to avoid this congestion (although this issue is a hot area of research and new products are appearing to create multiple classes of service).

The historical solution to this growth has been simply to throw bandwidth at the problem. In the past, this tactic was cost-effective. For example, major upgrades to backbone bandwidth tying together major American universities were made in the United States in 1987, 1992, and 1996. In 1987, the backbone was upgraded from 56 Kbps to T1 (1.544 Mbps), a 24 times increase in bandwidth with an associated threefold increase in cost. In 1992, the backbone was upgraded from T1 to T3 (45 Mbps), a 28 times increase in bandwidth at a ninefold cost increase. In 1996, the backbone was increased from T3 to OC3 (155 Mbps), a 3 times increase in bandwidth for a 2.9-fold cost increase.

As these figures indicate, the days of simply throwing bandwidth at the problem are over. It is no longer cheaper to opt for this "quick fix" than to structure the network more intelligently.

More recently, the growth in the Internet, Intranets, and Extranets has been largely fueled by the growth of the Web. The Web has exploded because it is easy to author content; the presentation is flexible and users have the ability to tie together text, graphics, and even multimedia; hyperlinks provide a means to link to referenced material at the click of a mouse; and the browsers needed by users to access content from a PC have become free. Even the author's wife, a real estate agent, has her own home page and domain.

Some of the cybercrawl problems have been exacerbated by antiquated network architectures and inadequate protocols (particularly the HyperText Transport Protocol [HTTP], which is used for Web access) that were not originally designed to scale to large networks such as the Internet. HTTP is on its way to being significantly improved by HTTP/1.1, which adds pipelining of requests and allows downloading of multiple objects and pages with one TCP connection rather than requiring multiple parallel TCP connections.

The network architecture problem is illustrated in Figure 5-1. This figure shows a typical browser user located in Europe, where Internet usage is growing faster than in the United States.

Our hypothetical user, who resides in Stockholm, uses a Netscape browser. He logs on to his local ISP and launches this browser. By default, the browser connects to Netscape's home page in California's Silicon Valley. The request from the browser is then sent across the Atlantic Ocean over constricted undersea cable facilities (probably) to the east coast of the United States and then across the North American continent. The response with the content to be downloaded is sent to our Swedish user back across the North American continent and the Atlantic Ocean to Stockholm. If our user used a Microsoft browser, the same thing would happen, except that the destination would be Redmond, Washington, rather than Silicon Valley. Netscape and Microsoft are both in the top three Web sites based on "hits" — that is, the number of electronic visits — due to the default connections when the browser is launched.

This set-up is obviously very inefficient. Not only does it send excessive traffic over network backbones but it also provides poor response times for the user. Caching and replication technologies are being used to help bring content

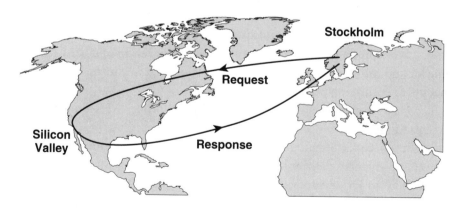

FIGURE 5-1

Web request-response

closer to the consumer so as to offload networks and servers and to reduce re-sponse times. Unfortunately, these proposals and implementations do not cur-rently use multicast technology, to their detriment.

5.1 CACHING AND REPLICATION: WHAT ARE THEY?

Caching is commonly used on local hosts by browsers. The browser user goes to a Web page that is pulled down by the browser and stored on that host's hard drive. The next time the user goes to that page, the browser pulls it off the local hard drive rather than going over the network, greatly reducing the response time, especially for larger blocks of data.

Network caching is the creation of network proxy servers that cache content based on demand. Under this scheme, multiple users may share the benefits from locally stored content, rather than just one user.

Mirroring or *replication*, in contrast, involves selection a priori of content to be replicated at other sites. In the early days of the Internet, File Transfer Proto-col (FTP) servers were commonly mirrored at multiple sites. Today, many large corporations have mirrored Web sites that serve international markets. Usually, the user must access the home site to find the location of the local site, as differ-ent locations often have different URLs.

5.1.1 Network Caching Systems

A great deal of research has focused on WAN caching. One of the earliest efforts to support caching in a WAN environment was the Domain Naming System (DNS) [5-1], the mechanism by which TCP/IP networks resolve names to IP ad-dresses. While not a general file or object cache, the DNS supports caching of name lookup results from server to server as well as from client to server, using timeouts to ensure cache consistency.

The Harvest cache system [5-2], funded by the Advanced Research Projects Agency (ARPA),* was the first to have a cache hierarchy. It uses timeouts for cache consistency—that is, after a timeout, the contents of the cache are deleted. Also, Harvest implements a general caching interface, allowing objects to be cached us-ing a variety of access protocols, such as FTP, Gopher, and HTTP. The Squid cache system [5-3] improved on Harvest and offers better performance.

---

*ARPA is now called the Defense Advanced Research Projects Agency (DARPA).

A new protocol, the Internet Cache Protocol (ICP), has recently been described [5-4]. ICP is a lightweight protocol used to find content from a mesh of caches. It has been applied to both the Harvest and Squid cache systems.

Network-based caches have been found to provide significant benefits in performance, based on the "hit" rate (that is, the number of requests from downstream users that can be satisfied by the cache versus from the source of content). Some studies have shown that the hit rate in today's network caching systems can approach 50%, resulting in significant performance boosts to users as well as significant reductions in network traffic.

Network caching is also becoming very popular in both public and private networks. A recent Forrester Report [5-5] surveyed *Fortune* 1000 companies and found that 54% deployed network caches today and 91% were planning to deploy network caches in two years. This finding suggests that this technology is destined to become pervasive. The primary reasons behind its success are its ability to cut down on network traffic and its advantages in improving performance for end users. For example, in the Forrester Report, an electronics company said deployment of network caches had reduced its network traffic by 30% to 40%.

The respondents in the report were also concerned about problems with network caching. If network caching is to realize its potential for greatly improving the performance of today's networks, these issues will need to be addressed.

As caching has been implemented primarily to improve performance for Web applications, it is worthwhile to review briefly the protocols used in the Web today and what is expected in the future. We will then describe how today's most common network caching systems work. Lastly, we will consider some of the issues with today's network caching systems and note how multicast technology can help solve these issues.

5.1.1.1   The Web

The simplicity of the Web model was one of the main reasons it succeeded. The Web model is based on URLs, HTML, and HTTP. A universal resource locator (URL) is the name and address of the site to be accessed from which an IP address is found using a DNS. Hypertext markup language (HTML) is the mechanism used to create Web content, and HTTP is the primary protocol used to transport content from a site to a user.

The Web was invented in 1990 by Tim Berners-Lee, a physicist from CERN, the European Laboratory for Particle Physics in Geneva, Switzerland. He envisioned it as a way to disseminate information more effectively within CERN. The Web exploded precisely because of this simplicity; creation of HTML documents is easy, hypertext links (first made available in commercial products from Apple Computer) embedded in content provide the means to link to a reference or other topic related to the subject matter via a URL, and HTTP is a simple protocol used to transport the content.

HTTP operates over TCP in the TCP/IP protocol stack, as shown in Figure 5-2. HTTP borrows heavily from other protocols; for example, it uses Multipurpose Internet Mail Extension (MIME) headers borrowed from e-mail.

The first version of HTTP (1.0) suffers from some limitations that are now being largely corrected in HTTP 1.1 [5-6]. The main issue is one of separate TCP connections for the transport of each object downloaded. A Web page consists of many objects—text, graphics, and even multimedia. In HTTP 1.0, each object requires a different TCP connection, even though the object may be very small (tens of bytes). This requirement creates excessive protocol overhead and places a greater burden on the server resources, and the TCP connection never gets out of slow-start mode (see Chapter 8 for an explanation of slow start); as a result, operation occurs at the slowest rate possible. Browsers have now evolved to download as many as four objects simultaneously with four separate TCP con-

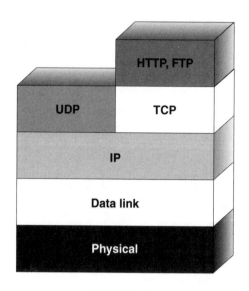

FIGURE 5-2

HTTP uses TCP

nections in an effort to improve performance within the constraints of HTTP 1.0. HTTP 1.1 pipelines requests and uses one TCP connection to download multiple objects, allowing the slow-start mode to hit a steady state for higher data rates and results in greatly reduced overhead.

Besides the limitations to today's HTTP, the network architecture issue illustrated in Figure 5-1 and excessive server load both contribute to congestion. Popular Web servers cannot be serviced with simply one server, so Web "clusters" are commonly employed to spread the load. Rather than distributing this load locally, it makes sense to spread it throughout the network to solve both the server congestion and network congestion issues simultaneously — hence, the desire for network replication and caching.

5.1.1.2 Today's Network Caching Systems

The first proxy network cache was created and used by CERN, where the Web originated. The CERN cache technology has been superseded by the Harvest cache, which was developed at the University of Colorado with ARPA funding. The Harvest system has been improved under a National Science Foundation (NSF) grant and is now known as the Squid cache.

Some commercial products have become available that are based on the Harvest or Squid cache. What follows is a description of the Harvest and Squid caches as well as the relatively new ICP, which is used by the Squid cache.

Harvest and Squid cache systems are organized into the hierarchy shown in Figure 5-3.

Desktop clients have browsers that are used to access the Web via HTTP or another supported protocol, such as FTP or Gopher. All commercial browsers have the ability to select a proxy, so that, depending on the configuration, all inquiries to the Web may go through the local proxy cache.

As the local proxy receives requests from desktop clients, it first checks whether the requests are for content that is cachable. A large class is not, such as requests requiring certain types of authentication, session-encrypted data, highly personalized responses, and certain types of database queries. When the proxy detects a noncachable request, it is forwarded directly to the content source for retrieval.

If the content is cachable, it is first checked for content in the local proxy; if the content is not found there, it requests the content from a *peer* — that is, a neighboring cache that is either a *parent* or a *sibling*. If a hit is detected from either peer, it retrieves the content from that cache, leading to a *resolved* hit. If a

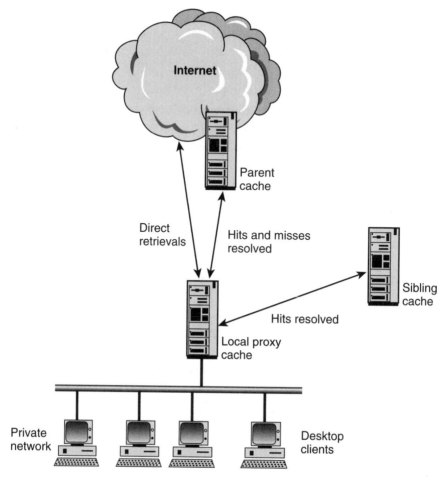

FIGURE 5-3

Harvest/Squid proxy cache hierarchy

miss occurs, the proxy sends the request to the parent and asks it to retrieve the content and forward it to the proxy, which in turn forwards the information to the requesting client. This situation is called "resolving the miss." Only parent peers in the cache hierarchy are allowed to resolve misses. Caches in the path of the retrieval store the content for possible use by a future client request.

Parent caches in the hierarchy are ideally located within or on the way to an ISP to be closer to the content source.

Cached content not only involves the content from the source Web site, but also includes meta-data that describe the content and DNS entries that are used to bind names to IP addresses. Examples of meta-data include tags that describe the size of the object retrieved, the time of its last change, and its expiration date.

Cached items are called *objects*. A particular Web page may consist of multiple objects, such as text and graphic images. Each graphic image is a separate, cachable object.

In Squid systems and some Harvest systems, the hierarchy of caches communicates using ICP. ICP is a lightweight protocol that can quickly determine in an efficient way whether any peer caches have requested objects and, if not, forward the request to the content source. This protocol can operate in a multicast mode to query peers simultaneously with one message; the ICP document, however, discourages use of multicast because no mechanism is available for the requester to determine whether the cache from which a requested object is received is valid.

Squid and Harvest allow for complex hierarchies. For example, it may be specified that a given neighbor be used only for a certain class of requests, such as URLs from a specific DNS domain. Similarly, parents may be configured to handle only certain domains so as to spread the load and avoid choke points.

Today's proxy caches do not depend on any cooperation with the content source. Web sites do not know whether requests come from client browsers directly or from an intermediary network proxy cache. Network proxy cache systems can thus be deployed without any change to today's rapidly growing number of Web sites.

This flexibility is both a benefit and a liability. The benefit is that network proxy cache systems can be deployed without any cooperation from the myriad Web sites already deployed; the liability is that the systems do not work all that well—or at least as well as they otherwise could. Let us now discuss some of these limitations.

Web pages are organized as a series of files, or objects. Each object can have attributes associated with it, including an expiration date or a mark to say that the object is noncachable. The network proxy cache intercepts all browser requests from downstream hosts, as previously described. As requests are made, the network cache first checks whether it has the object requested; if it does not, it sends a request to either another network cache or the source. The content received is stored in its network cache and sent along to the requesting host.

Although there is a mechanism to associate an expiration date with objects, most content on Web sites today does not bother to include one. As a result, the network cache rarely has knowledge of when content in its cache is stale. Instead, it simply uses a configurable timeout to age content and delete it after the timeout occurs. This process leads to the "stale content" problem.

5.1.1.3   Stale Content

As mentioned, Web objects seldom have expiration dates even though a mechanism is available to provide one. This situation is not necessarily a fault of the content creator; after all, he or she may not know when the content will change next. As a result, today's proxy caches must attempt to make educated guesses as to when to delete content.

Each object includes meta-data that describe when it was created. A common approach is to set the TTL of the cached object to be a percentage of the elapsed time from the content creation to the point when the object was cached; Harvest suggests 50%, for example, while Microsoft suggests 20%. This criterion is relatively arbitrary, however, and does not take into account the varying lifetimes of objects based on the object type.

A 1995 study [5-7] checked 4,600 HTTP objects distributed over 2,000 Web sites during a three-month period. It found that the mean lifetime of all objects was 44 days, though there was high variability based on type. HTML text objects averaged 75 days, image objects averaged 107 days, and unknown object types averaged 27 days. More than 28% of the objects were updated at least every 10 days, and 1% of the objects were updated dynamically. It is likely that today's objects change more frequently, as the Web has now become a strategic marketing and selling tool for many companies, and they must change content often to keep visitors interested. Consequently, TTL parameters will need to become increasingly shorter to reduce the probability of stale content. The flip side is that this system reduces the effectiveness of caching. In fact, some Web sites mark their content as uncachable to ensure that the content is never presented in a stale form.

A second possible approach involves "polling," where the cache periodically polls the Web site to determine whether the content is stale by using the HTTP "if-modified-since" request. This header field indicates that the Web server should return the requested object only if the object has changed since the specified date. This technique could potentially help the stale content problem, but the timing of polls remains an issue. Should it be based on object type? If the timing is made quite short so as to minimize stale content, it can generate considerable traffic back to the content source. Nevertheless, this approach is an improvement on simple guesswork.

It should be pointed out that local client caches use the HTTP "if-modified-since" command to check on content when the browser "Reload" (Netscape) or "Refresh" (Microsoft) button is activated.

To be fail-safe, an "invalidation" protocol is needed to ensure that cached copies never become stale. The server "pushes" out updates to caches when changes occur. The server must have knowledge of the caches with its content. Today's Web servers will need to change to carry out this work.

Reliable multicast can greatly help with this problem. A large number of proxy caches are likely to have content from a particular source. If they are all updated point-to-point from that source, it creates so much of a burden on the Web server and the network as to approach impracticality. It is much more effective to create a multicast group of those caches with content that needs updating and then send the update once. This approach saves not only server resources, but also network resources. It also means that all caches can be updated simultaneously, essentially eliminating the "stale content" problem.

5.1.1.4   *"Flushing" Algorithms (The "Garbage Collection" Problem)*

A problem related to stale content occurs with flushing, sometimes called "garbage collection." Storage is finite at the network cache. If cached content fills up the storage before some is deleted based on some staleness criteria, then a flushing algorithm is employed to create room for new requests.

Most flushing algorithms are either first-in-first-out or based on hits. With first-in-first-out, the oldest content is flushed first, without regard to any other parameters. With the hit algorithm, content with the least number of hits to the cache is flushed first, independent of age. Both of these strategies have limitations.

A recent paper [5-8] suggested a different algorithm to improve performance. It referenced a 1995 study [5-7] that analyzed the sizes of objects transferred over the Internet, which determined that most objects were actually quite small, in the range of 256 to 768 bytes. Another 1995 study [5-9] indicated that a small number of large objects, although they constituted only 1% of the object population requested, accounted for 28% of the data requested. The proposed algorithm suggested weighting the size of the object as well as how many hits it received to determine when to flush, suggesting it is more expensive to flush larger objects than smaller ones.

The object sizes have likely increased both for the smaller ones and the larger ones since these studies were conducted, but large objects still probably constitute a small percentage of the number of objects requested but a large percentage of the traffic.

5.1.1.5 *"Hit" Statistics*

Another major problem involves hit statistics and other information that is gathered about Web visitors. Many companies make money from advertising on their Web sites, and the amount they can charge depends on the number of "hits" recorded. Hits are equivalent to magazine subscriptions or TV viewership; the more hits occurring, the higher the price that can be charged to advertisers. Hits to network caches are lost, giving the Web host an undercount that can be substantial and which can mean less revenue to Web sites that include advertising. This problem explains why some sites mark their content as noncachable; they do not want their hit statistics to be lost.

It has been proposed to create a mechanism [5-10] to forward hit statistics to the content source and sample the hits to provide an estimate of their number. The latter technique is equivalent to the Nielsen ratings of television shows used to discover viewership for the purpose of determining popularity and thereby setting prices for advertising in the television medium.

5.1.1.6 *Security Issues*

Some observers have expressed concerns that network proxy caches offer significant chances for security breaches. Centralized caches of Web pages could potentially present a centralized target for hacking that could be vulnerable to outside alteration without permission of the source site. Secure sessions, however, pass through to the source and remain unaffected. Although invalid data could be inserted by an unscrupulous Web operator, this problem is no worse than the case with DNS servers; you have to trust the people in ISPs and other institutions operating proxy caches.

Of greater concern may be the possible misuse of cached statistical data. The information privacy policies of the originating Web sites mean nothing if the hit data collected by a cache regarding cached pages are under the sole control of that caching entity. This data can include sensitive information about sites and users viewing those pages and selecting particular links. Is the caching organization free to do whatever it likes with that information, such as sell it for marketing lists? Provide it for investigative purposes? Sell it to commercial databases? Although an originating site may have very strict policies regarding any information collected on sites or visitors to the Web server, a cache may have a completely different policy — or no policy at all. This area is one where new laws need to be drafted.

5.1.1.7 Copyright Issues

What about the copyrights of the original sites whose pages are cached? Can sites choose not to be cached? If so, will they suffer "access limitation" retaliation by some caches, making it difficult or impossible for users behind those caches to access those pages?

The question of copyrights was discussed in depth on the Squid mail list in August 1997. The conclusion reached was that automated operation of a Web cache may be considered like the operation of a long piece of cable; information is stored in it temporarily but is not considered "copied," much as multiple versions of television programs in transit in cable television systems are not copies. One respondent noted that draft German and possibly European Union legislation may address this issue. This situation represents a good example of the law not fully catching up to technology.

Proxy cache systems hold much promise for improving performance to the user in the form of shorter response times, while at the same time relieving strain on server and network resources. This advantage has been recognized by large companies as well; in the previously discussed Forrester Report [5-5], 91% of the respondents planned to deploy proxy caches in their networks. Still, significant issues must be resolved for this promise to be realized.

5.1.2 Commercial Network Proxy Cache Products

Despite the many unresolved issues, commercial companies are jumping into the market to offer network proxy caching products to the potentially huge market identified by the Forrester Report. Most of these products have been introduced only very recently. A brief survey of some of these products is given in this section.

The two giants of the Web, Netscape and Microsoft, both offer proxy Web caching products. The Netscape Proxy Server supports hierarchical caching and claims to have an "intelligent garbage collector" to manage the cache files. It is unclear whether this server is based on Harvest or Squid.

The Microsoft Proxy Server has specifications similar to those of the Netscape Proxy Server. Its documentation specifically mentions support for UDP protocols as well and also IPX.

Network Appliance, historically a company specializing in very efficient large network server products, bought Internet Middleware Corporation in March 1997; the latter firm was a start-up formed by some of the researchers who originally worked on the Harvest cache system and sought to commercialize Harvest. In June 1997, Network Appliance introduced NetCache, a product based on the work performed by Internet Middleware. Based on Harvest, NetCache uses ICP for communications between the hierarchy of network proxy caches. It also takes advantage of the efficient file management capabilities of the core set of Network Appliance technologies, resulting in high performance as measured by number of requests handled and response times.

In September 1997, Cisco Systems introduced a network proxy cache called the Cisco Cache Engine, which is based on Cisco's router hardware platform. The unique feature of Cisco's system is that a new protocol, the Cisco Web Cache Control Protocol, is supported initially in Cisco 7200 and 7500 series routers. Web requests can be automatically redirected to the Cache Engine rather than to the original site without configuring the browsers in the client, as shown in Figure 5-4.

The Cache Engine runs a real-time operating system rather than a general-purpose one, such as Windows NT or UNIX, to gain performance. Each Cache Engine supports up to 24 gigabytes (Gbytes) of storage, and a cluster of up to 32 can be created, giving a total of 768 Gbytes of storage.

A new company, Inktomi Corporation, introduced Traffic Server in October 1997. Traffic Server claims to be the first network proxy cache to support terabyte cache storage, based on "clusters" of proxy servers that add storage, CPU power, and fault tolerance. The Traffic Server product line is targeted at ISPs.

Mirror-Image, a Swedish company, offers a network proxy cache product called the FullSpeed Internet System. The network proxy cache at the edge of the organization's network also acts as an edge router. It intercepts client browser requests without requiring reconfiguration of browsers, in similar fashion to the Cisco Cache Engine system. Mirror-Image also uses polling to check on stale content rather than depending solely on "guessing."

5.1.2.1   Treatment of Clusters

Caches scale storage and gain computing power by creating clusters of hosts that act as a single virtual cache. The larger the cache size, the more likely it will

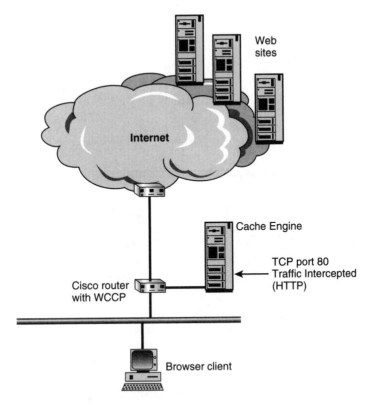

FIGURE 5-4

Cisco Cache director system

get a hit and not have to fetch from the source, as flushing is performed less often. Virtually all of the network proxy cache systems described previously include provisions for clusters of hosts to create a large system that appears as one entity. The same requirement applies to large Web sites that receive many hits.

A question then arises: How are queries directed to the individual hosts in the cluster? A proxy has the advertised IP address for the cluster and redirects it to an individual member of the cluster based on some load-balancing algorithm, as shown in Figure 5-5.

The most common algorithm used is simply a round robin, with each member of the cluster receiving requests on an equal basis.

A number of commercial products have been developed to address this problem in a more intelligent manner than via a round robin. Cisco Systems

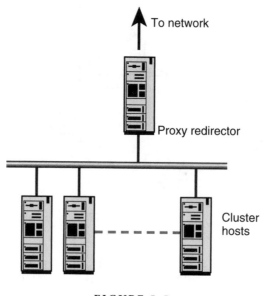

FIGURE 5-5
Cluster organization

offers LocalDirector; Checkpoint has ConnectControl; RND Networks, Ltd., has Web Server Director Pro; HydraWEB Technologies, Inc., has HydraWEB Load Manager; and F5 Labs, Inc., has BID/ip2. All offer algorithm choices from which the operator can choose for use in his or her network. Some are separate pieces of hardware—for example, the Cisco LocalDirector is based on Cisco's router hardware. Others operate on standard hosts such as Windows NT and UNIX.

If the cluster is a network cache, the individual hosts in the cluster will not usually have the same content in their cache as the other members of the cluster (if they did, the concept of a cluster is defeated!). Thus they often will need to use ICP to query other members of the cluster as a first step in the cache hierarchy if content does not reside on the host selected. In contrast, in a Web cluster, all hosts in the cluster are identical.

5.2 REPLICATION/MIRRORING

Another part of the network equation is replication/mirroring. Whereas caching moves content locally in response to a request, replication (mirroring) is totally server-driven. A content creator desires to make his or her content more accessible to consumers around the world and arranges mirrored servers in judicious spots for local consumption. In contrast to caching, replication ensures that all material from a particular site is duplicated. With caching, only the requested objects from a particular site are stored at the cache.

Replication is commonly used today by large Web sites. For example, both Netscape and Microsoft offer a number of international sites. These sites have different URLs, so a client must first connect to the home site to get the link to a local site. A number of other sites, such as that run by NASA, make mirrored sites accessible by first connecting to the home site.

It is especially desirable for busy Web sites to provide mirrored sites outside North America. The links usually involve undersea cable and typically are overloaded, providing an added incentive to develop local sites. Because the Internet is not multicast-enabled, these sites are currently kept in synchronization by a series of inefficient point-to-point transfers that limit the number of servers that can be mirrored. In some cases, it is desirable to create the mirrored sites with localized content, such as content in the local language. Often, a combination approach is used; parts of the site are localized, and other parts are the same as the content source.

It would be desirable to be able to find the closest mirrored site seamlessly, without identifying a different URL. For example, NASA has a large number of mirrored sites that are the same throughout the world, but you need to find the URL of the closest one to be able to access it.

Figure 5-6 shows the mirrored Mars Lander sites around the world. These sites, which are updated daily, provide large images of Mars. Another 30 or so mirror sites are located at corporations. Today, these sites are updated with point-to-point streams, so that the total update content is duplicated more than 50 times daily!

Reliable multicast can play a key role in this process. One daily transmission from the content source could be used to update all sites simultaneously, thereby keeping all sites in synchrony. In the example of the Mars Lander sites, the mirrored sites are situated worldwide and may be accessed most easily by satellite.

The next question is, "How do we make access to the nearest site seamless?" If mirrored sites are to become common, then the user should not have to take any special action, but should be automatically routed to the closest site or — even better — the closest site that is not "busy."

The first product on the market to address this issue was the Cisco DistributedDirector, which was introduced in March 1997. DistributedDirector

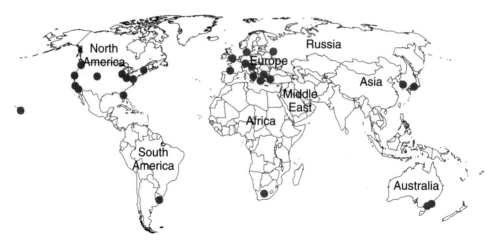

FIGURE 5-6

Mars Lander mirror sites worldwide

leverages routing table intelligence in the existing network infrastructure to redirect Internet traffic optimally to the most appropriate Web server. This "existing" network infrastructure, however, must consist of appropriately updated and configured Cisco routers.

Figure 5-7 shows the set-up for DistributedDirector. DistributedDirector can act as a DNS caching name server or as a HTTP session redirector on a per-host-name basis. When in DNS-caching mode, it returns an IP address of the best server to the client's local DNS. DistributedDirector maps a host name to several possible IP addresses and uses the intelligence of the Cisco router infrastructure (if so configured) to determine dynamically the best IP address to name binding for a given host name.

In HTTP-only mode, DistributedDirector masquerades as the requested Web server and returns an HTTP-specific status code that redirects client browsers to the topologically closest Web server.

DistributedDirector uses the Cisco proprietary Director Response Protocol (DRP) to query DRP server agents running in Cisco routers to obtain router protocol routing table metrics between the distributed servers and clients. These metrics are used to determine the appropriate server for the client request.

In Figure 5-7, two identical Web servers are located in San Jose and Brussels. Queries come to the DistributedDirector. If the query is from the client in Paris,

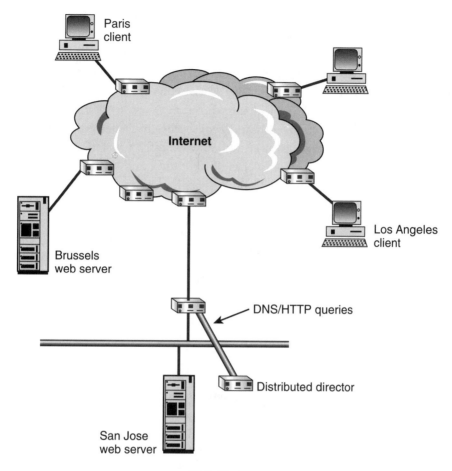

FIGURE 5-7
Cisco DistributedDirector system

it is redirected to the Brussels Web server. If it is from Los Angeles, it is redirected to the San Jose Web server.

Although DistributedDirector deserves recognition as first product to attempt to serve this market, it does have some shortcomings. For example, it appears overly complex and requires the use of a proprietary protocol and a changed router infrastructure, as well as a new box (the DistributedDirector).

Two other young companies also launched products in 1997 to solve this problem: Resonate, Inc., with its Global Dispatch Family, and Bright Tiger Technologies with its ClusterCATS.

Resonate's Global Dispatch product, announced in December 1997, is an extension to the company's Central Dispatch (formerly called "Dispatch") product that provides intelligent selection of a least-loaded server locally in a Web cluster. Global Dispatch allows multiple servers in a cluster to be geographically dispersed, with the direction of requests made based on the smallest response time.

Bright Tiger's ClusterCATS was introduced in October 1997. This software allows Web servers to be replicated and geographically dispersed in a network and have the optimal server be accessed automatically. ClusterCATS software resides on each server. A Java applet is downloaded to a browser client upon connection and keeps in touch with the servers to determine the optimum one for use by a particular browser client.

Use of multicast technology could conceivably solve this problem in a much simpler manner if the network were fully multicast-ready. Let us examine a couple of techniques that could be used to this end. Both require the mirrored sites to be a member of a multicast group, as shown in Figure 5-8.

In Figure 5-8, the replicated sites are in one region rather than distributed globally. In this case, they are found in the U.S. Southeast. Local sites are in

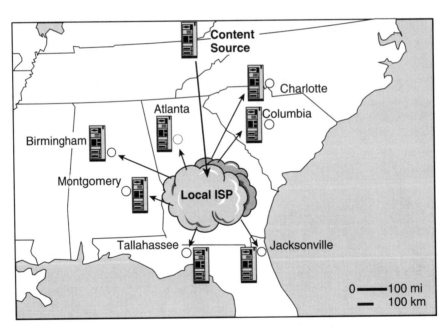

FIGURE 5-8
Locally replicated Web sites

Jacksonville, Tallahassee, Montgomery, Columbia, Atlanta, Charlotte, and Birmingham. The same replication concepts can be used regionally as well as globally. All of the sites are members of the same multicast group, including the source site.

Instead of returning an individual IP address, the DNS server returns the Class D multicast group address designated for the array of mirrored servers. In the first technique, the client browser recognizes that the address returned is Class D and sends a multicast query to that group address. The source address of the first response returned is thereafter used as an individual address. Note that this scheme takes into account not only network issues (it assumes that the fastest response is the closest; this assumption may not be true geographically but generally holds based on the number of hops), but also how busy a particular Web site is. A busy Web site will be slower to react. Note that the first query should be artificially small to minimize traffic, as all members of the group will respond.

Thus, if a user were located in an Atlanta suburb, the closest mirror site would be the one in Atlanta. Unless that site is very busy, the first response should be from that site and our user would be satisfied by it.

A second approach would be to use an *expanded ring search.* In this approach, the client again sends the query to the multicast address, but in this case with expanding TTL. The first TTL could be 2; if no response was received, then it would repeat with a TTL of 3, then 4, and so on, until a response occurred. This approach finds the nearest server, as the TTL limits the scope of the packet sent, as was discussed in Chapter 3.

Another approach would be simply to give the local DNS a different address to return that would be the local mirrored server rather than the content source. This scheme is generally regarded with disfavor because of the DNS configuration problems associated with it.

These replicated Web sites can also provide selected content for a particular organization on the local server for that organization, and block the members of that organization from either the rest of the Internet or only certain sites deemed "objectionable." For example, state educators and local teachers may decide on a set of material that is to be presented to students. Concern has arisen that students with the ability to surf the Net will spend all of their time finding pornography or sports sites and thus waste their time. In effect, the educators want to create a large electronic library and perhaps sort the material by subject. This goal can be accomplished by replicating desirable sites locally that may not be popular but may be very relevant to education.

This same concept could also be applied with commercial organizations. Many are concerned that their employees are wasting time by checking stock quotes or sports sites and may want to limit access to the general Internet.

5.3 SUMMARY AND CONCLUSIONS

It is essential to get content closer to the edge of the network and to the consumer if the Internet and its derivatives are to grow and prosper in the future. Much talk has focused on ever richer content, such as video. Video over the Internet will never become more than a novelty unless its quality approaches television's quality, the quality with which we are all familiar. This scenario cannot happen unless the content is closer to the consumer and can take advantage of the new high-speed, "last-mile" technologies, such as xDSL and cable modems.

Replication and network caching will be pervasive in the future. Multicast technologies—in this case, multicast routing and reliable multicast—are key enabling technologies that will allow this transformation to happen in a scalable way. Research and commercial products are appearing with increasing rapidity to address these issues.

What is the likely content distribution architecture in the Internet of the future? In all scenarios, both mirroring and network caching will play significant roles. But what will their relationship be?

Different scenarios are possible. In the first scenario, the largest 20% of the Web sites, which generate about 80% of all traffic, overwhelmingly decide it is in their interest to have many mirrored sites, perhaps thousands, located throughout the Internet and use one-way satellite or other suitable transport and reliable multicast to update and keep data in synchrony. The satellite providers also need to offer one-way satellite service at attractive prices for this situation to happen with satellite. In this scenario, mirroring dominates, and network proxy servers become an adjunct mostly at the very edges of the network (for example, at the gateways to private networks). Satellite operators are already starting to capitalize on the opportunities and the unique capabilities that satellite can offer—namely, multicast and high speed.

This model also applies if another phenomenon occurs—the emergence of the specialized electronic library. The Internet has become a boon to special-interest groups, which now have access to large amounts of detailed information over the Web. The problem is one of access and organization; it is difficult and time-consuming to "surf the Net" to find some particular information. This shortfall opens up opportunities for someone to organize the information from relevant Web sites and, in essence, create an electronic library Web site that houses this information. For example, educators may want certain information packaged for their students, law offices may want an electronic library created about the law, and medical doctors may want an electronic medical library. Many subjects are not covered in the most popular Web sites and most may not have commercial potential, but they can nevertheless be very important to particular interest groups. Distribution of this created information is more akin to replication than caching; multiple Web sites are combined and organized to form a much larger Web site that is filled with relevant information on a particular category. For example, there are thousands—perhaps hundreds of thousands—of law offices and doctors' offices just in the United States. This approach also means that rich content can be made available to be played on the local network only, which is not bandwidth-constrained. Electronic libraries could even include film clips of operations for doctors or famous trials for lawyers, for example.

As a third party is gathering content and copying it on other servers, the electronic library presents copyright questions. The third party gathering the information will need to obtain copyright permission from the original source. If the original sources are noncommercial, they rarely have any copyright restrictions.

In the second scenario, the large Web sites are less aggressive about mirroring their servers throughout the Internet. A number will probably mirror to network access points, (NAPs), which are the junction points tying together different ISPs. From the NAP sites, the different ISPs can upgrade their networks to be multicast-enabled and can use a hierarchical network cache system augmented with reliable multicast to ensure that content stays current. In this scenario, mirroring plays a relatively minor role, and network caching becomes the predominant mechanism to keep content as local as possible.

In either scenario, replication and network caching will become pervasive, both will use multicast technologies to scale, and both will increasingly be needed to prevent the Internet and its derivatives from reaching the breaking point.

In Chapter 6, we will look at "push" technologies to see how they can help users gain information from the wealth of sites on the Internet without an onerous search. This approach will not be possible on a large scale, however, without the use of multicast technologies.

REFERENCES

[5-1] Mockapetris P. DNS Encoding of Network Names and Other Types. RFC 1101, April 1989.

[5-2] Information on the Harvest cache can be found at http://harvest.transarc.com.

[5-3] Information on the Squid cache can be found at http://ircache.nlanr.net.

[5-4] Wessels D, Claffy K. Internet Cache Protocol (ICP), Version 2. RFC 2186, September 1997.

[5-5] Hannigan B, Howe C, Chan S, Buss T. Why Caching Matters. Forrester Network Strategies Report, vol. 11, no. 11. Forrester Research, Inc., October 1997.

[5-6] Fielding R, Gettys J, Mogul J, Frystyk H, Berners-Lee T. Hypertext Transfer Protocol—HTTP/1.1. RFC 2068, January 1997.

[5-7] Bestavros A, Carter RL, Crovella ME, Cunha CR, Heddaya A, Mirdad SA. Application-Level Document Caching in the Internet. Proceedings of the Second International Workshop on Services in Distributed and Networked Environments, 1995: 166–173.

[5-8] Yeung KH, Ng KW. An Optimal Cache Replacement Algorithm for Internet Systems. Proceedings of the 22nd Conference on Local Computer Networks (LCN '97), November 1997.

[5-9] Kwan TT, McGrath RE, Reed DA. NCSA's World Wide Web Server: Design and Performance. IEEE Transactions on Computers, September 1995.

[5-10] Mogul J, Leach P. Simple Hit-Metering and Usage-Limiting for HTTP. RFC 2227, October 1997.

URLS FOR COMPANIES MENTIONED IN CHAPTER 5

Bright Tiger Technologies	http://btweb2.brighttiger.com
Checkpoint Software	http://www.checkpoint.com
Cisco Systems	http://www.cisco.com
F5 Labs, Inc.	http://www.f5.com
HydraWeb Technologies, Inc.	http://www.hydraweb.com
Inktomi	http://www.inktomi.com
Microsoft	http://www.microsoft.com
Mirror-Image	http://www.mirror-image.com
Netscape	http://www.netscape.com
Network Appliance	http://www.netapp.com
Resonate, Inc.	http://www.resonate.com
RND Networks	http://www.rndnetworks.com

6

"PUSH" APPLICATIONS ("WEBCASTING")

In Chapter 5, we discussed how multicast technology can help solve one of the main problems with today's Internet—namely, poor performance—by providing more efficient ways to deliver content to the edges of the network closer to the consumer. In this chapter, we discuss possible solutions to another major problem with today's Internet—namely, the difficulty in finding the information you want among the myriad Web sites.

Currently, the Internet is organized for "pull" delivery of information. The user employs a browser to search the Internet for the desired information. There is little organization to this information, however. In addition, the number of Web sites is growing astronomically, from just 130 in June 1993 to 2.2 million in April 1998 [6-1]. Every organization, no matter its size or its nature, believes it needs a Web site to advertise its capabilities, to provide information about its activities, to conduct electronic commerce, and to carry out many other activities. Even though the Internet user has tools like search engines to find information, it still remains quite a chore to sift through the information available to find what is desired. This situation is akin to going to the store and "browsing" for something even though you know what you want, rather than having it delivered on a subscription basis. After all, a "browser" won its name for a reason; you browse the Internet much as we might browse through a store looking at goods.

Browsing has its place, but we do not want to employ this technique all the time. We would like to have the equivalent of a subscription service in electronic form. This approach describes "push," in which you subscribe to content and have it delivered automatically.

A number of companies have sprouted up to offer "push" services. Established companies in the Internet such as Netscape and Microsoft also offer "push" capabilities in their browsers. We will discuss these products here, as well as new technologies such as Channel Definition Format (CDF), which may very well be an enabler of new "push" services in the future.

Today's "push" companies use the architecture of defining content "channels" and providing mechanisms for the consumer to "tune in" to the channel to subscribe to the information. This approach resembles the broadcast television model, where different television stations have different content that is advertised somewhere (such as in the newspaper or on a special Prevue channel), and consumers tune in to the channel of their choice.

A second "push" architecture that is familiar to computer users is e-mail. Although e-mail is not called "push," it is like a true "push" because information is sent directly from the source without any "pull" component. Instead of tuning in to a channel, people subscribe to mailing lists and receive information based on the mailing list chosen. Delivery of information is asynchronous—that is, it may be sent at any time.

Various companies have focused on different business models for "push." The first is the content aggregator, and it is embodied in the most visible and successful "push" company, PointCast.

6.1 THE CONTENT AGGREGATOR

The business model for a content aggregator is to provide client software free to users, who can then receive content over "push" channels. The content is aggregated from many sources and packaged together for delivery over these channels. It is sorted into categories to fit these channels, and it typically includes the type of information you might find in a newspaper, such as general news, financial news, sports, and weather.

The content aggregator desires to make the content as appealing as possible because it makes money via advertising. The price that can be charged for this advertising depends on the audience, just as circulation for print media is largely the determinant of advertising rates for newspapers and magazines.

6.1.1   PointCast

PointCast, Inc., was founded in 1992 to provide current news and information services to viewers and corporations via the Internet and corporate Intranets. The PointCast Network was the first free network to broadcast up-to-the-minute news and information directly to a viewer's computer screen via the Internet. Viewers of the PointCast Network enjoy the ability to personalize the service according to their interests. The PointCast Network employs PointCast's SmartScreen technology, which automatically begins running headline news when a viewer's computer is idle—that is, it appears as a screen saver. Point-Cast gathers content from many sources, such as Reuters and other news organizations, to create the content it distributes.

The PointCast business model aims to make money from advertisements that come with the news and information services. PointCast client software is offered free, and millions of people have downloaded the software to date. Many people find it convenient to have the latest news on their desktop at all times.

The original service operated as shown in Figure 6-1. It still represents the model used in most organizations today.

Client software operates on the desktop host on which it is installed. In the background, the client goes to the PointCast content server and pulls down the content to which the client has subscribed, including the advertisements. Thus every client installed within an organization's network pulls down content that is often the same. Hence, if there are 1,000 clients within an organization, 1,000 individual pulls for content take place. Also, the news changes fairly rapidly, requiring frequent pulls of content. If a user turns off his or her host computer (for example, when leaving the office), when the user returns to the office the next morning and turns on the computer, the PointCast client immediately goes out for content. Other clients that were turned off for the night follow suit.

Note that this duplicate set of downloads occurs not only on the organization's network, but also through the connection to the Internet, and through the

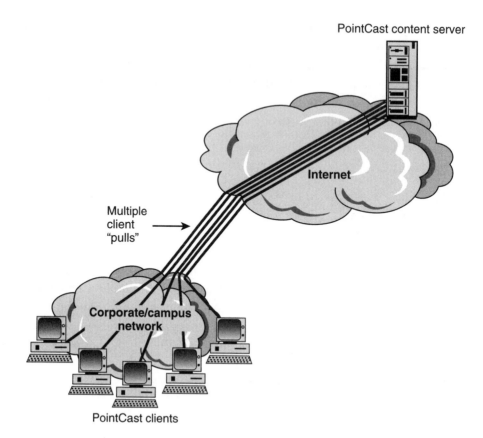

FIGURE 6-1

PointCast architecture

Internet to the PointCast content server site. As a result, network managers within large organizations have found that their organizations' networks were clogged up with traffic, caused by PointCast automated "pulls" from employees' desktop computers. Additionally, this traffic was clogging up their corporate Internet connections. Consequently, many major corporations have dictated that all PointCast clients be removed from desktop PCs within their organization. In fact, a 1996 study [6-2] that monitored Internet traffic found that more than 17% of the HTTP Internet traffic involved PointCast.

Realizing the problem created by this excessive traffic, PointCast responded with the I-Server. The I-Server is designed to be located just inside the organization's network, as shown in Figure 6-2. It pulls the content from the PointCast Web site for storage locally; the clients then pull content off of the local I-Server. This set-up reduces the multiple pulls of content through the connection to the Internet and over the Internet to just one for that organization, though it does nothing to reduce traffic on the organization's internal network.

PointCast initially intended to sell the I-Server to these organizations, but found so much antipathy toward PointCast that no organization would pay; it ended up offering the server to organizations free. The company has also opened up the I-Server so that organizations can create internal content into channels that can be distributed to the employees of the organization.

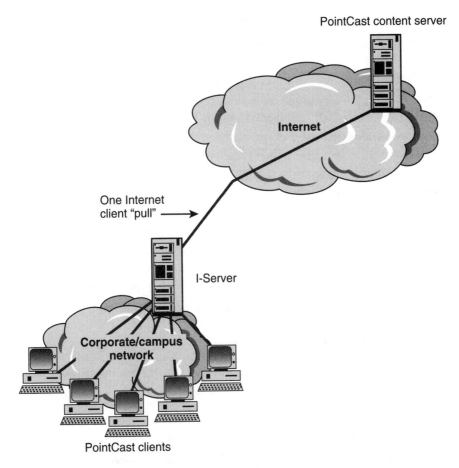

FIGURE 6-2

PointCast architecture with I-Server

PointCast had an estimated 1.2 million desktop clients at the end of 1997 [6-3]. Microsoft has included this service in its browser so that users of Microsoft Internet Explorer 4.0 can receive PointCast content without having to download a PointCast client.

PointCast recently announced support for reliable multicast based on the TIBCO protocol engine (see Chapter 8). However, this service will be used primarily internally by PointCast and does not provide help for consumers.

6.1.2   Other Content Aggregators

A number of other content aggregators offer subscription services to information that is usually industry-specific and delivered via e-mail (or fax). The content delivered is text only, ensuring that the data delivered does not overwhelm networks and users' e-mail systems. One of the most prominent of these companies is Individual, Inc.

Individual (now called NewsEdge, after a merger with Desktop Data in February 1998) provides an entire spectrum of customized, electronic information services for a fee, all aimed at delivering the most relevant, timely news to busy professionals around the world. These information services can be tailored to a workgroup, a department, an entire enterprise—or just an individual. Delivery takes place via a variety of methods—e-mail, delivery to an Intranet Web server, groupware, or fax. Most subscribers choose to receive delivery via e-mail.

Each weekday morning, the subscriber receives the relevant news in the preferred delivery medium. Individual is a single-point provider for hundreds of reputable sources that would be familiar to most consumers as well as more obscure sources. The company promotes its SMART agent technology and the industry expertise of its editorial managers to produce the most sophisticated text filtering available.

This approach has some advantages:

- It is information for a fee, so extraneous advertisements are eliminated.

- The information is textual, resulting in minimal data for download.

- The information is of importance to a business or organization, so the service will not be banned by the client's network operators.

- It uses e-mail (primarily), an established "push" method.

- Information is typically delivered at night, when networks carry little traffic.

6.2 PLATFORM PROVIDERS

Most of the other companies marketing "push" products hope to make money by selling software licenses that will provide a means to get information to the client company's employee base more efficiently over the company's internal Intranet. They typically offer a combination of the Internet and the company's Intranet or, in the case of Diffusion, a combination of the Internet and an Extranet (a set of multiple organizations that have a community of interest). These companies include BackWeb, Wayfarer,* Intermind, Astound, the aforementioned Diffusion, and Marimba. This list of vendors is not intended to be comprehensive; in fact, many companies, most of them new, operate in this market.

All of these companies offer somewhat different twists in their products. BackWeb, for example, strives to be an open platform that fills in the gaps for Webcasting among browsers, databases, and Internet sites. It intends to integrate tightly with environments such as Microsoft's Internet Explorer 4.0, Netscape's Constellation, Lotus Domino, electronic commerce engines, and legacy databases.

Intermind has recently ceased product development and is promoting the licensing of a new patent to be granted shortly. This patent covers a way to control and provide automated delivery of information between publishers and subscribers over a computer network, with a key tool being a special communications control file called a *channel object*. The company claims that a number of "push" products violate this patent and is now building its business based on patent licenses.

Astound is focusing on providing high-quality multimedia presentations by augmenting content from various Web sites to provide a "channel" for the presentations.

Marimba is creating channels for applications — that is, executable programs — rather than generalized content that would be viewed by a browser or some other application.

Another "push" category is "real-time" data "push." In this case, the content is not a Web page or some other defined piece of content, but rather a continuous stream of content that is continuously being created. The most obvious example involves stock and commodity tickers. A ticker consists of a continuous stream of stock or commodity symbols and the latest trading prices. As new trades occur, new content is created on the fly and transmitted. Because thousands of stocks and commodities are traded, these systems typically employ *subject-based addressing*, which is simply the ability to filter out the trades of

---

* Waferer was acquired by Vantive Corp in June, 1998

interest to the particular consumer based on subject. Companies providing "push" capabilities of this sort include TIBCO and Vitria (a spin-off of TIBCO).

Real-time multimedia content could also be "pushed" in a manner similar to broadcast television. Microsoft offers "NetShow" as a part of its Internet Explorer browser. NetShow handles multimedia events, such as Bill Gates providing a speech to his employees, that could be viewed by all on their desktop PCs. This transmission is treated as an "event" rather than a scheduled channel, so it is not usually considered as a "push" application.

The most significant "push" players, however, are the giants of the Web — Netscape and Microsoft. Many of the companies mentioned previously have provided methods to interface with the browsers of these two companies, so that channels may be subscribed and tuned to from within the browser. For example, PointCast has an agreement allowing its client to be integrated into Microsoft Internet Explorer 4.0. Likewise, Marimba technology is integrated into Netscape's Communicator as the NetCaster feature.

Virtually all of these solutions involve multiple point-to-point downloads to each individual client. As such, they do not scale and are thus doomed never to migrate to the mainstream. If 1.2 million PointCast clients can generate more than 17% of the HTTP traffic on the Internet, what would happen if "push" clients became as pervasive as browsers? The answer is an Internet meltdown. This scenario will not be allowed to become reality. The only way for "push" to scale is to use multicast for distribution; if not, this technology will become a wave of the past rather than the future. Most of the content that is now being pushed is viewed as noncritical by organizations — sports scores, general news, stock quotes, and so on. Corporations are increasingly viewing "push" with a jaundiced eye; in the Forrester survey quoted in Chapter 5, approximately 50% of the *Fortune* 1000 companies said they do not allow "push" products in their organizations.

6.3 PROPOSED "PUSH" STANDARDS

The biggest contributions made by the "push" pioneers could prove to be the proposed standards that might bring these concepts into the mainstream. These standards mostly deal with how content is packaged and organized, although the Marimba-sponsored Distribution and Replication Protocol (DRP) proposal deals with sending only changes in material in an effort to reduce the amount of content to be pushed, thereby improving scalability. These new standards are built upon the eXtensible Markup Language (XML), an extension of HTML, which is currently used to create Web pages. Both XML and HTML are subsets of the SGML language for content creation. Microsoft and other vendors are committed to XML in their future Web server products, and it is expected that a significant number of larger sites will convert to XML in 1998.

6.3.1 Channel Definition Format (CDF)

One of the most significant of these new proposals is the Channel Definition Format (CDF) [6-4], which was submitted by Microsoft to the World Wide Web Consortium (W3C) in March 1997 and revised most recently in September 1997. CDF can be viewed as an application of XML that can be used to define a "push" channel. CDF contains the following major elements:

- Channel — defines a channel.
- Item — defines a channel item, or a unit of information that is available from a channel.
- UserSchedule — refers to a client/user-specified schedule.
- Schedule — defines a particular schedule.
- Logo — defines an image to represent a channel or channel item.
- Tracking — defines user tracking parameters of a channel.
- CategoryDef — defines a category, possibly including a child category of another category.

Each major element has a number of child elements, (that is, subelements that are associated with it). For example, some child elements of Channel and Item are as follows:

- LastMod — last-modified date for the Web page.
- Title — title for Channel of Item.
- Abstract — short description summarizing an article (recommended to be 200 characters or less).
- Author — author of Channel or Item.
- Publisher — publisher of Channel or Item.
- Copyright — copyright status.
- Publication Date — publication date of content.
- Logo — visual logo for the channel.

- Keywords — comma-delimited keywords that match the channel.
- Category — category to which the Web page belongs.

CDF files reside on Web sites to allow the content creators to organize their sites by subject into channels. A CDF file may be posted on the Web site listing the URLs that might interest subscribers the most.

When visiting a CDF-enabled Web site, a Microsoft Internet Explorer 4.0 browser client (or other browsers, if they support CDF in the future) can subscribe to the site's channels by simply creating a hyperlink to the CDF files existing on the site, which define the elements of that channel on the site. Use of CDF requires no change to the organization of a site; it simply provides a means for translating the organization of the site into meaningful subjects that can be used to define a channel.

CDF does not preclude delivery of content using multicast technology. In fact, Microsoft promotes this approach as a means to reduce network traffic.

CDF has received endorsements from a number of companies other than Microsoft, including PointCast and a number of content creators.

6.3.2 Meta Content Framework (MCF) and Resource Description Format (RDF)

The Meta Content Framework (MCF) was one of the earliest meta-data systems on the Web, having been first introduced by Apple Computer in September 1996. It remains in use by hundreds of Web sites today. Netscape was among the first companies besides Apple to support MCF and submitted it to W3C in June 1997 [6-5].

MCF has been described as a tool to provide information about information. Its goal is to make the Web more like a library and less like "a heap of books on the floor." MCF attaches properties to objects on Web pages.

Although the tools to describe information are useful for creating "push" channels, MCF is not specifically focused on "push"; rather, it is a better tool with which to organize content. Netscape submitted the Resource Description Framework (RDF) [6-6] to W3C in September 1997. RDF is based on both MCF and XML and is claimed to be a single mechanism for organizing, describing, and navigating information on Web sites. As such, it is claimed to include a superset of the functionality provided in CDF. Also in September 1997, Netscape announced that it plans to introduce RDF into its product line in the near future.

RDF is essentially Netscape's answer to Microsoft's CDF in the continuing "browser wars" between these two giants of the Web.

6.3.3 Open Software Description (OSD)

The Open Software Description (OSD) [6-7] was submitted to the W3C in August 1997 by Marimba and Microsoft. It describes a new data-formatting scheme that will allow any company to update software over the Internet. OSD has been described as a vocabulary that defines the contents of a software package and its dependencies. It can be used with "push" to distribute software over a network to multiple receivers and provides the following three features:

- Hands-free installation.

- Easy and timely upgrades from a designated location.

- Cross platform—It provides cross-platform software or the correct version of platform-specific software. The user is guaranteed to receive working software in either case.

OSD can be used to deploy Java packages, Java stand-alone applications, or platform-native code. Like CDF, it is based on the emerging XML standard.

A wide range of companies support OSD, including Netscape. It provides useful, standardized techniques for distributing software and software updates, a nice application for "push." It is also a "killer" application for reliable multicast, as will be discussed in Chapter 8.

6.3.4   HTTP Distribution and Replication Protocol (DRP)

The HTTP Distribution and Replication Protocol (DRP) [6-8] was submitted to the W3C in August 1997 by Marimba, Netscape, Sun Microsystems, and @Home. The basic protocol comes from Marimba, and it is already found in that company's products. Marimba is offering this protocol for free to the Internet community.

DRP is used to update content. It sends only changes to the content rather than redundant data, thereby reducing network traffic and download times. This goal is a laudable one; Marimba, however, was sued in August 1997 by Novadigm, a desktop management company, for patent infringement relating to this technology. The dispute has clouded the future of DRP.

6.4 E-MAIL AS "PUSH" TECHNOLOGY

Classical e-mail represents a significant competitor to the new Web-based "push." As mentioned previously, companies like Individual sell information to both organizations and individuals, and the primary delivery method is via e-mail.

A significant difference exists between the model of "push" using channels such as is found with Web-based "push" and the asynchronous "push" exhibited by e-mail. With the former approach, the channel is advertised in some fashion and the client receiver decides to subscribe. In most cases, the sender does not know who the receivers are; it simply sends the content on the channel or the receiver requests that it be sent (automated "pull"). This set-up mimics the broadcast television model; receivers (television sets) tune to the channel but the sender (broadcaster) does not know who is viewing the content.

This model is satisfactory if the content has little value to an organization. It is offered free, as in the case of PointCast, or it resides within an Intranet, and the content is not critical to the organization.

In the case of e-mail, the sender has a list of all receivers and directs the content to those receivers. If a problem arises with the transmission, the sender is notified. This model is more appropriate when the content has significant value —that is, when the content is sold or the sender wants to be sure it was delivered. Because the sender knows the e-mail recipients, it can reschedule transmissions that fail the first time.

Many of the early reliable multicast applications (although not called "push") operate via a model similar to e-mail, except that the recipients are local servers rather than desktop hosts. These application case studies are discussed in detail in Chapter 8.

6.5 THE FUTURE OF "PUSH"?

"Push" applications address a problem that needs to solved if the Internet is to evolve into a more general information source for consumers. With print media, we sometimes buy newspapers and magazines at a store, but we also typically subscribe to certain magazines or newspapers that we want delivered on a regular basis. We should have this same choice for electronic media as well. "Push" provides the ability to subscribe to information and have it delivered to you. A new category of subscription service is also likely to emerge in the future: software delivery and update.

The information provided via subscription may be very important or simply nice to have, and the "push" delivery method may very well vary for these two categories. Channel-based "push" is more appropriate for information that is not critical, whereas a more robust version of the e-mail model with delivery confirmation is better suited to critical information.

All "push" applications, however, will never achieve mainstream status unless they are provided using multicast network services and reliable multicast. The fact that about 1.2 million PointCast clients generate more than 17% of HTTP Internet traffic illustrates that point.

The good news is that some of the early reliable multicast applications are, in essence, a form of "push," providing a precursor to an inevitable trend for "push" to become pervasive using multicast transports.

REFERENCES

[6-1] Zakon RH. Hobbes' Internet Timeline. http://info.isoc.org/guest/zakon/Internet/History/HIT.html.

[6-2] Graham-Cumming J. Hits and Miss-es: A Year Watching the Web. Sixth International World Wide Web Conference, Santa Clara, California, April 1997.

[6-3] Information on PointCast can be found at the company's Web site at http://www.pointcast.com.

[6-4] Ellerman C. Channel Definition Format (CDF). Submitted to W3C, March 9, 1997.

[6-5] Guha RV, Bray T, eds. Meta Content Framework Using XML. Submitted to W3C, June 6, 1997.

[6-6] Lassila O, Swick RR, eds. Resource Description Framework (RDF) Model and Syntax. W3C Working Draft, February 16, 1998.

[6-7] van Hoff A, Partovi H, Thai T. The Open Software Description Format (OSD). Submitted to W3C, August 13, 1997.

[6-8] van Hoff A, Giannandrea J, Hapner M, Carter S, Medin M, eds. The HTTP Distribution and Replication Protocol. Submitted to W3C, August 25, 1997.

URLS FOR COMPANIES MENTIONED IN CHAPTER 6

Astound	http://www.astound.com
BackWeb	http://www.backweb.com
Diffusion	http://www.diffusion.com
Individual	http://www.newsedge.com
Intermind	http://www.intermind.com
Lotus	http://www.lotus.com

Marimba	http://www.marimba.com
Microsoft	http://www.microsoft.com
Netscape	http://www.netscape.com
PointCast	http://www.pointcast.com
TIBCO	http://www.tibco.com
Vitria	http://www.vitria.com
Wayfarer	http://www.wayfarer.com

7

MULTIMEDIA
STREAMING
APPLICATIONS
AND TECHNOLOGY

Multimedia streaming applications are often associated with multicast networks. The combination of video and audio (and possibly other components) is called *multimedia*, as the stream consists of more than one medium. High-quality multimedia streams that include video have an incentive to use multicast if it is delivered to many recipients simultaneously because of the high bandwidths involved.

Figure 7-1 (which you may remember from Chapter 1) highlights these applications within the full spectrum of multicast applications. Note that audio applications, although they involve only one medium, are usually characterized as multimedia.

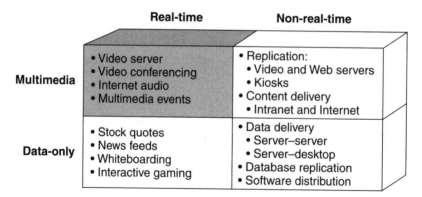

FIGURE 7-1

Real-time multimedia multicast applications

These multimedia streaming applications span the gamut of one-to-one, one-to-many, and many-to-many with very different bandwidth requirements. They include audio applications (one medium) and multimedia applications, which most often combine video and audio.

Table 7-1 further characterizes the major multimedia streaming applications. All of these applications are marked by a need for timeliness rather than absolute reliability. Note that Internet telephone conference calls are essentially the same application as audio conferencing.

The multimedia real-time streaming applications that fit best with today's Internet infrastructure and have the greatest value are the ones that are receiving the most attention today. For example, Internet telephony is viewed as a huge new use of the Internet. It does not require much bandwidth and is usually point-to-point, so today's Internet infrastructure can easily support this application. Additionally, Internet telephone products can be purchased in computer stores for less than $50, allowing the user to make telephone calls around the world to other so-enabled users of the Internet almost for free.

Similarly, audio on a Web site can provide added appeal for the site. Although Web site multimedia (for example, the inclusion of video with audio) may make the sites more interesting, the bandwidth constraints of today's Internet have limited its acceptance at this time.

In the one-to-many category of multicast applications, Internet radio channels are available over the Mbone and hint at the possibilities if the Internet be-

TABLE 7-1

MULTIMEDIA STREAMING APPLICATIONS

Application	Unicast	Multicast One-to-Many	Many-to-Many	Bandwidth Requirement
Internet telephone	X		X	Low
Web site audio	X			Low
Web site multimedia	X			Medium–High
Internet radio		X		Low
Remote training		X		Medium–High
Multimedia events		X		Medium–High
Audio conferencing			X	Low
Video conferencing	X		X	Medium–High
Virtual reality	X		X	Very High

came fully multicast-enabled. The most crucial one-to-many applications for business, however, remain remote training and multimedia events that would most often use a corporate Intranet rather than the public Internet as the underlying network infrastructure.

Both of these applications represent targets for Microsoft's NetShow, which is an integral component of Internet Explorer 4.0, Microsoft's Web browser. NetShow is essentially given away for free, as Internet Explorer 4.0 is bundled with Windows 95 and Windows NT (unless the U.S. Justice Department has its way).

With the rush of technology overwhelming us, training has become increasingly important. It is not always convenient to train all employees in the same location. Similarly, multimedia events are viewed as an important new tool that can facilitate communications between management and employees in large organizations. For example, a CEO could announce and discuss a new merger with all employees, and the employees could simply watch the event unfold on their desktop computers.

The financial industry has been among the earliest adopters to embrace multimedia events. Members of this field wish to know business news, such as mergers, acquisitions, and other fast-breaking developments, as soon as it happens; they also want to see both the body language of the presenter and the words associated with the event. For them, much money could be made by correctly judging the real message of the event.

Video conferencing is a many-to-many application that has been available for a number of years. It is relatively new as a multicast IP application, however, and appears destined to enter the mainstream as multicast IP becomes more pervasive in networks. Audio conferencing serves the same function as a telephone conference call, and it is likely to become relatively common when more network infrastructures support multicast.

Network-based virtual reality is more of a future application, though it holds promise as a great hands-on teaching tool. A demonstration at the general meeting of Internet2 (a consortium of more than 110 American universities working together to further network infrastructures and applications so as to facilitate teaching and research) in September 1997 showed a virtual human ear on which student surgeons could practice surgery without the use of a cadaver. The images were generated in Chicago, while the students were in Washington, D.C. The bandwidth requirements are high and the latency requirements are low for this application. Both of these stringent requirements will delay the widespread adoption of this technology.

In summary, today's most important multicast multimedia streaming applications are video conferencing, remote training, and multimedia events. These applications are driving the development of the technology that will bring these applications into the mainstream. Some actual case studies related to these applications are presented in Section 7.1.

Besides the giants of the Web, Microsoft and Netscape, smaller companies such as Icast, Precept Software, Starlight Networks,* and RealNetworks have been formed in the last few years to address real-time multimedia applications. Other start-ups, such as Vxtreme, have been absorbed by giants like Microsoft.

7.1 BUSINESS CASE STUDIES

The following sections detail some real business applications of multimedia streaming to multicast groups in Intranets.

---

* Icast was acquired by First Virtual in July 1998. Precept Software was acquired by Cisco Systems in March 1998. Starlight Networks was acquired by PictureTel in July 1998.

7.1.1 Paribas

Paribas is a financial institution based in London that specializes in trading, private asset management, equities, and other related financial services. With approximately 9,000 employees, the company operates in 60 countries. Today, Paribas uses streaming video from Starlight Networks to enhance its information delivery.

Recently, Paribas constructed a new building in London. In designing the building, the company focused on its technology requirements, technologies readily available today, and technologies expected to become important in the future. Paribas executives recognized that high-speed networks (ATM) and "digital everything" were the future because rich multimedia applications, including networked digital video, would be used to enhance their business processes.

In a pilot application, live feeds of Reuters and Bloomberg television are delivered directly to traders' desktop computers via Starlight Networks' streaming video software and multicast IP. As a consequence, traders no longer have to leave their desks to watch these broadcasts in a viewing room. Rather, they can keep abreast of late-breaking financial news and their investment portfolio activity simultaneously.

In the future, networked digital video will be used for internal communications among the company's various sites, supporting video conferencing to the desktop computer. Eventually networked digital video may be used to tape conferences involving high-level management and then stored on the server for later review by employees and customers.

7.1.2 Smith Barney

On February 17, 1998, Starlight Networks announced that Smith Barney, the United States' second largest retail brokerage firm, was implementing its Star-Cast software. The adoption represented an innovative move by Smith Barney to deliver real-time, video-based financial information to approximately 11,000 financial consultants and managers at nearly 500 remote branch locations across a satellite network. Smith Barney advisers will be able to receive live information from industry and market analysts directly on their desktop workstations; in the future, they will have access to commercial video feeds, custom-developed reports, and multimedia training material.

Smith Barney is seeking to harness the power of multimedia technology and video content and deliver it directly to financial consultants' desktops, enabling them to make quicker, better financial decisions for Smith Barney clients. As part of the Smith Barney NextGen program, which uses technology to improve communication and productivity, Smith Barney is taking advantage of streaming multimedia to deliver more value to its customers.

Smith Barney has been working with Starlight Networks for six months to complete the prototype system. The video rollout started in the second half of 1997. The primary video content will consist of analysts' daily briefings, which will be delivered directly and in real time to the desktop. A video encoder running StarCast Multicaster will send the feed to local desktops at the New York headquarters and retransmit the feed via Smith Barney's satellite network. At each receiving location, a video server running StarCast Recaster will then take the feed and multicast it to all local desktops. Financial consultants will be able to remain at their desks and view broadcasts on their PC desktops through the StarCast Viewer, without disrupting other applications or feeds.

In the past, financial consultants were briefed through audio broadcasts or had to go to VCR- and television-equipped rooms to watch video tapes of prerecorded briefings. Not only did productivity suffer, but the flow of business was also interrupted—and the video briefings were already outdated information.

In contrast, StarCast captures video and audio content from a live source or satellite and multicasts it over the LAN to an unlimited number of PCs. The content can include communications developed in-house (such as corporate presentations or training videos), stored information from a video server, or live broadcasts (such as CNN). Whatever the content, StarCast delivers it over Ethernet LANs, with a speed and in a quantity previously impossible to obtain. In addition, by working through a satellite delivery system interface, StarCast can extend the reach of a single broadcast to thousands of viewers, spread across multiple sites, with full-screen high-quality video at 30 frames per second.

Unlike other solutions, StarCast employs IP multicasting to reach the desktops throughout the routed enterprise network, not just within a LAN. In addition, StarCast provides full integration with StarWorks media servers in the areas of archive and on-demand playback and support for MPEG compression format and satellite delivery. This integration creates an open, standards-based solution that delivers high-quality video for mission-critical applications.

7.1.3   National Institutes of Health

The U.S. National Institutes of Health began deploying Precept Software's IP/TV multimedia multicast streaming software products in November 1997.

As of February 1998, it had approximately 200 desktop applications installed. Eventually, this number will grow to about 15,000.

The deployment of IP/TV has made possible the dissemination of fast-breaking information on events in the medical field. Scientific lectures and conferences on hot topics such as gene therapy and the latest information about newly discovered diseases and ways to treat antibiotic-resistant infections can now be conveyed to the research community at their desktops as data becomes available. These feeds may originate at the Center for Disease Control and Prevention in Atlanta or at some other location covered by IP/TV.

The technology is deployed over a multicast-enabled campus complex of approximately 40 buildings located in Bethesda, Maryland, which is linked to other sites in the Washington, D.C., metropolitan area with four FDDI rings. T1 links tie offices in Atlanta, Research Triangle Park, North Carolina, and Phoenix, Arizona, as well as other sites in Maryland and Montana, to the main campus network in Bethesda.

Although not fully deployed, the ability to multicast events in real time has made communications of medical events much quicker. As a result, medical personnel can be kept up to date on new events in the medical world as they happen.

7.1.4 Microsoft

Microsoft's NetShow Services provide built-in streaming services in Windows NT Server. The client portion of the solution, called Microsoft Media Player, is available free for Windows 95 and Windows NT. Microsoft is using its own product internally on its multicast-enabled Intranet to provide the following functions:

Training. Microsoft devotes substantial resources to training. Using NetShow Services to extend the reach of professional instructors through corporate intranets lets the company maximize the value of this investment. NetShow Services makes it easy for trainers to generate the content and for users to receive the training whenever and wherever they need it. For example, a recorded speech can be combined with the speaker's slides to form a NetShow broadcast. The training material can thus be provided so that all employees have the advantage of hearing the course as it was delivered by the speaker. Delivery of multimedia information and presentations over the corporate network eliminates the costs formerly incurred in distributing training materials and binders or CD-ROMs.

Corporate Communications. Every Microsoft employee, regardless of his or her geographic location, can hear important organizational briefings live. These presentations, such as CEO talks or presentations for the press or analysts, can also be captured for later playback. In this way, employees can view presentations at their convenience, and the company develops a library of available on-demand information for reference and training. NetShow Services reduce the burden of having to fly all employees to a central location for an announcement or training session; Microsoft can instead send the content over the network to each employee's desktop or to a portable PC for personnel on the road.

7.1.5   3Com

3Com was one of the first large companies to upgrade its terrestrial Intranet to be multicast-enabled. This move has allowed 3Com to enjoy the benefits of both multimedia streaming and reliable multicast applications. The reliable multicast application case study for 3Com is presented in Chapter 8.

3Com's Intranet is totally multicast-ready, with the exception of some small sales offices connected by low-speed lines. The company's major centers are located all over the world and its headquarters is found in Santa Clara, California. 3Com selected Real Networks to provide multimedia streaming solutions based on its belief that Real Networks's low bit rate codec can handle the lowest common denominator of line speed in the corporate network, namely 56 Kbps.

3Com has initiated a series of "CEO Forums," where Eric Benhamou, the company's CEO, speaks to employees using multicast multimedia transmissions sent over an Intranet. In the first session in March 1998, the transmission was received by 1,200 viewers on desktop computers, and about 2,000 employees participated. Employees in Singapore came to work at 2:00 A.M. local time to participate.

The second CEO Forum was scheduled for July 1998. 3Com expected that twice as many employees would participate in this conference compared with the first one.

The company also plans to offer remote training courses on a scheduled basis advertised to employees by a "video guide." For example, a course entitled "How to Use Microsoft Word" might be offered on a particular multicast channel at 9:00 A.M. on Mondays during the month of May.

This capability greatly enhances 3Com's corporate communications and provides the benefit of a convenient training tool for employees. This system would not be possible without multicast technology in the network and the application.

7.2 MULTIMEDIA PROTOCOLS AND FORMATS

Video and audio streams represent the core data sources for multimedia. Both are generated from analog signals by some form of sampling technique. In the case of audio, a transducer (microphone) converts sound energy into an analog electrical signal, and a speaker converts this electrical signal back into sound energy. The electrical signal is converted to a digital signal by a "sampler" and analog-to-digital converter, as shown in Figure 7-2. Conversely, a digital-to-analog converter at the receiver converts the digital signal back to analog form. According to the Nyquist theorem, no theoretical loss of information occurs if the sample rate is at least twice as high as the highest frequency of the analog signal.

The number of bits per sample determines the level of "quantization noise," or the error created when the number of bits cannot span the dynamic range of

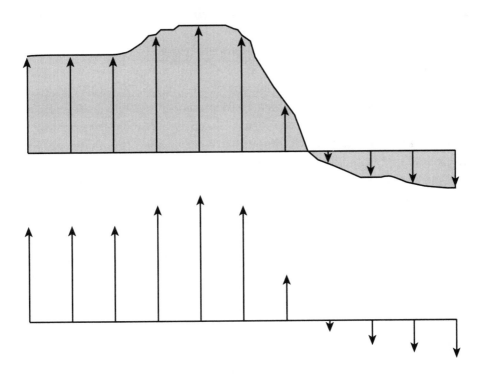

FIGURE 7-2

Sampled analog signal and samples

the analog signal accurately. Thus increased quality is achieved by increasing the bandwidth and the number of bits per sample. As an example, the telephone network characterizes voice with a 300 Hz to 3.3 KHz bandwidth sampled at 8 KHz with 7 bits per sample. This set-up yields the standard telephone voice channel data rate of 56 Kbps.

Video works via the *frames* concept. Each frame is essentially a picture, represented by a large number of bits using techniques more complex than simply sampling an analog signal (the technique used with audio). Frames employ a large number of bits to represent a still picture. Obviously, color images require more information than black-and-white ones, and thus many more bits are required to represent color than black-and-white. Differing amounts of data are also required to represent different levels of color quality.

Ideally, the frame *rate* is set so that the human eye perceives the incoming set of pictures not as a set of pictures but rather as motion. For example, broadcast television standards usually have frame rates of 30 frames per second, which is fast enough to fool the eye into believing it sees true motion.

Both video and audio contain considerable amounts of information redundancy. Compression techniques can therefore be employed to greatly reduce the data rate required for a given quality level. For example, telephone-quality speech can be achieved with compression at rates of less than 10 Kbps, rather than the 56 Kbps uncompressed standard present in the telephone network. Similarly, broadcast television quality can be achieved with 4 Mbps rather than the 6 MHz analog signal (which translates to more than 50 Mbps in digital form) that is standard in analog broadcast television. Considerable progress has been made in improving compression techniques for both audio and video in the last 20 to 30 years.

The compression/decompression device used for audio and video compression and decompression is called a *codec* (*compressor/decompressor*). A huge number of codecs are available using different compression algorithms. Some are intended to deliver broadcast-quality video and audio, such as MPEG (Motion Picture Experts Group); others target low-data-rate, low-quality video conferencing, such as H.261. Similarly, some audio codecs are directed at high-quality stereo/quadraphonic music audio, while others provide monophonic telephone-quality voice requiring lower data rates.

Codecs are considered part of the application, as shown in Figure 7-3. Regardless of the codec used, audio samples and video frames require constant arrival rates to reproduce an accurate signal for the ear or the eye to interpret correctly. For example, for an audio signal sampled at 8 KHz, samples should

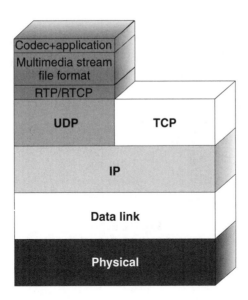

FIGURE 7-3

Multimedia streaming protocol and file format architecture

arrive every 125 microseconds (1/8,000 KHz). The variation in arrival rate is called timing *jitter*. Buffering in network elements can cause jitter because of the multiplexing of packets from many sources and the build-up of network element buffers, as shown in Figure 7-4. Additionally, network element buffers may overflow, causing packets to be lost with a corresponding change in timing relationships.

In Figure 7-4, the edge router receives packets from multiple sources on the subnetwork and combines them in a single stream for forwarding based on their destination addresses. These packets can come in different sizes; a large one can occupy the resource for longer periods and make packets from the multimedia server (shown shaded in Figure 7-4) wait for delivery. Additionally, as traffic increases, queues lengthen, further delaying the delivery and possibly dropping packets if the queue overflows. Packets to the same destination may also traverse different paths and arrive out of order.

Timing relationships for multimedia streams must be restored at the receiver to ensure coherent reception. This consideration is much more important than compensating for the loss of a packet, which may appear as a flicker on the screen (for video) or a virtually imperceptible silence (for audio).

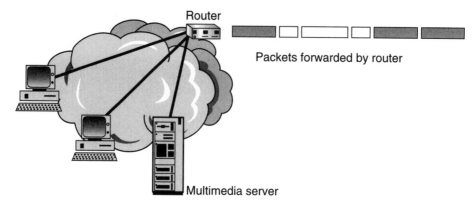

FIGURE 7-4

Rate timing lost through network

Collaborative applications such as video conferencing also have an absolute time delay limit. If network delay is too long, interaction between members of a conference becomes difficult and awkward. If the delay is excessive, human participants may become disoriented. For example, the telephone network has set a round-trip delay time limit of 400 milliseconds in their design standard.

7.2.1   Multimedia Codecs

As mentioned previously, codecs are compression/decompression devices used to reduce the amount of data needed to represent the multimedia data source. A huge number of codec types have originated from many different industries. Entire books have been written about this subject [7-1].

It is useful to understand at least the origin of the most popular codecs and the applications that they target. This section will introduce the most commonly used acronyms and describe the various codecs in broad terms.

The MPEG set of codecs came from the motion picture and entertainment industries. MPEG1 is intended to deliver video and audio for a CD-ROM-quality presentation at relatively high data rates. MPEG2 targets broadcast-quality compressed video and audio and is superseding the MPEG1 applications. MPEG2 has evolved into a large number of different quality levels and aspect ratios. It also serves as the basis for digital television, spanning quality levels that range from the equivalent of today's analog television to very-high-quality, high-definition television (HDTV). In addition, MPEG2 is commonly used to transmit high-quality multimedia streaming applications over TCP/IP networks.

Some new MPEG standards are being developed as well. To handle the specific requirements from rapidly developing multimedia applications, a new standard, MPEG4, likely will be approved in 1998 that will operate at low bit rates.

Motion-JPEG (Joint Photographic Experts Group) preceded MPEG and remains a standard for still pictures, where it is called JPEG. It is one of the two most common image formats used on the Web, with the other being GIF (Graphics Interchange Format, created by CompuServe).

The International Telephony Union (ITU, formerly CCITT) created the H.261 and H.263 standards. These standards focus on video conferencing applications. H.261 streams are designed to operate at rates that are multiples of 64 Kbps.

The H.263 video coding standard is a descendant of the methodology prevalent in several existing standards, including H.261, MPEG1, and MPEG2. It has emerged as a high compression standard for moving images that does not exclusively focus on very low bit rates. The improvements in H.263 relative to H.261 are mainly obtained via a more effective motion compensation scheme.

Audio codecs include G.723 and G.728, both ITU standards. Global System for Mobile Communication (GSM) is the speech codec used by the European-originated cellular telephone standard. Adaptive Differential Pulse Coded Modulation (ADPCM) is a compressed version of standard telephone speech. Musical Instrument Digital Interface (MIDI) is an audio codec for high-quality music that also supports stereo and quadraphonic multichannel sound. In addition, the audio portion of the MPEG2 codec may be used for audio only.

This list is by no means complete. Companies have also developed many proprietary codecs for audio-only and audio/video applications.

7.2.2   Real-Time Protocol and Real-Time-Control Protocol (RTP and RTCP)

The Real-Time Protocol (RTP) [7-2] is a protocol created to transport multimedia streams over IP networks. Its companion, the Real-Time-Control Protocol (RTCP), is used to monitor and control RTP sessions. RTP is on the standards track in the IETF.

RTP was primarily designed to manage multimedia conferences involving many participants, with a view toward accommodating other multimedia streaming applications. This protocol framework is deliberately incomplete;

companion "profiles" need to be specified to document fully how a specific application will be handled within RTP. The first of these profiles covered audio and video conferences with minimal control. Since its development, a number of other profiles have been defined, as shown in Table 7-2.

Although many of these codecs already combine video and audio, such as with MPEG1 and MPEG2, the two data types are separated and carried by different RTP streams or flows in the RTP profile. This approach was taken because it may be beneficial to treat the two flows differently. For example, audio requires less bandwidth than video.

We have seen that multimedia streams (or "flows") need to recover their time relationship at the receiver—that is, jitter needs to be removed to ensure coherent reception. To accomplish this goal, real-time data is buffered at the receiver for a sufficient time to remove the jitter added by the network and to recover the original timing relationships between the media data. To know how long to buffer to achieve synchronization, each packet must carry a timestamp that indicates the time at the sender when the data was captured. For audio and video data timing recovery, it is not necessary to know the absolute time when the data was captured, only the time relative to the other data packets.

RTP can simultaneously handle multiple flows that may have different characteristics, such as video and audio. As audio and video flows will receive differing jitter and possibly differing quality of service, audio and video grabbed at the same time at the sender may not arrive at the receiver at the same time. At the receiver, each flow will need a playout buffer to remove network jit-

TABLE 7-2

RTP PROFILES

Profile	Description	Document
Audio/video conferencing	Minimal control	RFC 18920
Sun CellB video	Sun video codec	RFC 2029
H.261	ITU low-speed video	RFC 2032
JPEG	Video	RFC 2035
MPEG1/MPEG2	Movie-quality video	RFC 2038
H.263	ITU X64 Kbps video	RFC 2190
Audio with redundancy	FEC added	RFC 2198

ter. Interflow synchronization can be achieved by adapting these playout buffers so that samples/frames that originated at the same time are played out simultaneously. The time base of different flows from the same sender must therefore be related at the receivers—for example, by making available the absolute times at which each flow was captured.

RTP's standard format packet header gives media-specific timestamp data as well as payload format information and sequence numbering. RTP does not provide or require any connection set-up, nor does it provide any enhanced reliability over UDP. For this protocol to provide a useful media flow, capacity in the relevant traffic class must be sufficient to accommodate the traffic. The method by which this capacity is ensured is independent of RTP.

Every original RTP source is identified by a source identifier (ID) that is carried in every packet. RTP allows flows from several sources to become mixed in gateways to yield a single resulting flow. In such a case, each mixed packet contains the source identifiers of all contributing sources.

RTP media timestamp units are flow-specific—that is, they are in units that are appropriate to the media flow. For example, the sampling clock of an audio signal is used to provide the timestamps. Consequently, interflow synchronization is not possible from the RTP timestamps alone.

Each RTP flow is supplemented by RTCP packets. A number of different RTCP packet types exist. RTCP packets provide the relationship between the real-time clock at a sender and the RTP media timestamps. They also provide textual information to identify a sender in a conference from the source ID.

In IP multicast, sources may send to a multicast group without being a receiver in that group. For many applications, however, it is useful to know who is listening to the transmission and whether the media flows are reaching receivers properly. Accurately performing both these tasks restricts the scaling of the group. Recall that receivers join multicast groups; as a result, no one knows the precise membership of a multicast group at a specific time. Discovery of this information may carry a high cost, including an implosion of messages that could cause many of them to become lost. RTCP therefore provides approximate membership information through periodic multicast of session messages that give, in addition to information about the recipient, information about the reception quality at that receiver. RTCP session messages are restricted in rate so that, as the membership of a group grows, the rate of session messages remains constant, and each receiver reports less often. A member of the group can never know exactly who is present at a particular time from RTCP reports, but it does have a good approximation of the group membership.

Reception-quality information is primarily intended for debugging purposes, since the debugging of IP multicast problems is a notoriously difficult task. It might also be possible to use reception-quality information for rate-adaptive senders, although it is not clear whether this information would be sufficiently timely to adapt to transient congestion.

RTP also includes a provision to support "translators" and "mixers." These devices interconnect different networks that may support different transports or codecs. A translator passes along data streams from different sources as separate entities, whereas a mixer combines them to form one new stream.

In Figure 7-5, a translator is used to change the encoding of a video conference for some participants who are on a network segment that cannot support the other participants' bandwidth. The translator converts the high-quality, high-bandwidth video and audio into lower-quality, lower-bandwidth flows, allowing participants in the network who have only low-bandwidth access to join the conference. Translators and mixers can also convert multicast addresses to

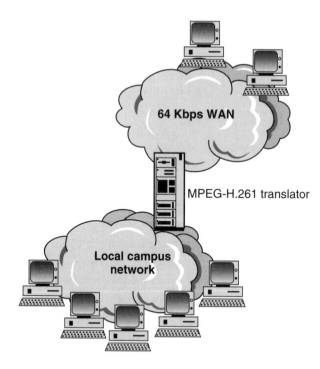

FIGURE 7-5

RTP translator

multiple unicast addresses so as to reach participants not on a multicast-enabled network, to convert from a secure session to an unsecured one, and so on. In general, these gateways can be tailored to provide different conversions for different purposes.

In Figure 7-5, most of the participants of a video conference reside on a local campus network with a bandwidth of 10 Mbps (Ethernet). Two remote participants, however, are connected via a WAN with bandwidth of 64 Kbps. Rather than degrade the quality of the video and audio for all participants to the lowest common denominator, the translator allows participants whose network can support higher quality with a higher-bandwidth network to do so; at the same time, it does not deny service to participants on a low-bandwidth, but connected network.

7.2.3 Quality of Service (QoS), Resource Reservation Protocol (RSVP), and Flows

As previously mentioned, a number of streaming applications require a minimum bandwidth to transmit the stream or "flow." The Resource Reservation Protocol (RSVP) [7-3] was created to allow a flow to reserve bandwidth hop by hop, from the receiver back to the source, so as to provide an acceptable quality of service (QoS) for the flow. Receiver initiation involves the same methodology as that employed in joining a receiver-initiated multicast group. RSVP is now on the standards track within IETF.

Before going into the details of RSVP and other QoS techniques, let us clearly define the problem that needs solving. Internet traffic is classified into two major categories—elastic and real-time—each of which has two subcategories.

Elastic traffic may be interactive or transaction-oriented and therefore sensitive to delay, or it may involve bulk transfer of data and therefore be sensitive to bandwidth. This class of traffic will be dealt with in Chapter 8.

Real-time traffic lacks elasticity, but it has definable average and peak data rates as well as loss and delay expectations. It either requires the network to lose traffic only rarely and deliver consistent performance, or it accepts some jitter and moderate loss of traffic in exchange for priority to maintain timeliness of delivery. These two subcategories are called *guaranteed delivery* and *controlled load*, respectively.

Multimedia flows must be delivered on a certain schedule (rate) or else they become useless. If delivered too late, multimedia traffic is worse than useless—it actually impedes delivery of later multimedia data. Multimedia applications account for variability in the network by buffering data. For voice, which can give acceptable quality at low data transmission rates, not much buffering is required for good performance; this level is easily accomplished by end-station hosts. For high-quality, high-speed multimedia data transfer — for example, MPEG at 12 Mbps — 1.5 Mbytes of data are needed for a 1-second buffer, which represents a significant amount of memory resource. When sufficient buffering is not available in the application, the application must request that the network induce less jitter and prepare to accept frame loss, if it becomes necessary to meet the requirement.

RSVP is the first documented specification to address QoS needs for real-time multimedia traffic, in which the host application requests the QoS level from the network. It offers two levels of service corresponding to the two subcategories discussed earlier: guaranteed delivery and controlled load. Guaranteed delivery service reserves a specific amount of bandwidth, and packets in this service's flow will not be dropped as long as the traffic in that flow does not exceed the reserved bandwidth. Controlled load service simply prioritizes the packets in the flow, ensuring that they do not wait too long in router queues as they cross the network. This option is essentially a best-effort service for priority packets; lower-priority packets are preempted but, if heavy congestion occurs, these packets could be dropped if no lower-priority packets are available to be sacrificed.

RSVP reservation requests are modeled as "flow descriptors" that, in turn, consist of a number of sub-elements, as shown in Figure 7-6. The "flowspec" specifies a desired QoS. It is used to set parameters in the node's packet scheduler or other Link-layer mechanism.

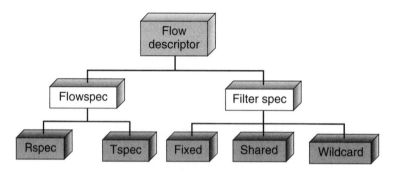

FIGURE 7-6

Flow descriptor attributes

The "filter spec" defines the flow that should receive the QoS defined by the flowspec.

The basic filter spec format defined currently in RSVP is restricted to the sender's IP address and UDP/TCP port number (generally UDP for multimedia flows). Wildcard filters implicitly select all senders in a particular session — for example, all members of a conference. Fixed and shared filters explicitly define the senders to which the reservation applies. A fixed filter applies it to only one particular sender. A shared filter creates a single reservation that is shared by selected upstream senders.

Both wildcard and shared filters create shared reservations and are suitable for applications such as audio conferencing, where generally only one member of the conference speaks at a time. Fixed filters, in contrast, would be suitable for video, such as when all members of a video conference need to simultaneously view all other participants; this application requires a number of reservations equal to the number of participants. Fixed filters are also suitable for one-to-many events of all types that involve a single sender.

Under the flowspec, Rspec defines the desired QoS and Tspec describes the traffic flow. Both are determined by the Internet service models defined in RFC 2210 [7-4].

RSVP is receiver-initiated hop by hop back to the source, as shown in Figure 7-7. Reservation requests originate at receiving hosts and are passed upstream to the senders. Reservation requests are unidirectional, moving from receivers to sender. These requests are made at each hop upstream to the sender. The RSVP process passes the request to *admission* control and *policy* control, both of which comprise local decision modules. Admission control determines whether the node has sufficient resources to supply the requested QoS. Policy control determines whether the requester has the administrative permission to make the reservation. If either test fails, the reservation is rejected and suitable error messages are sent to the receivers. If both succeed, the node is set to select the data packets defined by the filter spec; it also interacts with the appropriate Link layer to obtain the desired QoS defined by the flowspec.

As flows hit a replication point at a network node, they merge to form a single flow. They then proceed with reservation requests back to the source.

A number of unresolved issues characterize RSVP. For example, admission control and policy control are both administered locally. As a result, no coordination takes place between routing nodes in the network (unless it is performed manually), increasing the probability that a reservation request at a hop upstream

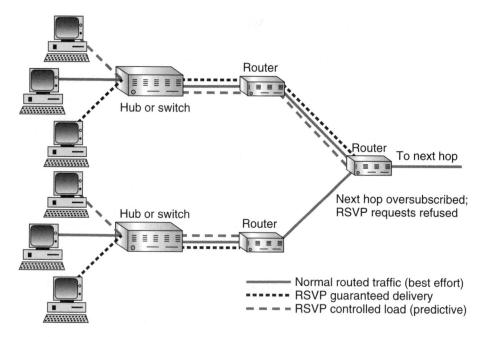

FIGURE 7-7

Receiver-based RSVP requests with one hop denying admission

to the source may refuse the request. In such a case, no mechanism is available for finding another route back to the source that can accept the request. Consequently, the application could be shut out and not receive any service. This problem was discussed in a *Data Communications* article [7-5] published in May 1997. A recent Internet RFC [7-6] discussed scaling issues of RSVP and questioned its use in high-speed backbones.

These issues have spurred a search for alternative methods to provide differing levels of QoS that are less resource-intensive in network nodes and that offer more broadly based policy and admission control architectures, which would therefore coordinate the nodes within an Autonomous System (AS) or networking domain. Researchers are also working to add QoS metrics to routing protocols to minimize blocking of RSVP requests.

These searches are being pursued by both researchers and commercial organizations, and products are already appearing that provide viable solutions to this problem. For example, a new algorithm [7-7] called Class-Based Queuing

(CBQ) provides good mechanisms to classify user traffic and assign bandwidth characteristics to each class. In effect, it operates as an engine to implement and enforce RSVP requests. Products incorporating CBQ are starting to appear, providing tools for network operators who want to implement QoS in their networks but who do not want to depend on RSVP. Rather, QoS is implemented with these products manually by network operators.

Work is ongoing for simpler mechanisms as well, the most prominent of which is described as Simple Differential Services [7-8]. This approach proposes to mark packets based on priorities using the Type Of Service (TOS) bits already present in the IP header but that go unused in today's practice [7-9].

Clearly, the topic of QoS in both Internets and Intranets is the subject of intense attention. The consensus among Internet researchers is that RSVP is suitable at this time primarily for Intranet use, but that even there administrative issues need more work.

The current state of QoS should be viewed as experimental and leading edge—and definitely not ready for mainstream use as yet. UUNet came to the same conclusion; it decided to forego the use of RSVP when it introduced its UUCast multicast service in September 1997.

7.2.4 Real-Time Streaming Protocol (RTSP)

The Real-Time Streaming Protocol (RTSP) [7-10] is a control protocol very similar to HTTP/1.1 that is used to establish and control one or more time-synchronized streams of continuous media, such as audio and video. In general, it does not deliver the continuous streams itself, although interleaving of the continuous media stream with the control stream is possible. Essentially, RTSP acts as a "network remote control" for multimedia servers, similar to a VCR control for television.

The set of streams to be controlled is defined by a presentation description. RTSP sessions are not tied to a transport connection, such as a TCP connection. During an RTSP session, an RTSP client may open and close many reliable transport connections to the server to issue RTSP requests. Alternatively, it may use a connectionless transport protocol such as UDP.

The streams controlled by RTSP may use RTP, but the operation of RTSP does not depend on the transport mechanism used to carry continuous media.

RTSP is intentionally similar in syntax and operation to HTTP/1.1, allowing most extension mechanisms to HTTP to be added to RTSP.

The protocol supports the following operations:

Retrieval of Media from a Media Server

The client can request a presentation description via HTTP or some other method. If the presentation is being multicast, then the presentation description contains the multicast addresses and ports to be used for the continuous media. If the presentation is to be sent only to the client via unicast, then the client provides the destination for security reasons.

Invitation of a Media Server to a Conference

A media server can be "invited" to join an existing conference, either to play back media into the presentation or to record all or a subset of the media in a presentation. This mode is useful for distributed teaching applications. Several parties in the conference may take turns "pushing the remote control buttons."

Addition of Media to an Existing Presentation

Particularly for live presentations, it is useful if the server can tell the client when additional media become available.

RTSP requests may be handled by proxies, tunnels, and caches, in a manner similar to HTTP/1.1.

7.2.5   Multimedia File Formats

Multimedia file formats were created to provide standard ways for storing digital multimedia content as files and a means for playback. Some have evolved to offer more full-featured capabilities, such as media types beyond audio and video, editing and creation capabilities, and the ability to mix multiple streams of audio and video together.

The oldest of these formats is QuickTime [7-11], which was introduced by Apple Computer in 1991. Microsoft later introduced Audio/Video Interleaved (AVI) as a simple audio and video file format for Windows PCs. Both formats were originally designed to provide formatting standards for storing multimedia on a CD-ROM for replaying by a user. Additionally, MPEG1/MPEG2 [7-12] not only are codecs, but also specify a file format for storing MPEG-compressed video on host computers.

In September 1997, Microsoft introduced specifications for the Advanced Streaming Format (ASF) [7-13]. This option was developed through a collaboration of Microsoft, Progressive Networks, Intel, Adobe Systems, and Vivo Software, Inc.

Audio file formats include the Audio Interchange File Format (AIFF) created by Apple Computer. Microsoft created the Wave file (audio files with a .wav extension), which is now common on PCs. Sun created the AU format. MPEG Layer 2 audio (just the audio portion of MPEG) is also a commonly used audio file format.

The two most significant of the multimedia file formats are probably Apple's QuickTime and Microsoft's ASF.

QuickTime has evolved over the years to the current version, Release 3. The latest release supports a plethora of codecs and supports animations, still images, text, music, three-dimensional images, and other data. It also supports mixing to create new kinds of effects by combining multiple media streams. In addition, it provides editing tools to allow a content creator to develop special audio and video effects and transitions. In summary, QuickTime is a format for directly capturing multimedia, for editing that data, for delivering it, and for playing it back. This format also includes a framework and a set of tools for the content provider. In March 1998 QuickTime was selected as the basis for a new ITU standard for streaming multimedia file format.

ASF is an open file format for storing streaming multimedia content. It is designed to become a key multimedia file format standard for Intranets and the Internet, replacing separate data types such as WAV and AVI. ASF provides for integration of different media types, optimization for delivery over lossy networks, and support of multiple bandwidths within a single media file. This format supports the synchronization of different media types on a common time line, enabling images, HTML pages, or scripted events to be synchronized with an audio track. Media servers, players, and authoring tools supporting ASF were expected to become available in early 1998, according to Microsoft. The latest version of NetShow, incorporated into Internet Explorer 4.0, Microsoft's Web browser, includes ASF.

Microsoft's creation of ASF represents an attempt by the company to develop a standard by using its industry domination to force its acceptance. This move is not bad; in fact, it is good for the industry, as other multimedia streaming companies have invented myriad new formats, resulting in an alphabet soup of acronyms such as VXF, RA, RMFF, and VIV. These proprietary formats, however, lock the customer into only one vendor's products.

ASF can be played not only from an HTTP (Web) server, but also from a separate media server. RTSP specifically includes this feature as one of its capabilities. This consideration becomes important for scaling, as the playing of media is very compute-intensive, especially when it involves a spectrum of individual transfers rather than a few multicast transfers. If this transfer took place on a Web server, it would soon be overloaded.

ASF defines seven core media types: audio, video, image, timecode, text, MIDI, and command. It is designed to permit the efficient delivery and play-back of powerful multimedia presentations involving the combination and syn-chronization of various types of media selected from these seven core media types.

The primary capabilities of ASF are as follows:

- Local and network playback
- Extensible media types
- Component download
- Scalable media types
- Prioritization of streams
- Multiple language support
- Environment independence
- Rich interstream relationships
- Expandability

Not all of these capabilities are unique to ASF; many are also available with QuickTime and MPEG1/MPEG2. It does appear, however, that ASF offers the most comprehensive set of capabilities.

7.2.6   Synchronized Multimedia Integration Language (SMIL)

The World Wide Web Consortium's (W3C's) Synchronized Multimedia (SYMM) Working Group created the Synchronized Multimedia Integration Language (SMIL) [7-14] specification. This XML-based language was designed for writing "TV-like" multimedia presentations for the Web. The SMIL specification was is-sued as a proposed W3C Recommendation in April 1998 by the Working Group. This Working Group includes such key organizations as Digital Equipment Cor-poration, Lucent/Bell Labs, Microsoft, Philips N.V., RealNetworks, and Produc-tivity Works, as well as a number of research and government organizations.

SMIL greatly facilitates synchronization of various multimedia components over time. A key advantage is that this language reduces the bandwidth of TV-like content, eliminating the need to convert low-bandwidth media types, such as text and images, into high-bandwidth video. Additionally, content creators can author content with a simple text editor under SMIL, following the success path blazed by HTML for Web pages.

SMIL is destined to facilitate the creation of multimedia content that possesses a highly varying character. This kind of content will likely become more prevalent in the future.

7.3 CONCLUSIONS

What can we conclude from the overview of multimedia streaming applications and technology presented in this chapter? Multimedia as a presentation tool is undoubtedly much richer than just text or still images, and it would be used extensively today if the appropriate infrastructure was in place and the price was right.

These criteria have not yet been met, however. Network operators are reluctant to turn on multicast in their network. To implement a QoS method requires an even further stretch, but one that is essential for high-quality video.

Users have a plethora of multimedia technologies from which to choose, a virtual alphabet soup of codecs to handle almost any data, and a range of multimedia file formats and mixing technologies. We have only one transport protocol, however, that is on the way to be standardized—RTP and its companion RTCP.

The first widespread penetration of multimedia is happening with audio. It can usually be used without a QoS, and many applications do not need multicast support, such as Internet telephony. Audio conferencing or video conferencing with very-low-bit-rate video could loom large if the Internet became multicast-enabled, as it would represent a cheaper alternative to telephone conference calls.

Until networks provide low-cost, high-speed connectivity that supports multicast and QoS, two of the mainstream multimedia applications—events and remote training—will be relegated to niches, albeit fairly significant ones. Additionally, satellite technology may boost this market, as will be seen later in this book.

Multimedia applications can also benefit from non-real-time delivery. In this case, they are delivered as a file to a local server, where users receive a high-quality multimedia experience over their high-bandwidth local network. This option could be especially useful for remote training, where students often do not want to view the course live, but would rather watch at their convenient time. In many of these applications, multimedia streams are individual rather than multicast, but are multicast as files and preloaded.

Another niche that is already becoming significant with early adopters relates to the financial industry. Two of our case studies involved financial applications

(Paribas and Smith Barney). The financial industry is willing to pay for the band-width needed to transmit high-quality video to the desktop, as it has compelling reasons to do so. Industry members can gain a measurable business benefit and competitive advantage by being able to watch industry events, whenever and wherever they happen, at employees' desktops, because financial decisions are often based on these events.

Some observers anticipate a merger of computer networking and broadcast entertainment, in which the Internet offers potentially thousands of content channels to compete with the broadcast television industry. This scenario could unfold in the future; this prospect will also be discussed later in this book. The technology discussed in this chapter will be crucial for the realization of this application, if it does emerge.

REFERENCES

[7-1] Buford JFK, ed. Multimedia Systems. Reading, MA: Addison Wesley Longman Publishing Co., 1994.

[7-2] Schulzrinne H, Casner S, Frederick R, Jacobson V. RTP: A Transport Protocol for Real-Time Applications. RFC 1889, January 1996.

[7-3] Braden R, Zhang L, Berson S, Herzog S, Jamin S. Resource ReSerVation Protocol (RSVP) — Version 1 Functional Specification. RFC 2205, September 1997.

[7-4] Wroclawski J. The Use of RSVP with IETF Integrated Service. RFC 2210, September 1997.

[7-5] Roberts E. RSVP: A Priority Problem? Data Communications May 21, 1997: 58–64.

[7-6] Mankin A, Baker F, Braden B, Bradner S, O'Dell M, Romanow A, Weinrib A, Zhang L. Resource ReSerVation Protocol (RSVP) Version 1 Applicability Statement: Some Guidelines on Deployment. RFC 2208, September 1997.

[7-7] Floyd S. Notes on CBQ and Guaranteed Service. Lawrence Berkeley Laboratory Report, July 12, 1995.

[7-8] Ferguson P. Simple Differential Services: IP TOS and Precedence, Delay Indication, and Drop Preference. Internet Draft, Work in Progress, draft-ferguson-delay-drop-00.txt, November 7, 1997.

[7-9] Prue W, Postel J. A Queuing Algorithm to Provide Type-of-Service for IP Links. RFC 1046, February 1988.

[7-10] Schulzrinne H, Rao A, Lanphier R. Real-Time Streaming Protocol (RTSP). RFC 2326, April 1998.

[7-11] Information on QuickTime may be found on Apple Computer's Web site at http://www.apple.com.

[7-12] Information on MPEG standards may be found on the MPEG home page at http://www.cselt.stet.it/mpeg/.

[7-13] Information on ASF may be found on Microsoft's Web site at http://www.microsoft.com.

[7-14] Synchronized Multimedia Integration Language (SMIL) 1.0 Specification. W3C Proposed Recommendation, April 9, 1998.

URLS FOR ORGANIZATIONS MENTIONED IN CHAPTER 7

Adobe Systems	http://www.adobe.com
Apple Computer	http://www.apple.com
Digital Equipment	http://www.digital.com
Icast Software	http://www.icast.com
IETF	http://www.ietf.org
Intel Corp.	http://www.intel.com
Internet2	http://www.internet2.edu
ITU	http://www.itu.org
Lucent	http://www.lucent.com
Microsoft	http://www.microsoft.com
National Institutes of Health	http://www.nih.gov
Netscape	http://www.netscape.com
Philips N.V.	http://www.philips.com
Precept Software	http://www.precept.com
Productivity Works	http://www.prodworks.com
RealNetworks	http://www.realnetworks.com
Starlight Networks	http://www.starlight.com
3Com	http://www.3com.com
Vivo Software	http://www.vivo.com
World Wide Web Consortium	http://www.w3c.org

8

RELIABLE MULTICAST APPLICATIONS AND TECHNOLOGY

The remaining multicast applications fit into the general category of *reliable* multicast. Although multimedia streaming applications are often almost viewed as being synonymous with multicast networks, most such applications actually deployed fall into the "reliable" multicast categories.

Reliable multicast applications encompass a large range of applications with very different requirements, as shown in Figure 8-1. In the figure, the three shaded quadrants indicate the range of reliable multicast applications.

The real-time data-only applications are very different than the non-real-time applications. Even within the real-time data-only category, many diverse requirements exist. We will first discuss these various requirements and the applications driving them before describing the reliable multicast protocols used to satisfy these needs. Some reliable multicast protocols attempt to achieve a generality applicable to all solutions, while others narrow their focus to particular applications to gain some benefit (usually scalability).

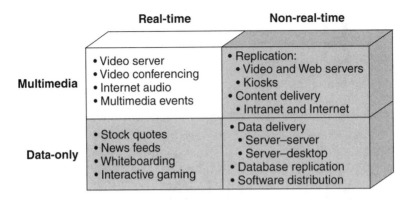

FIGURE 8-1

Reliable multicast applications

8.1 DATA-ONLY REAL-TIME APPLICATIONS

Data-only real-time applications appear in the lower left quadrant of Figure 8-1. They include a wide variety of applications, and many show some similarity to the multimedia streaming applications discussed in Chapter 7. Table 8-1 further characterizes these applications.

Ticker-tape feeds are a very common application. For consumers, they are simply a continuous stream of financial symbols that represent stocks, bonds, mutual funds, commodities, and their latest trading prices. Ticker-tape feeds are often shown on television screens along with news or financial programming. Similarly, financial Web pages often include this service. For consumers, this stream is purposely delayed for some time—usually many minutes—as the information is volatile. The fresher the information, the more valuable it is. Ticker-tape streams sent to consumers also do not need strict reliability, as the information is refreshed by the next trade of that security.

Traders in financial institutions have much stricter requirements regarding ticker-tape feed's reliability, latency, and concurrency. Reliability is needed for all data, as a missed trade could be a missed opportunity to buy or sell based on the financial instrument's price. Low latency is needed (in the range of one second), as timely knowledge means money in the financial business. Lastly, concurrency is important, as a service often provides the feeds to the financial industry, and the feeds should be delivered without favoritism shown to any of

TABLE 8-1

DATA-ONLY REAL-TIME APPLICATIONS

Application	Latency Requirements	Multicast		Bandwidth Requirements
		One-to-Many	Many-to-Many	
Ticker tape	Low–medium	X		Low–Medium
News feeds	Low–medium	X		Low
Whiteboard	Low		X	Medium–High
Network games	Low		X	Medium–High
Network simulations	Low		X	High

the recipients. These multiple, conflicting requirements have required financial institutions to create private networks that are overdesigned — that is, guaranteed not to be congested and characterized by built-in redundancy, which ensures that a single failure does not stop delivery. The trade-off is simply cost, and the financial industry is willing to pay the cost to obtain the reliability and low latency needed to handle its base business. Although many ticker-tape feeds used by the financial industry do not currently use multicast technology, they could benefit from its implementation.

News feeds are usually text-based and have characteristics similar to those of ticker-tape feeds. They are more akin to consumer ticker-tape applications, in that latency and concurrency are not crucial, but simply desirable. An example of news feeds includes the news stories "pushed" out by PointCast as discussed in Chapter 6.

As noted earlier, whiteboarding is essentially data conferencing. Members of the conference have a whiteboard, on which any member of the conference may draw images or write text that all members of the conference may see. Often, whiteboarding is accompanied by audio conferencing, so that the participants may speak to one another. The most prominent whiteboard is the "wb" tool created by Lawrence Berkeley Labs; it is commonly used by researchers over the Mbone. Both reliability and low latency are required, with the latter being a common characteristic of collaborative applications.

Network-based games constitute another collaborative many-to-many set of applications. Multicast war game scenarios have been created for use by the military. Additionally, network games might become a popular entertainment service over the Internet if the infrastructure were multicast-ready. Research institutions have carried out a number of experiments with network games using reliable multicast, the most prominent being the MiMaze multiuser game developed by Inria [8-1], a research institute in France. Network games require both reliability and low latency (approximately 100 milliseconds), although the data transferred may have different requirements for reliability.

Whiteboarding and network gaming are both collaborative applications where the scaling requirements are modest. For example, the group usually has less than 100 members and, more typically, less than 20.

Network-based simulation is attracting attention primarily for military usage. Its requirements are quite stringent, and investigation has spawned the Large-Scale Multicast Applications (LSMA) Working Group [8-2] in the IETF.

8.2 NON-REAL-TIME APPLICATIONS

The two right quadrants in Figure 8-1 both have essentially the same characteristics — non-real-time data delivery in the form of files or other data that is known before delivery. The only difference involves the data content: in one case, it is multimedia content, and in the other, it is data of some other kind.

In contrast to streamed data, the data being sent in these applications has a known beginning and ending, and its size is known beforehand. Virtually any amount of data can be sent, and the latency in sending it can be high.

Data is very often organized as files, with the Web being a prime example of this structure. Databases, which have data blocks of a known size, also fit in this category. Multimedia content is organized into files as well.

These applications are all one-to-many and the scaling requirements can be very large, conceivably as high as millions of recipients.

8.3 CASE STUDIES

Case studies of actual applications are illuminating to show the actual worth of technology to organizations. In Chapters 5 and 6, we discussed a set of applications that typically do not use reliable multicast but could to great advantage. These applications focus on Web server replication and network caching, which greatly improve performance of the network, and "push" technology, which can reduce the need for browsing the network to find information.

Only a few companies were selling reliable multicast solutions at the time of this book's publication. StarBurst sells toolkits and end-user products based on the Multicast File Transfer Protocol (MFTP). TIBCO sells solutions primarily to the financial community using a proprietary reliable multicast protocol that is based on message-stream technology and most suited to use on LANs because of the traffic it generates. The Analytic Science Corporation (TASC) sells military gaming solutions using the Reliable Adaptive Multicast Protocol (RAMP) protocol. GlobalCast sells protocol toolkits based on Scalable Reliable Multicast (SRM), Reliable Multicast Transport Protocol (RMTP), and RMP.*

8.3.1   A Major Telephone Carrier

This case study is described briefly in the *Bell Labs Technical Journal,* Spring 1997 edition. The organization is not revealed in the publication, but it is a major long-distance telephone carrier.

RMTP+ (the streaming version of RMTP, which will become integrated with the bulk data transfer version in the future to form RMTP II [8-3, 8-4]) is currently deployed in this carrier's LANs, which are connected by a WAN to distribute call detail information. The WAN consists of more than 100 switching nodes distributed across the United States. Each switching node collects call detail information and sends it to a distribution center. The distribution centers then distribute this information to several collection points (collectors) within the United States. RMTP+ has been partially deployed (with plans for full deployment) over a WAN to multicast the call detail information from each distribution center to all collection points.

Applications that tap into the RMTP+ multicast stream can be added easily, including more collectors. Unwanted data from the RMTP+ multicast stream is filtered out, and the remaining data is passed to the call detail application. Examples of call detail applications include billing, fraud management, and calling-pattern analysis.

---

*RMP is the Reliable Multicast Protocol. It is not described in this book, as it has gained only negligible commercial acceptance.

The call detail application's use of the data creates very stringent requirements for distributing call detail information in this network. For example, an application that bills for revenue on a per-call basis will lose revenue with every corrupted or lost billing record. Throughput on the order of hundreds of kilobits per second to megabits per second is required, while data loss cannot exceed one block per million.

During multicast operation, regular maintenance procedures that occasionally used the network would cause temporary, though serious network congestion. Initial configurations of RMTP+ suffered drastically reduced multicast throughput when this situation occurred, because RMTP+'s congestion avoidance mechanism was automatically activated, increasing the time between acknowledgments sent by receivers. (The time between acknowledgments is based on round-trip delays between the receiver and its designated receiver.*) To quickly return multicast throughput to its normal levels after such a temporary congestion, RMTP+'s congestion avoidance scheme was disabled. Round-trip time calculations were then modified to use the minimum measured round-trip time found in a sequence of consecutive round-trip measurements. The modified RMTP+ continued to operate as if congestion had never occurred in the network, and RMTP+ throughput and reliability remained high, as desired, despite the presence of this congestion.

8.3.2   3Com

As mentioned in Chapter 7, 3Com's corporate Intranet is fully multicast-ready, with the exception of a few small sales offices.

3Com selected TIBCO's TIB Rendezvous middleware product and reliable multicast engine to tie many of its corporate back-end business processes together. The company implemented a SAP Enterprise Resource Planning (ERP) system in late 1997, with the goal of tying together many of its corporate business processes to make the organization more efficient. A problem arose, however, because of the presence of other ERP systems at 3Com (for example, People-Soft in the Human Resources Department), as well as a number of legacy systems. All of these systems collected information, but did not have a good means of sharing it with the other systems.

3Com wrote the first module to interface its SAP Application Server in Santa Clara to the TIBCO Rendezvous Information Bus, thereby enabling the SAP

---

*See Section 8.4.2.1.2 for a description of RMTP operation.

server to send and receive data based on events. Modules were also written to tie other applications to the TIBCO information bus, including one Sun Solaris, ten Windows NT, and 21 Windows 95 applications in Santa Clara; 26 Windows 95 applications in Singapore, Boston, and the United Kingdom; and three Windows NT applications in Singapore. The system was considered to be in a pilot stage as of May 1998.

3Com is calling this internal system "InfoBroker," and it promises to speed up information delivery in the organization considerably and allow decision-making to occur before an event happens. Event triggers can automatically implement a predetermined "what-if" decision. The combination of multicast networking, reliable delivery, and TIBCO's middleware has allowed legacy systems to be linked to the newer ERP systems installed, which has significantly improved the company's business processes and made the organization more competitive. The applications have greatly enhanced the business processes in manufacturing and sales. They will eventually be expanded to cover business processes in all facets of the company.

8.3.3 Toys "R" Us

Toys "R" Us recognizes that technology can make its stores run more efficiently and has invested in information systems that enable it to service customers more effectively. Every Toys "R" Us store is equipped with PCs and a complete suite of Microsoft applications for tracking inventory, scheduling personnel, running registers, handling credit authorizations, and performing other important business functions. Approximately 250 of the company's 900-plus U.S. stores also have Windows NT servers.

Deploying, updating, and debugging so much software on so many machines at so many locations is a huge logistical undertaking, even with the VSAT network that links all Toys "R" Us stores with a corporate data center in Parsippany, New Jersey. Until recently, the company updated its software through point-to-point transfers that took days to complete and tied up large chunks of the VSAT network's bandwidth. In 1996, however, it implemented StarBurst Multicast, a one-to-many IP information transfer application that enables users to send large files from a central location to many receivers over any kind of network in one bandwidth-efficient session. Multicasting has significantly reduced unnecessary network traffic and slashed software delivery time from days to hours.

Toys "R" Us uses StarBurst Multicast in its stores to upgrade existing applications and deploy new ones. The company's network architecture is designed to relieve traffic on the WAN that links all the stores together by transferring software over the WAN to servers on LANs, which have more capacity. Each store then accesses the new software from the LAN, making the transfer and updating process less bandwidth-hungry.

According to Toys "R" Us, the long-range benefit of StarBurst Multicast will likely derive from the distribution of highly graphical customer service applications that are faster and easier for employees to use than the traditional character-based interfaces are. Graphical interfaces are replacing character-based interfaces in all industries. Installing and updating graphically sophisticated applications would have been a long and expensive process with the old point-to-point system, but Toys "R" Us expects StarBurst Multicast to make the process much easier.

8.3.4   The Ohio Company

The Ohio Company, an investment banking firm, is using the StarBurst Multicast application to deliver critical financial trading data to more than 200 investment executives (IEs) who operate out of 50 offices in five states. StarBurst Multicast provides the IEs with up-to-the-minute information that reaches all offices simultaneously and reliably.

The Ohio Company now multicasts a key financial information database to its branches. It will soon use multicasting to update its entire stock and bond inventory at all offices as transactions occur. This business-critical inventory tells IEs what they can sell and what has already been sold. The IEs can then avoid offering inventory that has already been purchased, as could happen under the company's previous point-to-point file transfer delivery system. Now, StarBurst Multicast automatically and simultaneously transfers information to local Sun Solaris servers at every Ohio Company branch via the company's VSAT network.

Before implementing reliable one-to-many IP multicasting, The Ohio Company distributed key financial data through sequential point-to-point file transfers. This method consumed network resources and time, and meant that IEs were rarely operating with the same information. When the company implemented a 300 Mbyte to 400 Mbyte financial information database, which needed to be updated weekly and completely replaced its monthly updates, its file transfer solution could not handle the increased traffic. The other immediate solution, mailing CD-ROMs, would be costly and inefficient. Consequently, the Ohio Company turned to StarBurst Multicast.

Simultaneous, reliable information distribution is vital when dealing with mission-critical data like a financial inventory; bonds can sell out in 20 minutes, and if point-to-point transfers are used, a broker at one branch may easily sell inventory that someone at another office already promised to a customer. The Ohio Company needed to guarantee its IEs that they would have equal access to the company's inventory. In addition, the company recognized that IEs cannot waste their time in downloading CD-ROMs or leafing through big, bulky books of database information. Although IEs need information, they cannot spend much time administering it.

In addition to freeing IEs to concentrate on sales, StarBurst Multicast has cut the company's costs by increasing network efficiency. Multicasting is a true server-push technology that enables a server to send a single stream of traffic to any number of clients, replicating information in the network rather than the server. This approach reduces unnecessary traffic and conserves network resources. StarBurst Multicast also allows users to save resources by regulating the amount of bandwidth they devote to transfers.

8.3.5   THE BOX

Reaching more than 30 million households worldwide, THE BOX (a subsidiary of THE BOX Worldwide, Inc.) is the first interactive, 24-hour, music channel. Unlike with any other music video channel, THE BOX's viewers dictate the channel's programming by choosing which videos play in their viewing area. The company's motto is "Music Television You Control" and, for this thriving Miami Beach-headquartered business, controlling how the latest, hottest videos reach the local channels is essential.

Because the music industry changes so rapidly and new video clips are released constantly, THE BOX needs to send new clips to local servers daily. Transmitting videos to local broadcast channels was a chore, however.

To keep its U.S. channels reliably stocked with music, THE BOX uses StarBurst Multicast running over a two-way, interactive VSAT network. The system distributes new videos efficiently as MPEG computer files to more than 100 Windows NT servers located across the country.

Videos are stored as MPEG files on servers at local cable or broadcast stations. Viewers choose videos from a constantly updated menu that includes as many as 300 choices, displayed either on their television or on THE BOX's Web site (http://www.thebox.com). They then dial a 900 number to order a selection.

When an order comes in, the server finds the video in the library and puts it in the broadcast queue behind other viewers' requests. MPEG2 decoders transform these digital files into high-quality music videos that are then broadcast to everyone in the viewing area. The cost of the video appears on the viewer's telephone bill.

For THE BOX, perhaps IP multicasting's biggest benefit is peace of mind. There is little administration, because transfers are automatically sent from Miami Beach and downloaded onto local servers. Multicasting saves employee time and ensures that every Wednesday at 12:01 A.M., the company provides new music for the masses.

8.3.6   General Motors

The GM Access program, which was deployed to provide dealerships with on-demand sales and service information, was not delivering data quickly or reliably enough. Salespeople had trouble finding the specific cars that their customers wanted, which put sales in jeopardy. Service personnel sometimes had to keep vehicles in the shop longer because they did not have up-to-date service instructions.

General Motors' old data distribution system caused most of these problems. Information such as car pricing and availability, dealer incentives, and service bulletins was sent point-to-point to each dealership; alternatively, it might be copied to disks and CD-ROMs and sent via overnight mail. Information sometimes took weeks to reach dealerships and even longer to get to employees as nontechnical dealers tried to install it on their computer systems.

Both General Motors and Electronic Data Systems Corporation (EDS), the system integrator for GM Access, knew the process had to change. EDS began looking for an information delivery system that could ensure that all dealerships received updated information reliably and regularly without devouring network bandwidth, consuming exorbitant sums of money, or flustering nontechnical employees.

To facilitate the GM Access program, EDS deployed StarBurst Multicast to send software updates simultaneously from EDS application servers in Auburn Hills, Michigan, to dealers via General Motors' existing satellite-based WAN.

General Motors wants dealerships to have the latest available information to ensure customer satisfaction, but dealers are not technical people; their job is to fix and sell cars, not load software. The easier that the company can make the information delivery process, the more successful that it will be in getting all of its dealerships in synch with updated information. Where it once took 30 minutes to send a 1 Mbyte file to a limited number of dealerships, General Motors can now send the same file to more than 500 dealers in three minutes.

8.4 RELIABLE MULTICAST PROTOCOLS — REQUIREMENTS AND EXAMPLES

Now that we have seen how commercial enterprises have actually benefited from using reliable multicast technology, we will examine the underlying reliable multicast protocols, including the requirements placed on them by the varied applications. Additionally, we will review TCP operation briefly to gain an understanding of what the research community expects from a "TCP"-friendly reliable multicast protocol.

Unlike the case in Chapter 7 where multimedia streaming became standardized on RTP/RTCP as a specialized transport, no such protocol or protocols have been standardized for reliable multicast. The subject is now being studied in the Internet Research Task Force (IRTF) [8-5]. The decision to have the subject of reliable multicast studied in the IRTF rather than the Internet Engineering Task Force (IETF), the body that works on Internet standards, was based on the fact that the technical issues are complex. It was decided that basic techniques should be recommended before standardization was pursued.

The main issues that the IRTF believes need to be resolved are congestion control and "fairness" to TCP. We will review the mechanisms of TCP operation in Section 8.4.1 to understand this issue better. TCP is designed to share fairly the available bandwidth with all other TCP sessions present. For example, if bandwidth B is available to n TCP sessions, then in steady-state each TCP session will occupy B/n of the bandwidth. TCP responds to congestion implicitly by backing off multiplicatively and recovering additively, a format that researchers have shown to be stable.

Today's reliable multicast protocols do not, in general, provide this characteristic. They are typically rate-based — that is, a rate for sending is determined at the sender and no feedback mechanism exists to reduce it if congestion arises. Some suggestions for congestion control in reliable multicast protocols have been made by researchers, however, and they will be discussed later in this chapter.

Scaling is another major issue and one that is fundamental to a successful reliable multicast protocol. Two issues related to scaling have emerged, complicating the ability to have large groups. The first and most significant is widely known as ACK/NAK implosion. As the number of receivers grows, the amount of administrative back-traffic to the sender eventually overwhelms the network's capacity to handle it. This problem is especially dire when timeliness is important, such as in collaborative applications. Additionally, the network at the sender site becomes congested from the cumulative back-traffic from the receivers.

The second issue involves retransmissions (often referred to as "repairs"). If the packet loss is uncorrelated at the receivers, retransmissions grow so that the data may need to be sent multiple times to satisfy all receivers. Measurements of the Mbone have shown that this loss consists of both correlated and uncorrelated parts. Satellite networks also exhibit a mixture of correlated and uncorrelated losses.

The ability to handle different network infrastructures also looms large. Mbone researchers who have been studying reliable multicast protocols have focused on the routed land-line-based Internet as the basic network infrastructure for their designs. A number of network infrastructures, however, are being added to this base.

One of the most prominent of these options is satellite. Because satellite is a broadcast network by nature, it has often been mentioned as a multicast overlay to the current land-line-based Internet, as shown in Figure 8-2.

The satellite link in the forward direction can be used for high-speed multicast downloads to the user. This approach is even feasible for consumer use, as satellite dishes for television usage are available at very low cost.

Satellite networks have two characteristics that are very different from land-line terrestrial routed networks. The first is high latency. All satellite systems in operation today are geostationary — that is, they are in fixed Earth orbit of approximately 22,600 miles (36,000 kilometers). This set-up results in a one-way delay of about 0.27 seconds caused by the speed of light.

The second characteristic of satellite networks is their asymmetric nature, where the back channel offers a different speed than the forward channel. In Figure 8-2, the back channel uses the terrestrial Internet; in two-way VSAT networks, this channel is over satellite, but its speed is usually much lower than the forward direction.

Another characteristic of satellite infrastructures is that large numbers of receivers (millions) can be connected with one transmission over this very flat network. This structure has implications for scaling, as will be discussed later.

Cable networks are also being built as extensions to the Internet. These networks do not experience high latency, though they do exhibit the same asym-

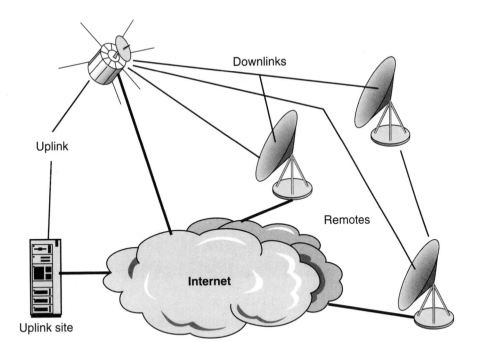

FIGURE 8-2

Satellite overlay to Internet

metric nature as satellite systems. The most prominent is the @Home network, which offers high-speed Internet access via cable modems. The @Home network was designed as a parallel network to the Internet and heavily depends on caching for service. It was also designed to be multicast-enabled from the start.

8.4.1   Brief Review of TCP

It is worthwhile to review briefly the operation of TCP. TCP is generally used to provide reliability in point-to-point (unicast) transmissions so we can have some context for the problem when it is extended to point-to-multipoint (one-to-many multicast) or multipoint-to-multipoint (many-to-many multicast).

As we recall from Chapter 1, the TCP/IP protocol suite has two choices, TCP and UDP, for the Transport layer (Layer 4 in Figure 8-3). Figure 8-3 illustrates the OSI model for communications as adapted for TCP/IP, where Layers 5 and 6 in the OSI model are subsumed into the Application layer. As mentioned

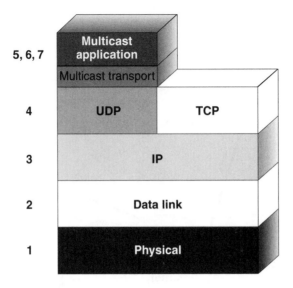

FIGURE 8-3
TCP/IP communications model

previously, all multicast applications must operate a specialized transport over UDP (or alternatively, to interface directly to IP using "raw sockets," in effect becoming an alternative Transport layer).

The Transport layer is responsible for end-to-end delivery of data from the source host (host A) to the destination host (host B), as shown in Figure 8-4. Most applications today choose to operate over TCP as a Transport layer due to the rich services it provides — namely, packet ordering, error correction, and port multiplexing. TCP also includes provisions for congestion control in the network. UDP, in contrast, provides only the minimal Transport-layer services of error detection and port multiplexing. If a UDP packet is detected in error, it is simply discarded.

For all of its rich services, however, TCP is only a point-to-point (unicast) transport protocol and does not support multicast. It is also an error-correction protocol and as such does not optimally support multimedia streams, even if they are only point-to-point.

When applications rely on TCP, they can focus on the application at hand as TCP is guaranteed to deliver data to the application in order and error-free.

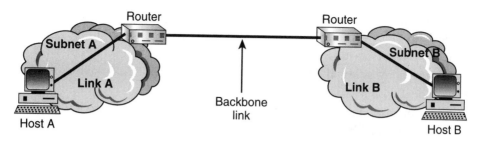

FIGURE 8-4

TCP provides end-to-end transport service

Such popular applications as File Transfer Protocol (FTP) and Hypertext Transfer Protocol (HTTP), which are used for transferring files and accessing the Web, employ TCP as their Transport layer.

TCP is surprisingly complex for a protocol which had simple origins. It has been enhanced a number of times in the past to help solve problems that emerged as the Internet experienced explosive growth. In fact, TCP is still being modified to help solve problems, the most recent of which involve coping with high-speed, high-latency networks.

TCP is a *window*-based protocol — that is, it uses a dynamic windowing method in an attempt to use all of the available bandwidth for transfer. At steady state, an attempt is made to optimize the window at the network round-trip time (RTT). Thus the network "pipe" will be filled with data to the fullest when the next acknowledgment is received, allowing the next window of data to be sent.

Modern implementations of TCP contain four intertwined algorithms that were only recently fully documented as Internet standards: *slow start*, *congestion avoidance*, *fast retransmit*, and *fast recovery*. RFC 1122 [8-6] requires that a TCP implementation include slow start and congestion avoidance. Fast retransmit and fast recovery were not documented until after the development of RFC 1122. Fast retransmit and fast recovery will not be described here; if the reader is interested in them, refer to RFC 2001 [8-7].

Slow start avoids the problem of overflowing buffers in intermediate routers. It operates by observing that the rate at which new packets should be injected into the network is the same rate at which the acknowledgments are returned by the other end.

Congestion can occur when data arrives on a high-speed link (for example, a fast LAN) and gets sent out a on a lower-speed link (for example, a slower WAN). It can also arise when multiple input streams arrive at a router whose output capacity is less than the sum of the inputs. Congestion avoidance is a way to deal with lost packets.

The congestion avoidance algorithm assumes that packet loss caused by errors is very small. Thus the loss of a packet signals congestion somewhere in the network between the source and destination.

What follows is not a complete description of how TCP's slow start and congestion algorithms operate; rather, it has been simplified so you can understand it relatively easily and see how it is not extensible to the reliable multicast problem. Additionally, this discussion will illuminate the context in which reliable multicast must coexist with the TCP traffic that makes up the bulk of the traffic on any TCP/IP network.

The two most important parameters are the congestion window, called *cwnd*, and the slow start threshold, called *ssthresh*. When a new connection is established with a host on another network, the congestion window is initialized to one segment (that is, the segment size announced by the other end, or the default, typically 536 or 512 bytes). Each time a positive acknowledgment (ACK) is received, the congestion window increases by one segment—that is, from one to two—and two segments can be sent. When each of those two segments is acknowledged, the congestion window increases to four. This process leads to an exponential growth and continues, assuming no lost packets, until cwnd equals ssthresh. At that time, congestion avoidance mode is entered and the congestion window begins increasing linearly rather than exponentially.

At some point, the capacity of the busiest link used between the two hosts will be reached, and an intermediate router will begin discarding packets. This action tells the sender that its congestion window has become too large. The congestion window will then be reduced by a factor of two.

If cwnd is less than or equal to ssthresh, TCP is in slow start; otherwise, TCP performs congestion avoidance. Slow start continues until TCP is halfway to the point where congestion occurred (as it recorded half of the window size that caused the problem). Congestion avoidance then takes over.

This approach is obviously not extensible to many recipients for a number of reasons. In slow start mode, positive acknowledgments (ACKs) are sent by a receiver every window setting, which is initially quite small (for example, 512 bytes). Even hundreds of receivers would soon overwhelm the sender with ACK traffic. Every receiver would also have its own window and negotiate with the sender—an obviously impractical scheme when it is desired to scale to millions of receivers.

As a result of these shortcomings, approaches to reliable multicast design have had to be completely different than the model that TCP provides.

8.4.2   Existing Reliable Multicast Protocols and Design Philosophies

Reliable multicast designers have adopted two basic philosophies. The most obvious one, and the one taken by most researchers and developers, is to attempt to create a generalized reliable multicast Transport layer that can handle all reliable multicast applications. This approach, in effect, is a multicast equivalent of TCP. As such, the reliable multicast protocol has all the requirements placed on it by all of the multicast applications. Thus it needs timeliness, packet ordering, error correction, and very high scalability—that is, the ability to handle millions of simultaneous receivers. Being able to satisfy all of these requirements represents a very tough problem for a single reliable multicast protocol. Additionally, this same protocol needs to be able to operate with many different network topologies.

A second philosophy is to focus the reliable multicast protocol on solving the needs of particular applications. For example, non-real-time bulk delivery does not need timeliness (within limits), which means that latency requirements can be relaxed in the protocol to gain other benefits, such as scaling. Similarly, conferencing applications do not need the same level of scalability as one-to-many multicast applications often require. Some data streaming applications, such as consumer ticker-tape and news feeds, need to be semi-reliable, but usually require very high levels of scalability.

The general consensus within the Internet community is that the second philosophy is preferable to the first and more practical. Some remain unconvinced that the "Holy Grail"—that is, a generalized protocol that can be a multicast TCP—is possible.

The result has been a matrix of application capability and network support. Protocols that support the broadest range of applications generally accommodate a more limited range of network infrastructures. Conversely, those that limit their application capability will generally support more network infrastructures. This division is shown in Table 8-2, where each protocol supports the shaded areas next to it. For example, MFTP is narrowly focused on bulk delivery applications, but can operate over any network infrastructure.

Note that some of the protocols in Table 8-2 could operate over network infrastructures shown as unsupported but with very limited scaling. Scalable

Reliable Multicast (SRM) could be adapted to provide bulk data transfer as well as an example.

Three protocols that attempt to be a generalized multicast TCP are discussed: SRM [8-8], which is now supported commercially with a toolkit product by GlobalCast Corporation; Reliable Multicast Transport Protocol (RMTP and RMTP+) [8-9, 8-10], which was created initially by Bell Labs researchers and is now commercially offered by GlobalCast Corporation; and Pragmatic General

TABLE 8-2

RELIABLE MULTICAST PROTOCOL APPLICATION AND NETWORK SUPPORT
(shaded boxes indicate support)

Protocol	Application	Network Type
SRM	Collaborative	LAN
	Message streaming	Symmetric routed WAN
		Asymmetric WAN
	Bulk data transfer	Satellite WAN
RAMP	Collaborative	LAN
	Message streaming	Symmetric routed WAN
		Asymmetric WAN
	Bulk data transfer	Satellite WAN
RMTP/RMTP+	Collaborative	LAN
	Message streaming	Symmetric routed WAN
		Asymmetric WAN
	Bulk data transfer	Satellite WAN
PGM	Collaborative	LAN
	Message streaming	Symmetric routed WAN
		Asymmetric WAN
	Bulk data transfer	Satellite WAN
TIBCO	Collaborative	LAN
	Message streaming	Symmetric routed WAN
		Asymmetric WAN
	Bulk data transfer	Satellite WAN
MFTP	Collaborative	LAN
	Message streaming	Symmetric routed WAN
		Asymmetric WAN
	Bulk data transfer	Satellite WAN

Multicast (PGM) [8-11], a new protocol created by Cisco Systems, which heavily depends on supporting routers in the network infrastructure to provide scaling. SRM is most focused on collaborative applications but can also support message streaming (and probably bulk data transmission), whereas the other two protocols support message streaming and bulk data transfer applications.

Two examples of specialized protocols are also described: Reliable Adaptive Multicast Protocol (RAMP) [8-12], created by TASC (now a division of Litton Industries), a company that targets military applications; and Multicast File Transfer Protocol (MFTP) [8-13], created by StarBurst Communications. RAMP was designed for use with network gaming applications and does not attempt to scale to more than about 100 recipients. MFTP was designed for bulk data delivery applications (the two right quadrants of Figure 8-1); it trades off low latency for high scalability with any network infrastructure.

TIBCO's reliable message streaming protocol will also be discussed in very general terms, as TIBCO is a dominant vendor of multicast streaming solutions. Its protocol is not described in public documents, but it is thought not to be very scalable and thus better suited to use in LANs or campus networks, where NAK implosion issues apply only to the sender rather than the network. Such applications tend to require relatively low bandwidth, meaning that senders may be able to handle more administrative back-traffic than forward-traffic. These limitations have led TIBCO to provide support for PGM as its basic reliable multicast protocol for the future.

Note, however, that a number of other reliable multicast protocols have been proposed; the ones discussed here are simply leading representatives of their relative classes. Information on other reliable multicast protocols may be found by accessing http://research.ivv.gov/RMP/links.html.

8.4.2.1   *Generalized Reliable Multicast Protocols*

Generalized reliable multicast protocols need to provide for packet ordering and error correction in a similar fashion as TCP. If all receivers sent ACKs and NAKs within a reasonable window size back to the sender, then the sender would soon be overwhelmed with traffic as the number of receivers grows, resulting in low scalability. SRM and RMTP have taken different approaches to resolving this scalability problem.

Collaborative and streaming applications also have intermittent flows of data punctuated by significant gaps of no data before more data arrives. Some protocols use mechanisms to let other group members "know" a sender is still there if these gaps extend beyond a certain length.

8.4.2.1.1 Scalable Reliable Multicast (SRM)

Internet researchers would probably take exception to a description of SRM as a general-purpose multicast TCP, as it is actually a *framework* for supporting all reliable multicast applications. For example, in its first application as the reliable multicast protocol used with Lawrence Berkeley Labs' "wb" whiteboarding tool, it does not provide packet ordering, but rather requires the application to perform this function.

This "framework" architecture was first suggested by Clark and Tennenhouse [8-14] and has been called Application-Layer Framing (ALF). Recall from Chapter 7 that RTP requires a series of companion specifications to document the protocol set needed to support that particular application. With SRM, the framework is general; additional specifications need to be created to specialize it to the particular application—hence the ALF concept.

SRM depends on the concept of repair by any receiver that has the data to gain scalability in reducing administrative back-traffic to the source. This approach charges receivers with the responsibility of ensuring that they get missed data.

Group members send low-frequency *session* messages to the group so that their neighbors can learn their status, measure the delay among group members and learn group membership, and detect the last packet in a burst. These messages are similar to the RTCP status messages described in Chapter 7. Session messages are designed to handle only about 5% of the traffic in the session.

Receivers that identify missing data wait a random time period before issuing repair requests, allowing suppression of duplicate requests via a mechanism similar to the one that IGMP uses on its subnet (see Chapter 3). The process for making the actual repairs also closely resembles this request process. The random back-off time for both repair requests made by receivers and for repairs made by senders is a function of "closeness" to the sender and requesting receiver. Thus those closest to one another time out first and make the repair request or the actual repair, thereby keeping repairs as local as possible. Receivers, seeing the first request and determining that it is the same that they would have made, stay silent, reducing potential redundant requests. The requester continues to send repair requests until the repair takes place.

Any receiver may satisfy the repair request, as all are required to cache previously transmitted data. Any receiver that can satisfy the request is prepared to take that step. A random back-off timer is used before a repair is sent; if it sees the repair coming from another group member, it stays silent to reduce the likelihood of duplicate repairs.

One major issue with sending repair requests to the group and with sending the actual repairs to the same group address is the potential for both the repair requests and repairs to be propagated throughout the network span of the group. For example, consider the example in Figure 8-5. The link depicted by the dotted line is a congested link, and hosts H3, H4, and H5 need the same repair. One of those three hosts sends the repair request, depending on the random times generated for each host. The request is transmitted via the same multicast group address as normal session traffic and is propagated to all group members.

Host S is the original source of the data and, with H1 and H2, may satisfy the repair request. Based on which host has the smallest random timeout, one— for example, H2—sends the repair. This repair is propagated to all group members, including those that do not need it. Its reception by members that need the repair terminates requests for that repair.

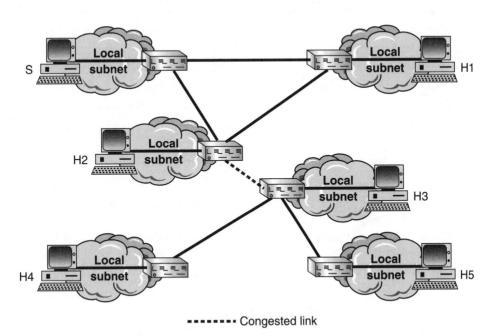

▪▪▪▪▪▪▪▪ Congested link

FIGURE 8-5

SRM configuration

Hence, the initial sender is relieved of the burden of NAK implosion and effort is taken to keep the traffic generation local. On the other hand, no limitation applies to traffic flow within the group as there is no scope limit for group traffic. Although suggestions have been made about ways to limit the scope of repair requests and the repairs, this area remains the subject of study by researchers.

Though some problems persist and SRM continues to evolve, it is still the framework that many Internet researchers believe should be used to build a reliable multicast set of standards. Some of these extensions will be discussed later in this chapter, including mechanisms for limiting the scope of the traffic within the group.

Even with emerging improvements, there are flaws with SRM. Looking again at our satellite example in Figure 8-2, we see that the closest group member with the repair is the sender, negating all of the scaling benefits. Additionally, SRM includes timers that assume that the forward and back channels are of the same speed, which is normally not the case in satellite and cable networks. In its current form, then, SRM is incompatible with asymmetric network infrastructures.

Additionally, in certain commercial environments, it will be unacceptable for repairs to be made by other receivers that may not be in the same network domain as the receiver needing the repair. For example, suppose the information being multicasted had group recipients who were competitors. One receiver could be J. P. Morgan, another Salomon Brothers, and so on. They may be subscribers of the same financial information yet fierce competitors who are not willing to depend on repairs being sent from a host located at a competitor's site.

This commercial issue can be skirted by creating certain neutral "repair retransmitters," which forfeit generality and require more network infrastructure.

8.4.2.1.2   Reliable Multicast Transport Protocol (RMTP)

The Reliable Multicast Transport Protocol (RMTP) was developed at Bell Labs when it was the research arm of AT&T; it became part of Lucent Technologies when Lucent was spun off out of AT&T in 1995.

RMTP gains scalability by providing consolidating nodes, called Designated Receivers (DRs), that collect status messages from nodes in a local RMTP domain and provide repairs, if available. Thus, the DR provides both local recovery and consolidation of control traffic to the next DR in the hierarchy if the data requested is not available, as illustrated in Figure 8-6.

There is a novel election process to determine the designated router (DR) for each RMTP domain. The data source and DRs periodically multicast special SendAckToMe messages. All SendAckToMe messages are sent with the same time to live (TTL). Each router hop decrements the TTL number by one; the SendAckToMe message with the largest TTL value is then selected by the local receivers and downstream DRs as the DR to which they should unicast control messages, as it is the closest DR to those receivers. DRs need to be placed into the network architecture manually.

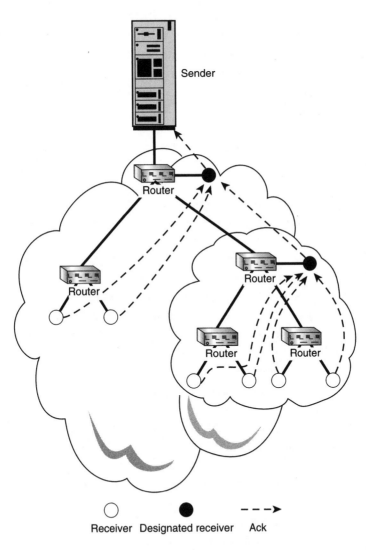

FIGURE 8-6

RMTP designated receivers

In this way, RMTP overcomes some of SRM's deficiencies; control traffic is unicast to DRs, preventing the proliferation of control traffic throughout the group. Local repair is attempted first at the closest DR to the receiver and, if it is not available, is then sent to the next DR up the hierarchy on the way to the sender. In this respect, the DRs act in similar fashion as the network caches in a hierarchical architecture, as described in Chapter 5.

RMTP was originally designed only for bulk (file) transfer, but was upgraded to add message streaming capability with a "transmit window" in a new version called "RMTP+." The RMTP+ version has since been added to the original RMTP bulk transfer version to provide a superset of both capabilities, which is called RMTP II [8-3, 8-4].

Status messages contain a bit mask preceded by the first in-sequence packet number that is not received among the packets in a "window" of data. They also indicate to which window the status message applies. Repairs contain only the marked bad packets as indicated by the bit map, invoking a *selective repeat* retransmission. The DR consolidates status messages from the nodes in its domain, so that only one is returned up the hierarchy.

Repairs may be sent via either unicast or multicast, depending on a settable threshold. This flexibility keeps repair traffic to a minimum when the number of receivers needing repairs is small.

RMTP also has a congestion control mechanism that attempts to emulate TCP's slow start algorithm (see Section 8.4.1). RMTP receivers and Designated Receivers periodically send acknowledgments to the DR selected to invoke a measurement of round-trip delay, as shown in Figure 8-6. This measurement is used to optionally invoke a slow start and congestion avoidance algorithm, similar to the case with TCP. In the one documented commercial application, however, congestion control needed to be disabled because it slowed down the delivery of critical information in the application (see Section 8.3.1).

RMTP has a number of desirable characteristics. Its main flaw is its dependence on hierarchy for scaling. Referring to the satellite example in Figure 8-2, we find that flat network infrastructures, such as that present with satellite, have no place for relays or Designated Receivers because the destination receiver is most often tied directly to the satellite network.

In land-line routed networks with multiple hops, however, RMTP includes a number of desirable characteristics. These capabilities can also be beneficial in hybrid land-line/satellite networks that include land-line extensions to the satellite network.

RMTP was updated in April 1998 to RMTP II, as mentioned previously, through a series of Internet Drafts. This update consolidated the streaming and bulk data delivery.

8.4.2.1.3 Pragmatic General Multicast (PGM)

Pragmatic General Multicast (originally Pretty Good Multicast) was first publicly documented in January 1998 in an Internet Draft [8-11] from Cisco Systems and first presented at the Reliable Multicast Research Group meeting of IRTF in February 1998. This general protocol can handle all reliable multicast applications except collaborative ones, where scaling is dependent on active assistance of network elements (that is, routers).

Design goals for the creators of PGM included simplicity and the ability to optimally leverage routers in the network to provide scalability. PGM bypasses UDP and interfaces directly to IP via "raw" sockets, as shown in Figure 8-7.

PGM provides no notion of group membership. Rather, it simply provides reliability within a source's transmit window from the time a receiver joins a group until it departs.

PGM has only a few defined data packets:

ODATA—original content data

NAK—selective negative acknowledgment

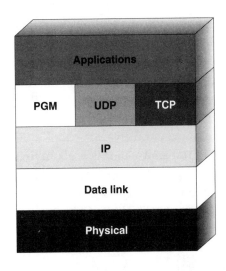

FIGURE 8-7

PGM interfaces directly to IP

NCF—NAK confirmation

RDATA—retransmission (repair)

SPM—source path message

Each PGM packet contains a transport session identifier (TSI) to identify the session and source of that data, so multiple sessions may be easily identified by PGM-aware routers and receivers. ODATA, NCF, RDATA, and SPM packets flow downstream in the distribution tree, while NAK packets flow upstream toward the source.

PGM is designed to serve real-time applications as well as to be highly scalable. As such, it has a high need for timeliness, which is handled by the *transmit window*. The transmit window defines a sliding window of data such that, if no NAKs are received by the sender or a designated local retransmitter when the window ends, the data is simply not available for repairs.

PGM is totally NAK-based, so the scaling issue is to reduce the number of NAKs sent back to the source, while simultaneously protecting against lost NAKs. The router assist plays a role in this process, as shown in Figure 8-8.

NAKs are unicast from PGM router to PGM router initiated by a receiver that lost data when sending a NAK to its nearest PGM-aware router. The first PGM router responds to the NAK by multicasting an NCF downstream and forwarding the NAK upstream to the next PGM-aware router, which performs the same operation. Each PGM-aware router keeps forwarding NAKs until it sees an NCF or RDATA, which indicates that a repair is on its way. NAK suppression is provided by a receiver's subnet PGM-aware router, and all PGM-aware routers eliminate duplicate NAKs upstream to the source.

The unicast path back to the source must follow the same path as the downstream multicast tree. Source path messages (SPMs) are interleaved with ODATA packets and sent downstream to establish the path state for a given source and session. PGM-aware routers use this information to determine the unicast path back to the source for forwarding NAKs. SPMs also alert receivers that the oldest data in the transmit window is about to be retired and thus will no longer be available for repairs from the source. These messages are sent by a source at a rate that at least equals the rate at which the transmit window is advanced and that provokes "last call" NAKs from receivers; they also update the receivers' window state.

PGM-aware routers keep state information on the NAKs' origins in the distribution tree, enabling them to constrain the forwarding of RDATA repairs to only those ports generating NAK requests for repairs. This set-up eliminates the

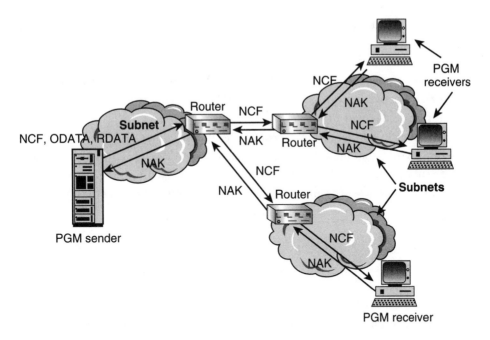

FIGURE 8-8

PGM NAK/NCF dialog

transmission of repair data to parts of the distribution tree that do not need the repair.

PGM also has the optional provision to redirect NAKs to a designated local retransmitter (DLR) rather than the source. A DLR announces its presence to provoke the redirection of NAKs for that session and source.

The first description of PGM did not include any flow-control mechanism, although the PGM Internet Draft [8-11] suggests possible methods that could be used. In the first version, the source rate limits the traffic, including the RDATA repairs, to a settable rate.

Obviously, network elements in the form of routers are intimately involved in the operation of PGM and are essential for scaling. Routers also have the normal tasks of routing packets over the network—their primary mission, and a complex one at that. If all packets flowing through a PGM-aware router needed to be examined to determine if they were PGM and thus required processing, it would impose a huge burden and would severely impact the normal routing functions. As a result, PGM specifies that SPM, NCF, and RDATA PGM packets must be transmitted with the *router alert* function outlined in RFC 2113 [8-15]. This option gives Network-layer entities, such as routers, an indication at the Network layer that a marked packet should be extracted from the routing functions for more detailed processing.

Although PGM has no field experience, it does show promise in land-line routed networks that include PGM-aware routers in the infrastructure. It offers the advantages of simplicity and scalability combined with timeliness, which allow it to address a wide range of applications. The protocol is still new, however, and will have to go through a maturation stage before being ready for prime time.

PGM is heavily dependent on support from the infrastructure. Some may view this approach as a violation of duties; routers should concentrate on Layer 3 routing functions, they will say, rather than worry about transport issues. There is a real issue here, however. The IETF is hard at work on developing the IPsec specifications discussed in Chapter 10. IPsec will be the basis for the creation of Virtual Private Networks (VPNs), an area of great interest. IPsec provides mechanisms that can be used to encrypt all layers above the IP layer, Layer 3. Thus the PGM layer would be encrypted if IPsec were used, making it unrecognizable by the network elements that are crucial to PGM operation.

Another practical issue also arises with PGM. Windows NT and Windows 95 as of May 1998 do not support interfaces to raw sockets, forcing implementers to use a totally separate TCP/IP protocol stack to support PGM in these operating systems. It remains unknown whether Microsoft will support raw sockets in its future versions of operating systems.

It should also be obvious that no scaling benefits accrue in satellite infrastructures, unless the network encompasses significant land-line extensions. Nevertheless, satellite is destined to be a major infrastructure supporting multicast services.

A number of companies has pledged support for PGM, including TIBCO and GlobalCast Communications. TIBCO needs a scalable reliable multicast protocol to support its real-time messaging applications. GlobalCast plans to offer a PGM toolkit to augment its line of protocol toolkits. Microsoft, Intel, and StarBurst have publicly stated that they are studying PGM and may support it in the future.

Products with PGM technology are unlikely to reach the market before late 1998 or early 1999. Cisco's router-assist code, for example, needs to be implemented first in a future release of its router software. Maturity will take longer than that.

8.4.2.2   Specialized Reliable Multicast Protocols

Specialized reliable multicast protocols focus more narrowly upon specific applications to gain some benefit. Two examples will be presented: RAMP, which targets collaborative applications where group sizes are usually less than 100 and thus gains timeliness as a major benefit, and MFTP, which focuses on non-real-time reliable delivery, which is traded off for high scaling over all network infrastructures.

TIBCO, a significant vendor in financial markets, will also be discussed, even though its protocol is not publicly documented. Nevertheless, some of its characteristics can be ascertained.

8.4.2.2.1   Reliable Adaptive Multicast Protocol (RAMP)

RAMP was developed by TASC and was originally described in RFC 1458 [8-12]. It was designed for military collaborative applications such as simulated war games; consequently, it was designed to provide low latency and reliable delivery. RAMP was also developed to operate at very high speeds over the ARPA-sponsored Testbed for Optical Networking (TBONE) project, an optical, circuit-switched network operating initially at 800 Mbps. In this environment, congestion in the network is virtually nonexistent and packet loss primarily comes from host buffer overflow in receivers.

RAMP, like most other reliable multicast protocols, operates over UDP, as shown in Figure 8-9.

With this protocol, the sender has complete knowledge of group members. Receivers notify the sender in the event of a failure, and senders notify all receivers in the event of a sender failure.

RAMP has an interesting ability to support two unreliable modes. In the first mode, the sender simply delivers unreliable data as a stream and no feedback occurs. In the second mode, the sender supports reliability, but some or all of the receivers may operate in an unreliable mode. This latter example may be used to benefit when, for example, images are delivered to receivers with differing needs—that is, when certain receivers, such as image archives, require total reliability, whereas other receivers may be able to tolerate some data loss, such as the loss of higher-resolution data in hierarchically encoded images. Both sender and receivers may freely switch between both reliability modes.

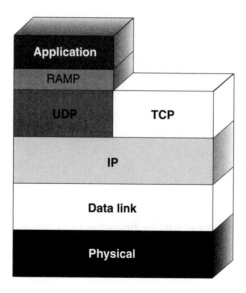

FIGURE 8-9

RAMP operates over UDP

RAMP breaks up the data sent into *bursts*. A burst is defined as a series of data messages where the interval between any two consecutive messages is less than some defined time (for example, 0.5 second).

A RAMP sender may send data in either the *burst* or *idle* mode and can switch between the two modes as the number of receivers changes. Burst mode minimizes network traffic from the sender to receivers at the expense of more control traffic from receivers to the sender. Idle mode introduces extra messages into the data flow, but minimizes the control traffic that receivers return to the sender.

In burst mode, the sender marks the start of the burst by setting an ACK flag in the RAMP header. When the sender reaches the end of a burst, it sends a single RAMP "idle" message, informing receivers that the sender will remain silent until the beginning of the next burst. Whenever a reliable receiver observes an ACK flag, it is required to acknowledge receipt of the message by sending an ACK message containing the segment number back to the sender. Receipt of a data message with an ACK flag set by receivers confirms that the forward data connection has not deteriorated during the sender's quiet interval between bursts. Receipt of the ACK response by the sender confirms that the unicast connection from receiver to sender has not deteriorated in that same quiet period.

If the sender does not receive an ACK message from one of the known reliable receivers, then it knows that data—and possibly a connection to that receiver—have been lost.

In idle mode, a series of idle messages are sent in the gap, rather than just a single one. These messages inform the receivers that no additional data is available, but that the sender will not be silent for longer than the defined burst time. The idle messages eliminate the need to send explicit acknowledgments at the beginning of a burst. All control traffic from receivers to the sender is sent unicast.

To date, RAMP has been confined to military applications, and it has not appeared in general commercial applications. Thus it has not had significant deployment.

8.4.2.2.2 TIBCO

TIBCO (The Information Bus Company) has been in the business of supplying message-based middleware for message streaming applications for a number of years. TIBCO has enjoyed its greatest success in financial markets but has extended the applications to the manufacturing floor. It is now seeking to extend its products to even more applications.

TIBCO's middleware family is called TIB/Rendezvous. It includes a reliable multicast message streaming protocol that is not publicly documented in the TIB/Rendezvous daemon. This protocol is probably not very scalable over WANs, as their applications require timeliness that quickly leads to more administrative back-traffic to the source. In fact, the bulk of the applications in which TIBCO products have been deployed run on local campus networks, such as financial trading floors.

The company promotes two concepts, *publish/subscribe* and *subject-based addressing*. These concepts are not related to a reliable multicast protocol, but are important to understand and will be discussed in Chapter 9.

TIBCO is now actively supporting PGM for its message streaming applications, as it needs to be able to extend its middleware to be scalable over WANs.

8.4.2.2.3 Multicast File Transfer Protocol (MFTP)

MFTP was developed by StarBurst Communications and refined with the help of engineering personnel from Cisco Systems. It was first publicly documented in an Internet Draft in February 1997, and a new Internet Draft was submitted to the IETF in April 1998 [8-13]. Products based on MFTP have the greatest penetration in commercial WAN applications and represent the largest reliable multicast installations.

MFTP operates over UDP in the Application layer, like most other multicast transports. It is targeted to non-real-time bulk transfer of data, usually in the form of files, from one to many with reliable delivery. This protocol takes advantage of the non-real-time nature of the delivery requirement to gain extra scalability and universal operation over all network infrastructures, including satellite and other asymmetric networks.

StarBurst announced a variant of MFTP that supports real-time message streaming with lower scaling capability in its toolkit product launched in early 1998. This version adds a transmit window similar to the mechanism found in RMTP.

MFTP can also accommodate sender-based group creation, with different group models and a group set-up protocol to notify receivers to join the group. This process is discussed in detail in Chapter 9.

In addition, MFTP includes some diagnostic tools. For example, it specifies an application-layer "multicast ping" that a sender can use to determine the reachability of group members. It also identifies delays in getting a response from the sender application through the multicast tree to the receiver Application layer and unicasts back to the sender.

The basic MFTP protocol breaks the data entity to be sent into maximum size "blocks." By default, a block consists of thousands or tens of thousands of packets depending on the maximum transfer unit (MTU) size selected, as shown in Figure 8-10.

MFTP is a "NAK-only" protocol; that is, if data is received correctly in a block, nothing is sent back to the sender. If one or more packets are in error or missing in a block, receivers respond with a NAK that consists of a bitmap of the bad packets. This *selective reject* mechanism bears some similarities to RMTP.

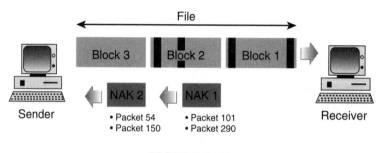

FIGURE 8-10

MFTP blocks

The main difference is that MFTP explicitly attempts to make the block as large as possible for scaling purposes.

NAKs are normally unicast back to the source, unless aggregation to improve scaling using enabled network routers is employed. In that case, the NAKs are multicast to a special administrative traffic group address.

MFTP does not make repairs after each block, however. It takes advantage of the non-real-time nature of the application for benefit. The data entity, such as a file, is sent initially in its entirety in a *first pass*. The sender collects the NAK packets for a block from all of the receivers. One NAK packet from a receiver can represent thousands or even tens of thousands of bad packets, which reduces NAK implosion by orders of magnitude. The collection of NAKs received by the sender from all of the receivers is ORed together to represent the collective need for repairs for the receiving group. These repairs are sent by the sender in a *second pass* to the group. If certain receivers already have the repair, it is simply ignored. This process is repeated until all repairs are received by all receivers or until a configurable timeout occurs. Thus packet-ordering services are not provided and holes in the data caused by dropped or erroneous packets are filled in as they are received.

The sender is *rate-based*; that is, it transmits at a data rate that the operator sets to be less than or equal to what the network can handle. The protocol is thus very efficient with high-latency networks, such as satellite, and is impervious to network asymmetry. It also attempts to be as scalable as possible on one-hop networks, such as satellite, and it provides for extensions so that network elements may aggregate downstream responses to increase scalability further, depending on the network configuration.

Figure 8-11 shows this aggregation capability. The network element, which can be a router, collects MFTP administrative back-traffic, which is sent to a multicast address where appropriately equipped routers are members. These routers aggregate back-traffic from all nodes downstream in the multicast tree from the source, including Registration, NAK, and Done messages. Registration and Done messages are used by MFTP's group set-up protocol and are described in Chapter 9.

This configuration is vulnerable to a limited form of the same problem that hampers SRM; back-traffic will be proliferated throughout the group, except for the router port from which it received the downstream administrative traffic. It is thus more limiting than the general SRM implementation, though excess proliferation still occurs. Depending on the network configuration, however, this aggregation capability can improve the scalability of MFTP by orders of magnitude.

The upper limit to scalability when no network aggregation of administrative traffic occurs is in the tens of thousands of receivers. For example, for an MTU of 1,500 bytes (the Ethernet maximum), the default block size is more than 11,000 packets. If the number of receivers is 11,000 and each receiver has at least one bad packet per block, then a total of 11,000 NAK packets about that block will come back to the sender from the group, or roughly the same number of packets as was sent in the forward direction in that block. MFTP provides for a NAK back-off timer to spread the NAKs out in time to the sender, thereby

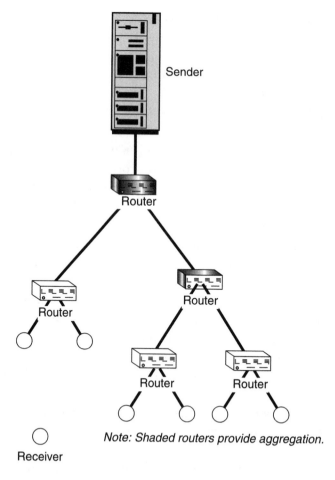

FIGURE 8-11

Routers as network aggregators

avoiding bursts. If the bandwidth is symmetric at the sender, then the sender should be able to handle this maximum NAK load. In many situations, the amount of back-traffic could even exceed forward-traffic.

MFTP also includes a provision for a crude congestion control mechanism. The sender at the beginning of a session sends Announce messages. These messages are used for many functions, including the setting up of groups, as described in Chapter 9. Additionally, the sender conveys a packet-loss parameter to all receivers. Receivers may use this packet-loss threshold parameter to leave the group if the packet loss exceeds the threshold. Leaving the group prunes the distribution tree, relieving the congestion in that section.

The majority of commercial reliable multicast installations over WANs, including the largest ones, use MFTP. The largest is for the General Motors dealer network mentioned in Section 8.3.6, where 8,500 receivers are served by one sender. As this application is a pioneer, it is worth exploring the field experience with its installation.

General Motors' dealer network included about 8,500 receivers as of early 1998. The network is bidirectional VSAT, with Demand Assignment Multiple Access (DAMA) back channels. The forward channel rate is 512 Kbps, and there are multiple 128 Kbps DAMA back channels, with one allocated for approximately 200 receivers. DAMA channels are contention-based, so that 200 receivers share the back channel based on demand in this configuration. Thus, each receiver has only about 650 bps of shared bandwidth on average.

Multiple traffic sources use the VSAT network. MFTP is typically used to send multiple files in the range of 70 Mbytes to 120 Mbytes (occasionally files are as large as 220 Mbytes) every night and sometimes during the day. File transmission is usually set to 300 to 360 Kbps (lower during the day) to leave bandwidth available in the 512 Kbps channel for other traffic.

As can be expected from satellite systems, the forward error rate is very good—better than 10^{-10}—resulting in about 70% of the receivers receiving the file error-free on the first pass. Errors are mostly uncorrelated among receivers and generated almost exclusively from the independent downlinks, which are typically geographically dispersed.

The benefits of reliable multicast delivery to thousands of receivers simultaneously have been realized. Information previously sent via CD-ROM by mail can now be sent over the network in about an hour. Performance is considered excellent. Session timeout is set to 200%—that is, after twice the time allocated to send the file once, the session terminates regardless of whether the transmission is complete to all receivers. Often a small percentage of receivers has not completed before session timeout occurs; this issue is not considered a major problem, however, as a separate session can be created for these receivers to send them the missing data.

The largest issues to date have related to the contention-based back channel. Initial implementation of MFTP did not include NAK back-off, causing correlation of NAK and Done messages (used in the MFTP Closed Group model for positive confirmation of completion). As a result, some receivers were locked out of the back channel for a period of time. The protocol recovers from this lockout, however, at the expense of extra time for completion.

A second issue involves simultaneous traffic from other sources on the back channel that can lock out some receivers. Implementation of NAK back-off has increased the availability of the back channel to receivers, but simultaneous traffic continues to make the back channel less available to some receivers. Back-channel traffic is continuously monitored by the user, and sources with excessive traffic are being managed to minimize their traffic. To date, the MFTP back-traffic has been only a minor component of the aggregate traffic flow.

Another issue involves the set-up of groups. This application uses the MFTP Closed Group model (see Chapter 9). When a group is initially set up, host lists are sent to direct particular receivers to join the group. With thousands of members, this list can become quite large and take more time (approximately 15 minutes) than desirable for set-up. A future release of MFTP will correct this issue by a mechanism called "host list pruning" (discussed in Chapter 9).

As noted earlier, MFTP has the most, and largest, commercial installations of reliable multicast over WANs. The basic protocol offers the benefit of simplicity and network infrastructure independence, two attractive characteristics. It gains these benefits by focusing more narrowly on the applications that can be served, thus restricting its scope of use.

Some sentiment in the Internet community calls for the standardization of a "bulk transfer"-type reliable multicast protocol in the future. MFTP could serve as a good foundation model if that desire comes to fruition.

8.5 RESEARCH ACTIVITIES AND TOPICS IN RELIABLE MULTICAST

As mentioned previously in this chapter, reliable multicast protocols are not standardized, nor are any on a track to standardization. Currently, reliable multicast techniques are being studied by the Reliable Multicast Research Group

(RMRG) [8-5] of the Internet Research Task Force (IRTF). RMRG has been operating since early 1997. IRTF groups recommend techniques to use to solve difficult problems; they do not work on particular standards.

This research group is unusual in the IRTF in being open; in the past, most such groups have been closed, consisting of Internet researchers who were selected to study a particular problem and recommend techniques to be used by the Internet Engineering Task Force (IETF) in formulating future standards. When the work of the IRTF's reliable multicast group is completed, it will similarly hand over the recommended techniques to an IETF working group, which will use them to create standard reliable multicast protocols.

An Internet Draft dating from November 1996 (now expired), "IETF Criteria for Evaluating Reliable Multicast Transport and Application Protocols," has served as a basis for the RMRG's work. This document expresses particular concern about the issue of congestion control.

The language from that document expressing concerns about effective congestion control for reliable multicast protocols is quoted here:

> *A particular concern for the IETF (and a dominant concern for the Transport Services Area) is the impact of reliable multicast traffic on other traffic in the Internet in times of congestion (more specifically, the effect of reliable multicast traffic on competing TCP traffic). The success of the Internet relies on the fact that best-effort traffic responds to congestion on a link (as currently indicated by packet drops) by reducing the load presented on that link. Congestion collapse in today's Internet is prevented only by the congestion control mechanisms in TCP.*
>
> *There are a number of reasons to be particularly attentive to the congestion-related issues raised by reliable multicast proposals. Multicast applications in general have the potential to do more congestion-related damage to the Internet than do unicast applications. This is because a single multicast flow can be distributed along a large, global multicast tree reaching throughout the entire Internet.*
>
> *Further, reliable multicast applications have the potential to do more congestion-related damage than do unreliable multicast applications. First, unreliable multicast applications such as audio and video are, at the moment, usually accompanied by a person at the receiving end, and people typically unsubscribe from a multicast group if congestion is so heavy that the audio or video stream is unintelligible. Reliable multicast applications such as group file transfer applications, on the other hand, are likely to be between computers, with no humans in attendance monitoring congestion levels.*

In addition, reliable multicast applications do not necessarily have the natural time limitations typical of current unreliable multicast applications. For a file transfer application, for example, the data transfer might continue until all of the data is transferred to all of the intended receivers, resulting in a potentially unlimited duration for an individual flow. Reliable multicast applications also have to contend with a potential explosion of control traffic (e.g., ACKs, [NAKs], status messages) and with control traffic issues in general that may be more complex than for unreliable multicast traffic.

The design of congestion control mechanisms for reliable multicast for large multicast groups is currently an area of active research. The challenge to the IETF is to encourage research and implementations of reliable multicast, and to enable the needs of applications for reliable multicast to be met as expeditiously as possible, while at the same time protecting the Internet from the congestion disaster or collapse that could result from the widespread use of applications with inappropriate reliable multicast mechanisms. Because of the setbacks and costs that could result from the widespread deployment of reliable multicast with inadequate congestion control, the IETF must exercise care in the standardization of a reliable multicast protocol that might see widespread use.

Shortly after the publication of this document, the RMRG was organized. One statement from this discussion, however, the author finds specious:

First, unreliable multicast applications such as audio and video are, at the moment, usually accompanied by a person at the receiving end, and people typically unsubscribe from a multicast group if congestion is so heavy that the audio or video stream is unintelligible. Reliable multicast applications such as group file transfer applications, on the other hand, are likely to be between computers, with no humans in attendance monitoring congestion levels.

This argument is very weak; it is not reliable to depend on a human to turn off a nonfunctioning event. Have you ever seen a child leave on the television when he or she exited the house? Or left the room to do something else? In contrast, some of the reliable multicast protocols, such as MFTP, have the sense of a finite session; they automatically time out and leave a group, even if all group members did not receive all of the content.

The aforementioned document also provides criteria for analyzing differing reliable multicast protocol proposals, as described on the next page:

a. *Analyze the behavior of the protocol. The vulnerabilities and performance problems must be shown through analysis. Especially the protocol behavior must be explained in detail with respect to scalability, congestion control, error recovery, and robustness.*

    For example, the following questions should be answered:

- *How scalable is the protocol to the number of users in a group, number of groups, wide dispersion of group members? If appropriate, how scalable is the protocol to the number of senders?*
- *Identify the mechanisms which limit scalabilty and estimate those limits.*
- *How does the protocol protect the Internet from congestion? How well does it perform? When does it fail?*
- *Under what circumstances will the protocol fail to perform the functions needed by the applications it serves?*
- *Is there a congestion control mechanism? How well does it perform? When does it fail?*

b. *Include a description of trials and/or simulations which support the development of the protocol and the answers to the above questions.*

c. *Include an analysis of whether the protocol has congestion avoidance mechanisms strong enough to cope with deployment in the global Internet and, if not, clearly document the circumstances in which congestion harm can occur. How are these circumstances to be prevented?*

d. *Include a description of any mechanisms which contain the protocol within limited network environments. It is likely that some answers to (a) and (c) will mean that such mechanisms are required. We recognize that the confinement of Internet applications is an open research area.*

e. *Show that the protocol can use IPsec or other mechanisms for secure operation. (General requirement with specific ramifications for reliable multicast that are outside the scope of this memo.)*

IPsec refers to IP security, a mechanism to secure transmissions at the IP layer. There is an IPsec working group in IETF.

    With this background charter, we will now discuss some of the techniques that have been presented and debated in the IRTF's reliable multicast group and describe how they can be used to solve the three major problems of congestion control, TCP fairness, and scaling.

8.5.1   Forward Error Correction (FEC) Techniques

FEC techniques have been used in the data communications industry for many years. In fact, the author's first job in the data communications industry was with Codex Corporation (now part of Motorola), which was founded in the 1960s with an original charter to provide FEC solutions to the military.

With normal FEC, redundant (parity) data based on certain codes [8-16] is added to the data stream to allow some of the transmission errors or lost packets to be corrected at the receiver without having to ask for retransmission from the sender. The penalty for this capability is that more data must be sent initially, resulting in waste if no errors occur. FEC techniques are commonly used in wireless systems at the Link layer to improve the link's effective bit error rate.

Another technique often used with FEC is *interleaving*. FEC codes do not handle burst losses well; they perform better when correcting single errors or single lost packets. Interleaving rearranges the packets (or bits) in a prearranged way so that any bursts are spread out and will likely appear as single packet losses, allowing FEC codes to correct more of the data lost in transmission.

It has not been proposed that FEC be used in this way with reliable multicast protocols. Rather, FEC has been suggested as a way to help increase scaling in some instances and as a method to aid certain congestion control proposals. A recent paper [8-17], however, suggests using FEC with the original data where the overhead in the original transmission reduces the repairs for applications where low latency is important and the network suffers loss.

8.5.1.1   Erasure Correction

The first application of FEC techniques to reliable multicast provides scaling help in reducing the amount of repair traffic needed when a large number of receivers are present and the loss at the receivers has a large uncorrelated component. Measurements [8-18] on the Mbone have revealed the presence of a combination of both correlated and uncorrelated losses. With uncorrelated losses, repairs that are sent to the multicast group reach receivers that already have those repairs, wasting bandwidth and receiver resource. A simulation [8-19] showed that, for certain reasonable assumptions about network losses, a group of 10,000 receivers would need to receive the data sent about 2.5 times on average for all receivers to get it correctly. For example, if 16 receivers were sent a block of data consisting of 16 packets, and each lost one packet, but the 16 receivers each lost a unique packet in the set of 16, then the repair retransmitter would have to resend all 16 packets.

A promising technique to reduce the amount of repair data that needs to be retransmitted has been proposed by a number of researchers. It uses FEC techniques, but does not send FEC packets except for repairs. It has been variously described as "integrated FEC," "erasure correction," and "type II hybrid ARQ" [8-19, 8-20].

This technique (we will call it *erasure correction*) can significantly reduce the amount of repairs that need to be resent if the packet loss is largely uncorrelated at the receivers. In our previous example, an FEC code is used to generate one parity packet from the 16 data packets that are originally sent. This parity packet can correct any one missing data packet from the set of 16 data packets by making calculations with the 15 received data packets and one parity packet. Thus the repair can consist of the one parity packet rather than all 16 original data packets.

If the loss is correlated, then many of the receivers lose the same data and erasure correction offers no benefit. However, there is also no penalty, except for the need for computing power at both the sender and the receivers to perform the FEC calculations. Simulations [8-17] have shown that a greater than 2:1 reduction in the number of repairs needed to be sent with 10,000 receivers. This benefit will be even greater when group sizes exceed tens of thousands.

8.5.1.2 *Layering Using FEC for Congestion Control*

Perhaps a more significant application for FEC is a congestion control technique known as *layering*. Many proposals for layering have been put forth [8-21, 8-22, 8-23]. With layering, a number of groups are set up by the sender, all with different rates, as shown in Figure 8-12. For this scheme to work without sending data redundantly, the number of parity packets created must be very large compared with the number of data packets.

For example, a Reed-Solomon Error Correction code can be used to generate the parity data. For a set of k data packets that are P bits long, the code generates a set of h parity packets, each P bits long. For a particular receiver, the following happens:

- If all k data packets are received, then no decoding is needed at the receiver.

FIGURE 8-12

Congestion control by layering

- If $l < h$ of the k data packets are lost, the data can be recovered and the decoding overhead is proportional to l.

With layering, the number of parity packets, $h >> k$; that is, the number of parity packets greatly exceeds the number of original data packets. To recover the data at the receiver, any k of the $h + k$ total (data plus parity packets) can be used to reconstruct the original data at the receiver. Receivers that can sustain the highest rate of traffic join all of the layers and combine the data from them to receive the content. As congestion occurs, different layers are left, relieving the congestion.

Having many more parity packets than original data packets creates great flexibility in the types of layering that can be used. In Figure 8-12, there are two layers and eight original data packets; thus $k = 8$. Layer 1 sends at twice the rate of Layer 2, and its data packets are transmitted first. Receivers that subscribe to both layers, assuming no loss, complete in time T after receiving the original eight data packets; receivers subscribing only to Layer 2 complete in time $3T$. No duplicate packets are sent.

Researchers have pointed out additional issues with the layering approaches, however. For layering to be effective, the routing tree should be identical for the different groups; otherwise, congestion will not be relieved on a part of the tree. This structure may not always be the case, especially in sparse-mode routing protocols, where the rendezvous point or core is selected based on group address.

Even if the same distribution tree is used for the different layers, leaves of hosts downstream from a congested link should be coordinated; otherwise, the action of less than all of them has no effect on congestion. Additionally, a receiver could cause congestion by adding a layer that another receiver could interpret as congestion, causing it to drop a layer with no effect.

Thus layering using FEC is an interesting technique that shows promise for use in congestion control. Issues associated with it still need to be worked on by researchers, however.

Layering has also been proposed as a congestion control mechanism for multimedia streaming applications [8-24]. Subscribers to lower numbers of layers receive lower-quality transmissions. At some point, video capability is dropped altogether, leaving only audio in severely congested links.

8.5.2   Bulk Feedback

Another technique that has been proposed for congestion control is bulk feedback to the sender. If the sender receives an excessive number of NAKs from receivers, it drops the sender's transmission rate via an algorithm that attempts to emulate TCP behavior. This strategy is an obvious approach, as it represents an extension of the process in which TCP falls back in the face of congestion.

Two basic problems arise with this approach. First, delays occur, because the sender needs to get feedback from the multitude of receivers before it acts. This lag can be considerably longer than in the case of TCP, which needs feedback from only one receiver.

Second, one errant receiver can effectively penalize the whole group, as this sender reduces the rate to the total group.

Bulk feedback is not viewed as a viable solution for these two reasons. In fact, a general consensus exists that congestion control decision-making will be required at the multiple receivers rather than at the single sender for both scaling and timeliness reasons.

8.5.3   Optimized Local Repair

Internet researchers generally believe that local repair is the primary means by which a reliable multicast protocol can scale to the global land-line Internet. The first prominent protocol to attempt local repair was SRM, which was first documented in 1995 [8-25]. SRM has some issues associated with it that were previously discussed—for example, an inability to operate in asymmetric networks and the unnecessary propagation of repair requests and repairs throughout the group because all members use the same multicast group address. In recent years, many researchers have strived to improve upon the mechanisms that SRM pioneered.

One of the earliest works was from the University of Karlsruhe in Germany, which first documented the "Local Group Concept" (LGC) in English in 1996 [8-26]. The initial work on LGC actually occurred independent of knowledge of SRM and at the same time that development of SRM was taking place. Nevertheless, it did not gain much visibility, as the earliest technical papers were available only in German. LGC was further refined in papers delivered in 1997

[8-27], and a presentation was made at the RMRG meeting in February 1998 on the latest research results.

LGC uses two protocols, the Local Group Multicast Protocol (LGMP) and the Dynamic Configuration Protocol (DCP), the details of which are still not documented in English. The basic idea in LGC is that local subgroups are formed dynamically with a local Group Controller, which transmits repairs for a local subgroup using a different multicast address. Considerable research has been performed to determine the optimal sizes of the subgroups and which receiver should be the subgroup group controller. DCP is used to dynamically create the subgroups and designate a Group Controller for each subgroup; it also handles changes in the composition of subgroups as membership in the overall group shifts. LGMP is the protocol that actually ensures reliability after configuration of subgroups occurs under DCP. Note that the Group Controller shares some similarities with RMTP's Designated Receiver.

One major advantage of LGC is that network infrastructure changes are unnecessary, as only end-system hosts are involved. The price for this advantage is that many more multicast groups need to be set up. Additionally, mechanisms to implement congestion control at the local level are also envisioned, but more research will be needed to optimize the algorithms involved.

Considerable discussion at the September 1997 RMRG meeting focused on other local repair techniques that do not require separate subgroup addresses. These techniques first try to identify nodes in a group just upstream from a congested link that could be used to send repairs locally to the nodes downstream from the congested link. This technique [8-28] does not specifically address the response to congestion; rather, it attempts to optimize and constrain local recovery, thereby reducing redundant traffic, and to accomplish this goal with low latency. Amazingly, in this era of acronyms no acronym was created to name this technique!* We will simply call it "optimized local repair."

The creators of "optimized local repair" identified five major unresolved problems in reliable multicast. They are described below, as they correctly identify the basic issues involved:

Request Implosion: This so-called ACK/NAK implosion occurs when the loss of a packet triggers simultaneous repair requests from a large number of receivers, overwhelming the sender and possibly other receivers (depending on whether ACK/NAK messages are sent via unicast or multicast).

Duplicate Replies: Multiple repairs may be sent in protocols that attempt local repair, such as SRM, when many respond to a request.

---

* This was recently named Lightweight Multicast Services (LMS).

Recovery Latency: The latency experienced by a receiver lasts from the instant a loss is detected until a repair is received. This consideration is important in collaborative and some data streaming applications with low latency requirements; it is not important in non-real-time data delivery applications.

Recovery Isolation (or Exposure): This problem is essentially the desire to keep local repair truly local to those receivers that actually experience the loss. It is especially applicable to *correlated* loss—that is, when a group of receivers experiences the same loss caused by an upstream congested link.

Adaptability to Dynamic Membership Change: This parameter measures how quickly steady state is reached after changes occur in group membership and topology.

The key idea in "optimized local repair" is to confine local repair so that it becomes a retransmitter that may be found just above a link congestion point, as shown in Figure 8-13. The key problem is gaining enough knowledge of the network topology to locate a receiving host with the repair data that is willing

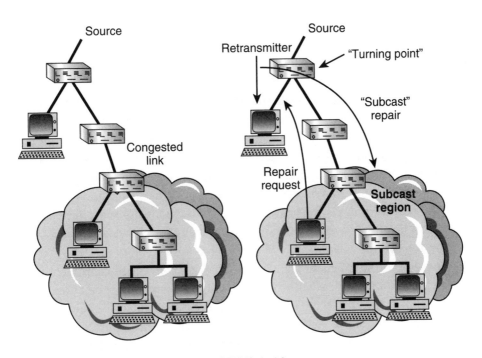

FIGURE 8-13

Optimized local repair

to retransmit, and containing the repairs within the region of the network that lost the original transmission.

The proposal would ask for assistance from the network routers. They know the topology and could be used to find the closest willing retransmitter that has the repair. The routers could also direct the repair to only the affected region, a strategy called a *subcast*.

Further schemes [8-29] to improve on the subcasting approach were presented at the RMRG meeting in February 1998. These options would reduce the assistance provided by routers.

All of these techniques can be considered an extension of concepts originally proposed in SRM and independently created in LGC to provide local recovery. They make the assumption that most loss is caused by congested links, and that uncorrelated loss is caused by a series of mildly congested links with few group members. This model is probably acceptable for land-line routed networks, but it may be problematical with other network infrastructures.

Nevertheless, these interesting proposals merit further research effort. Local repair is destined to be an important tool for meeting the goal of improved scalability with minimal traffic overhead.

8.6 SUMMARY AND CONCLUSIONS

Reliable multicast is clearly a surprisingly complex subject, with widely varying requirements being placed on the transport mechanisms by the widely varying requirements in the application. Internet researchers place a high premium on congestion control mechanisms and "fairness" to TCP. Scaling is also difficult, especially if all kinds of network infrastructures are considered, rather than just the traditional symmetric, highly meshed, land-line model that the bulk of today's Internet employs. Indications are that, increasingly, there will be alternative network infrastructures that will need to be considered in the future.

Some of the solutions to the hard problems of congestion control are innovative but need more research work. One major question must be asked about these options: Are they too complex? The more complicated the solutions, the more likely they are to have problems. Network operators are already concerned about anything that could disrupt their networks and will be loath to deploy any scheme that is not fully proven.

One new protocol, PGM, is relatively simple and has general applicability. Unfortunately, it relies on router infrastructure for scaling, which limits this solution to the traditional land-line routed network infrastructure. Additionally, the criteria set up for evaluation of reliable multicast protocols dictates that IPsec should be feasible; this security option is not possible with any router assist that requires the examination of source packets, as the contents of an IP packet may be encrypted. Such encryption precludes the recognition and manipulation of packets at the Transport and Application layers by network entities.

MFTP is also simple and operates with all network infrastructures, but it is narrowly focused on non-real-time reliable delivery. RMTP has some nice hierarchy characteristics that provide scaling and has been adapted to cover virtually all applications; hierarchy is not possible in some of the alternative network infrastructures, however. SRM provides a framework similar to RTP and pioneered the concept of local recovery.

Multiple reliable multicast protocols will therefore be used to satisfy different applications and different network infrastructures. Some of the best features of the different protocols will likely be combined to enhance their benefits. There have already been significant deployments in private IP networks, and scaling to tens of thousands of group members has been shown to work in demanding commercial environments.

Despite the numerous technical issues raised, which have given the RMRG's researchers plenty of work to complete before standardization efforts commence, reliable multicast applications will probably face less of a deployment barrier in WANs than streaming multimedia applications. There is no need for RSVP. No minimum bandwidth requirement exists for applications in most cases. Finally, the application benefits of deploying reliable multicast are usually more compelling—albeit less "sexy"—for early-adopter business users.

As a result, reliable multicast solutions will continue to penetrate into private networks, including many similar to the case studies described in this chapter. The corporate network managers, in these cases, will manage the bandwidth of their multicast applications rather than depend on an automatic congestion control mechanism, much as they do today. A telling sign can be gleaned from the fact that the congestion control mechanism in RMTP needed to be disabled in the major carrier case study described earlier in this chapter.

Public ISPs also have an opportunity to offer reliable multicast services, even if the reliable multicast protocol does not include proven congestion mechanisms. If the ISP can control the data transfer rate, it can largely eliminate the fear of one multicast launch crashing the network. Already, ISPs with early offerings, such as UUNet, are providing bandwidth-limited access points for multicast service, thus limiting the chance of damage to the network. Data streaming applications such as ticker tape and news feeds usually call for relatively low bandwidth and are inherently similar to a multimedia stream. They can therefore be configured with minimal network bandwidth consumption (in fact, the configuration will reduce duplicate point-to-point transmissions and save bandwidth).

Interestingly, many of the early ISP networks supporting multicast do not support collaborative applications. These applications are likely to be the last ones to find wide deployment.

Non-real-time reliable multicast applications could be deployed as service offerings by ISPs. Consumers could request content that could be delivered at a time determined by the ISP, thus providing different service levels at different prices to the consumer—all of which would remain under the ISP's control. Some of this delivery could take place overnight, when the network is not congested. ISPs and carriers have historically not been innovative in offering value-added services, however, so it remains to be seen if this opportunity will be recognized. This paradigm is very different from a consumer directly launching the application from his or her host computer; in the former case, the consumer requests a service from the network with his or her host computer, and the "network" provides that service.

This opportunity could be recognized sooner by alternative carriers, such as digital satellite and cable carriers, which possess networks that already have a broadcast infrastructure and can thus inherently support multicast. This prospect will be discussed further in Chapter 12.

Reliable multicast protocols and applications are in their early stages of development and deployment. Early installations have yielded huge benefits for the organizations sponsoring them. Events are happening quickly, and we can expect activity in this area to accelerate as more land-line networks are upgraded to support multicast. We are witnessing a period of dynamic change in a young market, and new applications that have not yet been anticipated are likely to appear in the future.

In Chapter 9, we discuss how to set up the groups to which content is delivered via reliable multicast or with multimedia streaming applications. Very different group set-up mechanisms are available to match the varying application requirements.

REFERENCES

[8-1] Information on MiMaze may be found at http://www.inria.fr/rodeo/MiMaze/.

[8-2] Information on the LSMA Working Group can be found at http://www.ietf.org/html.charters/lsma-charter.html.

[8-3] Whetten B, Basavaiah M, Paul S, Montgomery T, Rastogi N, Conlan J, Yeh T. The RMTP-II Protocol. Internet Draft, Work in Progress, draft-whetten-rmtp-ii-00.txt, April 8, 1998.

[8-4] Whetten B, Basavaiah M, Paul S, Montgomery T, Rastogi N, Conlan J, Yeh T. The RMTP-II Protocol Appendices. Internet Draft, Work in Progress, draft-whetten-rmtp-ii-app-00.txt, April 8, 1998.

[8-5] Information on the RMRG can be found at http://www.east.isi.edu/rm/.

[8-6] Braden R, ed. Requirements for Internet Hosts—Communication Layers. RFC 1122, October 1989.

[8-7] Stevens W. TCP Slow Start, Congestion Avoidance, Fast Retransmit, and Fast Recovery Algorithms. RFC 2001, January 1997.

[8-8] Floyd S, Jacobson V, Liu C-G, McCanne S, Zhang L. A Reliable Multicast Framework for Light-weight Sessions and Application Layer Framing. IEEE/ACM Transactions on Networking, November 1996.

[8-9] Buskens RW, Siddiqui MA, Paul S. Reliable Multicasting of Continuous Data Streams. Bell Labs Technical Journal, Spring 1997.

[8-10] Paul S, Sabnani K, Buskens R, Muhammad S, Lin J, Bhattacharyya S. RMTP: A Reliable Multicast Protocol for High-Speed Networks. Proceedings of the Tenth Annual IEEE Workshop on Computer Communications, September 1995.

[8-11] Speakman T, Farinacci D, Lin S, Tweedly A. Pretty Good Multicast (PGM) Transport Protocol Specification. Internet Draft, Work in Progress, draft-speakman-pgm-spec-00.txt, January 8, 1998.

[8-12] Braudes R, Zabele S. Requirements for Multicast Protocols. RFC 1458, May 1993.

[8-13] Miller K, Robertson K, Tweedly A, White M. StarBurst Multicast File Transfer Protocol (MFTP) Specification. Internet Draft, Work in Progress, draft-miller-mftp-spec-03.txt, April 1998.

[8-14] Clark D, Tennenhouse D. Architectural Considerations for a New Generation of Protocols. Proceedings of ACM SIGCOMM '90, Sept. 1990: 201–208.

[8-15] Katz D. IP Router Alert Option. RFC 2113, February 1997.

[8-16] Lin S, Costello DJ. Error Correcting Coding: Fundamentals and Applications. Englewood Cliffs, NJ: Prentice Hall, 1983.

[8-17] Rubenstein D, Kurose J, Towsley D. Real-Time Reliable Multicast Using Proactive Forward Error Correction. Proceedings of NOSSDAV '98, Cambridge, UK, July 1998.

[8-18] Handley M. An Examination of Mbone Performance. ISI Paper presented to RMRG Group, January 10, 1997.

[8-19] Nonnenmacher J, Biersack J, Towsley D. Parity-Based Loss Recovery for Reliable Multicast Transmission. Technical Report 97-17, University of Massachusetts, Department of Computer Science, March 1997.

[8-20] Vicisano L, Crowcroft J. One to Many Reliable Bulk-Data Transfer in the Mbone. Proceedings of the Third International Workshop on High-Performance Protocol Architectures (HIPPARCH '97), Uppsala, Sweden, June 1997.

[8-21] Vicisano L, Rizzo L, Crowcroft J. TCP-like Congestion Control for Layered Multicast Data Transfer. Research Paper from University College, London, and Università di Pisa, Italy, September 1997.

[8-22] Nonnenmacher J, Biersack EW. Asynchronous Multicast Push: AMP. Internal Report, Institut Eurecom, Sophia Antipolis Cedex, France, September 9, 1997.

[8-23] Hanle C, Hofmann M. Performance Comparison of Reliable Multicast Protocols Using the Network Simulator ns-2. Submitted to Local Computer Networks Conference, Boston, MA, October 11–14, 1998.

[8-24] Taubman D, Zakhor A. Multi-rate 3-D Subband Coding of Video. IEEE Transactions on Image Processing, September 1994:572–588.

[8-25] Floyd S, Jacobson V, McCanne S, Zhang L, Liu C. A Reliable Multicast Framework for Light-weight Sessions and Application Layer Framing. Proceedings of ACM Sigcomm '95, September 1995:342–356.

[8-26] Hofmann M. A Generic Concept for Large-Scale Multicast. Proceedings of International Zurich Seminar on Digital Communications (IZS '96), Zurich, Switzerland, February 1996.

[8-27] Hofmann M, Rohrmuller M. Impact of Virtual Group Structure on Multicast Performance. Proceedings of Fourth COST237 Workshop, Lisbon, Portugal, December 1997.

[8-28] Papadopoulos C, Parulkar G, Varghese G. An Error Control Scheme for Large-Scale Multicast Applications. Submitted to Infocom '98, September 1997.

[8-29] Levine BN, Paul S, Garcia-Luna-Aceves JJ. Deterministic Organization of Multicast Receivers Based on Packet-Loss Correlation. Submitted for publication; presented to RMRG meeting, February 1998.

URLS FOR ORGANIZATIONS MENTIONED IN CHAPTER 8

@Home	http://www.home.com
THE BOX	http://www.thebox.com
Cisco Systems	http://www.cisco.com
General Motors	http://www.gm.com
GlobalCast	http://www.globalcast.com
IETF	http://www.ietf.org
Inria	http://www.inria.fr
IRTF	http://www.irtf.org
Lawrence Berkeley Labs	http://www.lbl.gov
Lucent	http://www.lucent.com
The Ohio Company	http://www.ohioco.com
PeopleSoft	http://www.peoplesoft.com
SAP	http://www.sap.com
StarBurst Communications	http://www.starburstcom.com
TASC	http://www.tasc.com
3Com	http://www.3com.com
TIBCO	http://www.tibco.com
Toys "R" Us	http://www.toysrus.com

9

THE CREATION
OF GROUPS

I n Chapter 3, we learned that the joining of groups is receiver-initiated
and employs the Internet Group Management Protocol (IGMP). However, mechanisms must be in place to entice receivers to actually join a
group.

Different models are used for group creation. The Multiparty Multimedia Session Control (MMUSIC) [9-1] working group of the Internet Engineering Task Force (IETF) has been the body developing most of the official protocols and architecture for group creation. The architecture created by MMUSIC
encompasses the concept of channels, as briefly described in Chapter 6, which
discusses "push" applications. These channels are advertised on a Web page, a
special content advertising group, or via e-mail.

A second model is that of tight centralized control. It is embodied in one of
the group creation models that is part of the MFTP protocol.

Additionally, the concepts of publish/subscribe and subject-based addressing will be described in this chapter. These terms have been heavily marketed
by TIBCO and are associated with that company's solutions to group set-up and
discovery in data message streaming environments.

9.1 THE IETF MMUSIC GROUP CONFERENCING ARCHITECTURE

MMUSIC stands for Multiparty Multimedia Session Control, which encompasses both many-to-many conferencing applications as well as "events"—that is, "electronic crowds gathered around an attraction."

The MMUSIC architecture [9-2] is shown in Figure 9-1 with the protocols. This architecture also includes not only *set-up* and *discovery*, the main topics of this chapter, but also *conference course control*, or the rules for operation in a many-to-many conference.

Conference set-up and discovery protocols provide the tools to set-up and discover "conferences," in the form of either many-to-many conferences or events. Conference course control provides the means to control the conference. RSVP is used in multimedia applications to provide a quality of service for the multimedia streams used in a conference. Distributed control refers to the rules of controlling a many-to-many conference—for example, when someone can transmit or modify shared data in a data conference. The "agents" are the transport protocols used to deliver the content to the members of the conference.

The protocols for set-up and discovery were created by the MMUSIC IETF working group—in particular, the Session Description Protocol (SDP) [9-3], Session Announcement Protocol (SAP) [9-4], and Session Invitation Protocol (SIP) [9-5]. The presence of HTTP [9-6] in Figure 9-1 refers to the ability of a user with a browser to access a Web page using HTTP and find a listing of content that can be "tuned," just as you tune in to a television channel. The Simple Mail Trans-

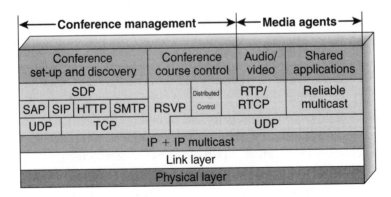

FIGURE 9-1

Internet multimedia conferencing protocols

port Protocol (SMTP) [9-7] is the Internet protocol used for e-mail; it indicates that a user could be notified by e-mail of the presence of a conference.

The architecture developed by the MMUSIC working group has defined *loosely coupled* sessions. In a loosely coupled session, the sender need not know beforehand who the receivers are. It may discover them later, but it is not required to do so. This architecture fits with the historic nature of the Internet, where events are open to all and any users may join and participate. It also enables a higher level of scaling, as less control is needed.

The researchers in the Mbone have designed a tool called session directory (SDR)* [9-8], which uses SAP to announce (advertise) sessions over a low-bandwidth stream and SDP to describe the conference or event. SDR acts as a "Prevue Channel" to advertise content, much like the Prevue Channel used in many cable television systems. A low-bandwidth stream, SDR is constantly transmitted as shown in Figure 9-2 over a well-known multicast address. If a user wants to discover events, he or she tunes to this multicast address to find a listing of events and the address and time to "tune" in to this event. This model resembles subscription television, where a channel continually lists programming, and the user can then tune his or her television to the desired channel.

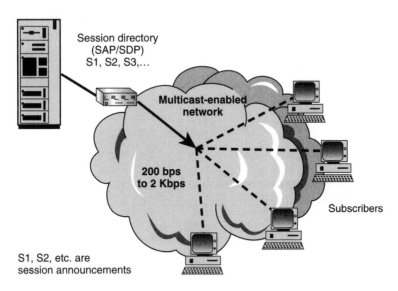

FIGURE 9-2

Use of SAP and SDP to announce conferences and sessions

---

* SDR is the latest version. The original was called SD.

SIP is used to invite members to join a conference, where the conference could be many-to-many or one-to-one. In the latter case, it can be used for IP telephony.

Conferences can still be advertised using SAP and SDP in a tool-like SDR, augmented by SIP to specifically invite certain members to join the conference.

9.1.1   Session Announcement Protocol (SAP) and Session Description Protocol (SDP)

SAP provides for multicast announcement of sessions described in its payload using SDP. Receivers may "tune" to the well-known multicast address and UDP port to read the session description defined by SDP, which describes the parameters of the session and the application needed to view the session.

The announcement is multicast with the same scope (as defined by a group address range, in the case of administrative scoping, or by TTL) as the session it announces. This approach ensures that the recipients of the announcement can also be consumers of the session. The time period between one announcement and its repetition depends on the TTL scope of the session and the number of other sessions being announced. The goal is to keep the total bandwidth used below a predefined level for each TTL scope. The recommended bandwidth limits for each TTL are as follows:

TTL	*Bandwidth*
1–15	2 Kbps
16–63	1 Kbps
64–127	1 Kbps
128–255	200 bps

This arrangement keeps the SDR channel to a low bandwidth, avoids consuming bandwidth unnecessarily, and reduces the amount consumed as the scope becomes larger.

The multicast address used by SAP depends on the scope of the address. For administratively scoped addresses, it normally uses the highest multicast address in the relevant administrative scope zone. For example, if the scope range is 239.16.32.0 to 239.16.33.255, then the convention is that 239.16.33.255 be used for session announcements. No default UDP port has been defined.

For TTL-scoped announcements, the well-known address is 224.2.127.254 and the UDP port is 9875. If different media in an announcement are given different TTLs, then multiple announcements are necessary to ensure that any receiver joining the session can receive data for each medium employed. For example, an announcement could be made for both video and audio at TTL 63 and a separate announcement containing only audio could appear at TTL 127. This strategy is somewhat like layering; those far away can get only audio, whereas those closer can receive the video as well.

SAP also provides for security, so that private sessions may be announced. The distribution of encryption keys, however, is considered to be performed external to SAP.

The payload—that is, the data field of SAP—is used by SDP to describe the session being announced. The SDP payload in a SAP packet is limited to 1 Kbyte in length.

The information conveyed by SDP about the session includes:

- The session name and purpose
- The time(s) that the session is active
- The media constituting the session, such as video and audio
- Information needed to receive those media (for example, addresses, ports, formats)

Optionally, information about the bandwidth to be used by the conference and contact information, such as an e-mail address and telephone number, for the person responsible for that session may be conveyed.

The media information includes the type of media (for example, video and audio), the transport protocol used to convey the media (for example, RTP), and the format of the media (for example, MPEG). For multicast sessions, the multicast address and port for the media are provided. In similar fashion, a remote unicast address and transport port are provided for unicast sessions.

Timing information provided may be in the form of start and stop times or repeat times, such as "every Monday at 10 A.M. for one hour." Timing information is in a form that is globally consistent.

Additional information may be provided as well. For example, URLs may be provided at which the user can find more information about the session on the Web.

There is also provision to indicate the conference control policy in many-to-many conferences, although there is still some debate in the community as to how this should be communicated.

SAP and SDP as embodied in SDR are supported by most of the companies supplying multimedia applications as described in Chapter 7.

The MMUSIC architecture shown in Figure 9-1 also includes means to advertise sessions on Web sites using SDP or e-mail. This tactic is just an alternative mechanism to advertise content availability. Web advertisements are the most common way that "push" channels as described in Chapter 6 are advertised.

SAP and SDP were obviously created with multimedia conferences and events as the target applications for advertisement, although the "wb" whiteboarding tool that uses SRM is also defined in SDP as a "medium." Other reliable multicast protocols and applications could certainly be added.

The most important point about the MMUSIC architecture is that the sessions are loosely coupled; the sender need not know the members of the group. This approach essentially follows the broadcast television model; the consumer of the information sent decides whether to "tune" in or not, and the sender does not know who is listening.

9.1.2   Session Invitation Protocol (SIP)

Whereas SAP and SDP are used to advertise sessions and their content, SIP is used to "invite" participants to a session. Like SAP and SDP, it has been designed primarily for multimedia sessions rather than reliable multicast sessions.

These multimedia sessions include multimedia conferences, distance learning, Internet telephony, and similar applications. SIP can invite a person to both unicast and multicast sessions; the initiator does not necessarily have to be a member of the session for which an invitation is issued. Media and participants can be added to an existing session. SIP can be used to "call" both persons and devices — for example, to invite a media storage device to record an ongoing conference or to invite a video-on-demand server to play a video into a conference using the Real-Time Streaming Protocol (RTSP) (RTSP was described in Chapter 7). SIP can be used to initiate sessions as well as to invite members to sessions that have been advertised and established by other means, such as SAP and SDP.

SIP supports personal mobility telecommunications intelligent network services. Personal mobility is based on the use of a unique personal identity (that is, a "personal number"). Personal mobility complements terminal mobility — that is, the ability to maintain communications when moving a single-end system from one network to another.

SIP supports the following five facets of establishing and terminating multimedia communications:

- User location: determination of the end system to be used for communication.

- User capabilities: determination of the media and media parameters to be used.

- User availability: determination of the willingness of the called party to engage in communications.

- Call set-up: "ringing," establishment of call parameters at both the called and calling party.

- Call handling: management that includes transfer and termination of calls.

This protocol may also be used in conjunction with other call set-up and signaling protocols. In that mode, an end system uses SIP exchanges to determine the appropriate end-system address and protocol from a given address that is protocol-independent. For example, it may be used to determine that the target is reachable via the public switched telephone network (PSTN) and indicate the phone number to be called, possibly suggesting an Internet-to-PSTN gateway to be used.

SIP does not offer conference control services, such as floor control or voting, and does not prescribe how a conference is to be managed. Nevertheless, it can be used to introduce conference control protocols.

As can be seen, SIP is an all-encompassing protocol for use in inviting participants to all kinds of multimedia sessions. These sessions can be multiparty, multicast-based, or point-to-point.

9.2 MFTP GROUP CREATION

The Multicast File Transfer Protocol (MFTP) [9-9], discussed in Chapter 8, is one of many reliable multicast protocols. One major difference between it and all other reliable multicast protocols is that MFTP was not developed by the academic research community; rather, it was developed by a commercial company (StarBurst Communications) with input from potential commercial users as to desirable characteristics of a product.

The customer input resulted in the inclusion of group creation tools within this protocol that were not available from the Internet research community. Additionally, the MFTP group creation tools were explicitly designed to support bulk data transmission. In particular, the group model most desirable is the MFTP *Closed Group*. The Closed Group model creates a *tightly coupled* one-to-many session.

The Closed Group enables a sender to completely define a multicast group and direct members to join the group using IGMP; the new members then "register" back to the sender to indicate that they have actually joined the group. At the end of the session, all receivers confirm delivery or, if the session timed out, the sender is informed which members did not receive the information. Another major difference between this model and the MMUSIC model is that senders may schedule transmissions at any time without advance knowledge of receivers. This ability is especially useful when the receiving site is unmanned, such as when transmissions are sent during the night when networks are lightly loaded. It is also desirable when the remote sites do not have competent technical personnel on the premises.

The Closed Group model is important when organizations wish to deliver critical information from their home offices to many scattered remote locations. These organizations desire to control and support the delivery of critical information and software to the remote locations without stationing scarce and costly technical support personnel at those remote sites.

MFTP also defines two other group models, *Open Limited* and *Open Unlimited*. With the Open Limited model, the announcement message acts as an advertisement; receivers are not directed to join. After joining, however, receivers register with the sender and the sender then can track the transfer and confirm delivery. The Open Unlimited model acts more like the MMUSIC model in that receivers join but do not register, resulting in a loosely coupled session.

9.2.1   MFTP Announce/Registration and Completion Phases

Like SDR using SAP/SDP, MFTP Announce messages are usually sent on a special "well-known" multicast address and UDP port that is constantly being monitored by the population of potential receivers. The Internet Address Numbers Authority has assigned UDP port 5402 to MFTP for this purpose, though no specific multicast address has been designated. In the normal mode of operation, the Announce message contains the "private" multicast address for the data transfer. The receivers that join the group then access this address, which is typically used only for the duration of the session and then given up for use by other transfers. This architecture is shown in Figure 9-3.

9.2.1.1   *Closed Groups*

With Closed Groups, the sender creates a list of receivers that comprises a subset of the receivers listening to the Announce multicast address. Receivers are

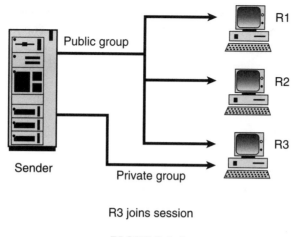

R3 joins session

FIGURE 9-3
Announce and join

identified by their IP addresses or, alternatively, by special global IDs. Such an ID takes the form of a Class E IP address (IP address space not currently used). Global IDs are useful in situations when receivers may not have a permanent IP address but are assigned one whenever they connect to the network.

Receivers receive Announce messages and look for their IP addresses or Global IDs if so configured. If present, the receiver responds with a Registration message. Multiple Announce messages are sent during this phase, with subsequent ones serving as confirming messages to newly joined receivers. Two main operational parameters are associated with this phase: announce frequency and announce duration.

The announce frequency determines how often the Announce messages are sent in the Announce/Registration phase. The announce duration determines how long this phase lasts. For example, one typical parameter sets the announce frequency at once per second and the announce duration at one minute, resulting in the transmission of 60 Announce messages during the duration of the Announce/Registration phase. If all receivers in the group have registered, the phase is terminated. If all receivers have not registered when the announce duration ends, the transmission commences; the sender knows who did not register, however, and can take action at a later time as desired for unregistered receivers.

The Announce message conveys more information to receivers than simply the list of receivers that it wishes to join for the session. The following list describes this information:

Server address
Server port
Response address
Response port
Private address
Announce duration
Announce options
Application reference
Block size
Data rate
Product name
Data transfer duration
DTU size
Products size
Error threshold
User data
Host list

The first four parameters are needed only when aggregating entities exist in the network—that is, when responses from receivers are aggregated by routers in the network. The private address is the address for which the data transmission will occur. The data rate at which the sender transmits and the size of the data being sent for the session are also conveyed. The Announce options communicate to the receivers what type of group is being formed, whether to leave the private address when the session ends, whether the transmission is an initial one or a "restart," and whether to overwrite an existing file of the same name.

The restart capability provides for a means of sending only data not completely transmitted in a previous session that had been terminated by that receiver or data it had not completed when the session ended.

The data transfer duration determines the session time limit, based on the theoretical time to send the data in the session, expressed as a percentage. For example, the amount of data and the rate at which it is sent are known; a data transfer duration of 200% would indicate that twice the theoretical minimum time for the transfer is allowed before the session ends.

The user data field allows a user to put in any descriptor up to 64 bytes. It can describe the data further and be used as a criterion for acceptance by receivers.

The receiver uses the error rate threshold to measure its own packet error rate and to make the decision to leave the group should this packet loss exceed the threshold. This parameter provides a timely method of congestion control, where the dropouts must obtain the data in some other fashion.

For improved scaling, a technique called "host list pruning" is employed to reduce the amount of data needed to identify the hosts directed to join the group. This approach is illustrated in Figure 9-4.

The first Announce message includes the total list of hosts directed to join. This number could be 10,000 or higher. For a maximum transmit unit (packet size) of 1,500 bytes (a common number as it is the maximum for Ethernet), about 60 Announce packets need to be sent to reach all 10,000 host list members. After the first Announce message, the sender collects Registration messages until the second Announce message is due to be sent. The sender sends the total host list again to confirm reception of Registrations to those members that joined and to solicit Registrations from those not received. Again, the sender collects Registrations until the third Registration message is due to be sent. This time, however, the host list is "pruned" to eliminate receivers that registered in the period between the first and second Announce messages, reducing the number of packets

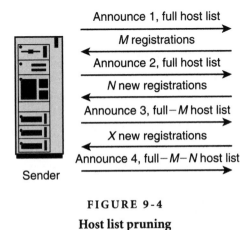

FIGURE 9-4

Host list pruning

needed for the third Announce message. This process continues until all receivers have registered or the Announce duration has expired. It results in the
host list being pruned further with every subsequent Announce message.

Thus the time needed to set up the group grows as the number of receivers
increases. This trade-off is acceptable when a highly sender-controlled group
set-up mechanism is desired.

Registration messages are sent from receivers to the sender or to the response address contained in the Announce message. The latter address is usually that of the sender, but it could be a response multicast address used by
routers when aggregating responses to reduce implosion. It could also identify
a designated responder somewhere in the network.

Receivers in a Closed Group may register and decline with a reason. For example, the receiver may not have enough storage space to store the data being
transferred. Alternatively, the receiver may not want to receive the data transmitted based on the description in the user data field, or it may not want to receive data from that sender. In these cases, the receivers essentially indicate they
are available but unable to join the session for some reason. The sender captures
this information and can deal with it as desired.

At the end of a session, receivers complete receiving all of the data and respond with a Done message, which is essentially one ACK to signal complete
reception. Done messages are also confirmed by the sender via Completion
messages. Host list pruning is used to reduce traffic in a similar fashion as in the
Announce/Registration phase.

9.2.1.2   *Open Limited and Unlimited Groups*

With Open Limited Groups, the sender does not define the group members.
Rather, an Announce message is sent to the Announce address and acts as an advertisement. Receivers that are interested, based on the name of the data delivered
or some other criteria, register that they are listening with the sender. The sender
then tracks the progress of the session and confirms delivery in similar fashion as
with Closed Groups. This Open Limited Group model provides tight control of
the session but allows receivers to decide whether or not to join the session. Done
messages are sent to the sender as receivers complete; the sender acknowledges
their finished state with Completion messages, exactly as happens with Closed
Groups.

Open Unlimited Groups have no sense of registration at all. The sender
does not know the listeners, creating a loosely coupled session.

9.3 TIBCO'S PUBLISH/SUBSCRIBE AND SUBJECT-BASED ADDRESSING

TIBCO provides message streaming middleware software solutions, historically targeting the financial industry. As mentioned in Chapter 8, TIBCO has a proprietary reliable multicast protocol and is strongly supporting Cisco's efforts to promote its own new reliable multicast protocol, PGM.

TIBCO promotes two concepts, *publish/subscribe* and *subject-based addressing* [9-10]. These two concepts are tied in with how the company promotes the methods to create groups.

Publish/subscribe is just a fancy name for send and listen. The term "publish" implies that when the event occurs (that is, when the content becomes available), it is sent (published). Receivers that are interested in that content then listen (subscribe) to the content.

Content is identified by subject-based addressing. Subject-based addressing is simply a naming context similar to that used in the Internet — for example, ckm@eng.starburstcom.com. Subjects are resolved into multicast addresses by TIBCO's subject name server, as shown in Figure 9-5. If multiple subjects are present in a stream of information on one multicast address, subject-based addressing can be used for filtering, enabling receivers to pick out the information desired from the stream.

This technology has been extensively deployed in financial brokerage houses for distribution of ticker-tape information to brokers. The ticker-tape feed comprises a data stream that is multicast by a sender continuously; brokers subscribe by tuning in based on the subject. This subject could be broad, like commodities, or more narrow, in the case of particular commodities. The former could resolve into a multicast address from the name server; the latter could perform as a filtering function at the receiver.

This model more closely resembles the MMUSIC model than the MFTP Closed Group model; the sender does not direct members to join. TIBCO, however, supports two levels of reliability with its message streaming middleware, which it labels "reliable" and "certified." "Reliable" indicates that the sender does not know the receivers and it is the receiver's responsibility to ensure that the data is delivered. This approach is similar to the MFTP open unlimited group model.

With "certified" delivery, receivers "register" with the sender, and the sender keeps track of all receivers. The sender gets explicit confirmation of delivery from every receiver, and the sender notes which messages were delivered and which

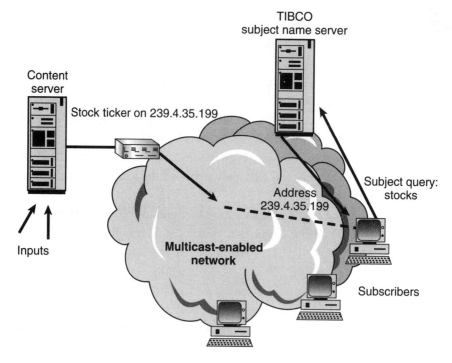

FIGURE 9-5

TIBCO publish/subscribe architecture

were undeliverable to which recipients. This model represents a message stream-ing version of the MFTP Open Limited Group model, providing for a tightly coupled session designed for the needs of message streaming applications.

The TIBCO products are not end-user products, however. Thus they require the user to develop application software on top of the TIBCO middleware to provide a complete product.

9.4 CONCLUSIONS

For multicast applications to be useful, mechanisms must be in place to allow the applications to join groups intelligently. We have seen previously that many different multicast applications exist, and these applications logically need dif-ferent mechanisms for group set-up and discovery.

A number of group set-up mechanisms have been defined to serve the various applications.

The MFTP closed group model provides a means to create groups at the sender location and to direct receivers to join that group, thus creating a tightly coupled session. The sender then tracks transmission and confirms delivery or nondelivery. This model is very important for the delivery of critical information from an organization's central headquarters to its remote offices. In many respects, these applications are the ones that the Information Technology group within an organization views as critical and would spur the company on to upgrade its Intranet to be multicast-ready. Many of the case studies in Chapter 8 attest to the importance of centralized control.

Both the TIBCO model and the MFTP Open Limited Group model provide for a tightly controlled session in applications where receivers of information should make the decision about receiving information. The receivers then want to receive certification from the content source that this data was in fact delivered.

Another major group creation model is based on the same model employed by broadcast television. Content is advertised either through a Prevue Channel or by some other means (for example, from a Web page). Any receiver that wishes to receive the content simply "tunes" to the multicast address, much as a television viewer tunes a television to the desired program. The sender does not know who is listening in this model. This group model is appropriate for the distribution of noncritical content, such as content that individuals within an organization may find desirable but whose delivery is not measurable as a dollar-benefit to that organization.

Many-to-many conferences also need a means of "inviting" participants to a conference, such as video, audio, or data, using a protocol such as SIP.

These group set-up and management tools are essential in providing complete multicast application solutions. Multicast applications will not enter the mainstream without them.

One major shortcoming in these applications is the lack of security in multicast applications. In Chapter 10, we will discuss the security issues relevant for multicast applications and networks.

REFERENCES

[9-1] Information on the MMUSIC working group in the IETF can be found at http://www.ietf.org.

[9-2] Handley M, Crowcroft J, Bormann C, Ott J. The Internet Multimedia Conferencing Architecture. Internet Draft, Work in Progress, draft-ietf-mmusic-confarch-00.txt, July 1997.

[9-3] Handley M, Jacobson V. SDP: Session Description Protocol. Internet Draft, Work in Progress, draft-ietf-mmusic-sdp-07.txt, April 2, 1998.

[9-4] Handley M. SAP: Session Announcement Protocol. Internet Draft, Work in Progress, draft-ietf-mmusic-sap-00.txt, November 19, 1996.

[9-5] Handley M, Schulzrinne H, Schooler E. SIP: Session Initiation Protocol. Internet Draft, Work in Progress, draft-ietf-mmusic-sip-04.txt, November 11, 1997.

[9-6] Berners-Lee T, Fielding R, Frystyk H. Hypertext Transfer Protocol—HTTP/1.0. RFC 1945, May 1996.

[9-7] Postel J. Simple Mail Transfer Protocol. STD 10, RFC 821, August 1982.

[9-8] Information on MBone tools, including session directory, may be found at http://pipkin.lut.ac.uk/~ben/video/.

[9-9] Miller K, Robertson K, Tweedly A, White M. StarBurst Multicast File Transfer Protocol (MFTP) Specification. Internet Draft, Work in Progress, draft-miller-mftp-spec-03.txt, April 1998.

[9-10] Information on publish/subscribe and subject-based addressing may be found at the TIBCO Web site at http://www.tibco.com.

URLS FOR ORGANIZATIONS MENTIONED IN CHAPTER 9

IETF	http://www.ietf.org
StarBurst Communications	http://www.starburstcom.com
TIBCO	http://www.tibco.com

10

SECURITY SYSTEMS APPLIED TO MULTICAST APPLICATIONS

S ecurity becomes important in data transmission when traversing public networks—in particular, the Internet. We have all heard stories of
hackers infiltrating large organizations via the Internet. We are all familiar with computer viruses that may be spread through e-mail at-
tachments sent over the Internet to an organization's private Intranet.
Sensitive information often needs to be kept confidential from potential eaves-
droppers. In addition, electronic commerce involving the sale of goods over the
Internet has spurred the use of security techniques to protect transactions.

There are many facets to security. ISO 7498 [10-1] defines them as follows:

Confidentiality: Confidentiality requires that nontrusted third parties be
prevented from accessing data. It is usually implemented by encrypting the data
via an encryption key employing some cryptographic algorithm.

Integrity: Integrity means that the data cannot be altered in transit over the network without detection.

Access Control: Access control provides the mechanisms to allow only authorized users to access resources—for example, to enter a network. The most common form of access control is the use of passwords. This technique, however, provides only minimal protection.

Authentication: Authentication requires that the received data be actually sent by the claimed sender. Authentication systems are often used in conjunction with access control systems to verify the identity of a user who is attempting to access a network or other system.

Nonrepudiation: Nonrepudiation enables the recipient to prove that the sender did send particular data, even if the sender denies transmitting it.

Protection Against Denial-of-Service Attacks: Denial of service occurs when an attacker performs some act that results in the system becoming unavailable to other users. Denial of service has become a large issue in the Internet, where servers have been brought down during an attack. The servers then become unaccessible to all other users of that particular network.

Today's security systems were designed originally for unicast traffic, which involves only two participants in a session. As a result, the security key exchange needs to involve only the two participants. With multicast, in contrast, the session involves the multicast group; at its extremes, this group could conceivably encompass thousands or even millions of recipients. Even worse for security, this group can be dynamic, with new members joining and leaving during a session without the sender's knowledge. This system creates some unique problems for security.

In this chapter, we shall investigate some multicast applications that could potentially use a multicast-enabled public Internet to provide services requiring some form of security. Applications on the Internet are inevitably "consumed" by business users who reside on private corporate Intranets, requiring traversal of the firewalls used to protect the corporate networks from malicious attacks. Additionally, some extra opportunities to "hack" and cause other forms of maliciousness become easier with multicast, which increases the need for protective measures.

A brief discussion of security technology in general is provided as a background. The IETF IPsec specifications and the application of multicast support to virtual private networks (VPNs)—private networks that are carved out of the Internet—are discussed as well. Finally, the multicast group key management problem is described.

10.1 MULTICAST APPLICATIONS NEEDING SECURITY

As ISPs begin offering multicast support in their networks, they must deal with the need to provide security for the multicast applications offered. Not all multicast applications will need such security, however.

We have discussed multicast applications many times in previous chapters. Which ones could use security if used on a public network? With one multicast transmission of a virus or other piece of malicious data, millions of recipients could be infected, making it easier for hackers to cause damage. Multicast transmissions will also need to traverse both the public Internet and private Intranets, requiring mechanisms to cross firewalls without breaching the security in the Intranets provided by those firewalls.

10.1.1 Collaborative Applications

Collaborative applications include video and data conferencing and network-based games. All may require security. For example, different companies may collaborate on technical projects and want to have periodic cyberspace meetings over the Internet that could be based on video or data conferencing. The participants would likely want to keep this technical collaboration secret from the Internet as a whole, yet use the Internet as a common networking medium.

Network gaming has long been thought to be a major money-making vehicle of the Internet. For application providers to turn a profit, the participants in the game need to be authenticated as having paid for the service using security techniques.

10.1.2 Multimedia Streaming Applications

Multimedia streaming applications are classified as either scheduled programming or asynchronous events. Many regard scheduled programming as an alternative viewing medium to broadcast television that adds the equivalent of many more channels of content viewing. If this proposed application becomes reality, many channels will be public and free to all, just as public television is. Providers of this content will gain revenue from advertising, just as free television does. An equivalent to pay (cable and satellite) television is also likely to emerge, in which channels of content are available without advertising. Additionally, there would likely be an equivalent to "pay per view," in which a scheduled event, such as a special sporting match, was made available to viewers who paid for it. The latter two examples would need to include security to prevent nonpaying viewers from gaining access to the content.

These kinds of events are already occurring [10-2] over the Internet, and their numbers are predicted to increase dramatically in the future. The types of events suited to the Web are classified as sports, concerts, and science events (for example, the Pathfinder landing on Mars). Some of these will be pay-per-view events and will need to have mechanisms to restrict viewership to paying subscribers. Similar mechanisms are used in the satellite broadcast television industry to scramble satellite television broadcasts so that only paying viewers can unscramble the signal and access the content.

Other events can be considered business-oriented rather than consumer-based. For example, financial institutions could pay to subscribe to business events, such as the 1998 Microsoft–Justice Department tussles, or to talks about major mergers, such as the takeover of MCI by Worldcom. Such events could be transmitted using security techniques that restrict access to only the paying subscribers.

Similar events can be contemplated in education. Remote educational courses could be taught over a multicast-enabled Internet to thousands of paying students. Again, security techniques would be needed to restrict access to this classroom to those students who have legitimately paid to join.

Even publicly available events targeted to business consumers have an element of security attached to them. The viewers inevitably reside inside a corporate Intranet, and the content would need to traverse the corporate firewall. This process needs to be accomplished without breaching the security offered by the firewall. This topic is discussed further in Section 10.4.

10.1.3   Data Streaming Applications

Data streaming applications such as ticker-tape stock, bond, and commodity feeds and news feeds could be either offered publicly or specialized versions could be offered on a paid subscription basis. The latter type of application will need to employ security to restrict access to valid subscribers.

Business consumers of free content will also have the same firewall issue described in section 10.1.2.

10.1.4   Bulk Data Transfer Applications

Bulk data transfer applications could also be offered as a subscription service. For example, software updates could be provided over the Internet based on a subscription service. Informative content, such as electronic magazines or newspapers, could be delivered electronically to paying subscribers as well. Again, there would need to be security controls in place to restrict the content to valid subscribers.

The same issue of firewall traversal is applicable to free content that is delivered via bulk data delivery.

10.2 MALICIOUS ATTACKS USING MULTICAST

Many have worried that multicast's ability to access many remote receivers with only a single transmission could be a hacker's dream. For example, desired content could be advertised by a hacker on a particular multicast address (channel). The hacker could then use this vehicle to distribute viruses to many unsuspecting hosts, creating an "epidemic." Similarly, a hacker could send viruses or other malicious material to the same address occupied by a well-known channel, such as SDR, thereby infecting all of those viewers.

Even worse, a hacker could send a stream at a very high rate to a well-known multicast address, such as SDR, characterized by many receivers. This data flow would traverse the multicast tree and overload the entire tree, denying service to all hosts downstream from the hacking source.

Both of these scenarios can be prevented with the use of the proper security procedures.

10.3 BRIEF REVIEW OF SECURITY TECHNOLOGY

Security is a complex subject that is covered in whole books [10-3]. We do not intend to add a treatise about security in this book, which focuses on multicast networking and applications. Nevertheless, understanding the particular issues relevant to security for multicast applications requires an understanding of the fundamental security technology being used today. Hence, this section will give a brief overview of security technology.

Forms of security involving encryption of data (secrecy) and authentication use cryptographic technology, which has been around in some form for centuries.

Encryption is the transformation of data into a form unreadable by anyone without a secret decryption key. It ensures privacy by keeping the information hidden from anyone for whom it is not intended—even those who can see the encrypted data. For example, one may encrypt files on a hard disk to prevent an intruder from reading them.

In a multiuser setting, encryption allows secure communication over an insecure channel. The general scenario, illustrated in Figure 10-1, is as follows: A wishes to send a message to B so that no one else except B can read it. A encrypts the message, which is called the *plaintext*, with an encryption key; the encrypted message, called the *ciphertext*, is sent to B. B then decrypts the ciphertext with the decryption key and reads the message. An attacker, C, may try to obtain the secret key or recover the plaintext without using the secret key. In a secure cryptosystem, the plaintext cannot be recovered from the ciphertext except via the decryption key. In a symmetric cryptosystem, a single key serves as both the encryption and decryption keys.

Until 1976, all cryptography was based on the sender and receiver of a message knowing and using the same secret key—that is, the sender uses the secret key to encrypt the message, and the receiver uses the same secret key to decrypt the message. This method is known as *secret-key* cryptography. The main prob-

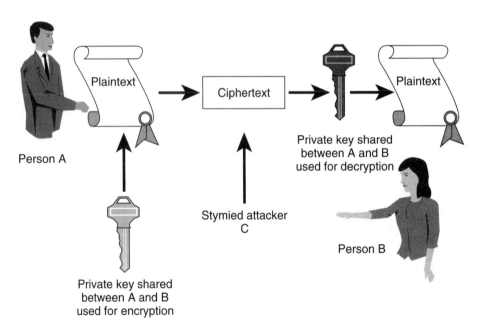

FIGURE 10-1

Symmetric cryptosystem

lem lies in getting the sender and receiver to agree on the secret key without anyone else finding out. If the two parties reside in separate physical locations, they must trust a courier, a telephone system, or some other transmission system to not disclose the secret key being communicated. Anyone who overhears or intercepts the key in transit can later read all messages encrypted using that key. The generation, transmission, and storage of keys is called *key management*; all cryptosystems must deal with key management issues. Secret-key cryptography often has difficulty providing secure key management.

Public-key cryptography was invented in 1976 by Diffie and Hellman [10-4] to resolve the key management problem. In this system, each person gets a pair of keys, called the *public* key and the *private* key. Each person's public key is published; the private key remains secret. The need for sender and receiver to share secret information is eliminated: All communications involve only public keys, and no private key is ever transmitted or shared. It is no longer necessary to trust some communications channel to prevent eavesdropping or betrayal. Anyone can send a confidential message using public information, but the data can be decrypted only with a private key that is in the sole possession of the intended recipient. Furthermore, public-key cryptography can be used for authentication (digital signatures) as well as for secrecy (encryption).

Figure 10-2 illustrates how this system works for encryption: When A wishes to send a message to B, A looks up B's public key in a directory, uses it to encrypt the message, and sends the message to B. B then uses a private key to decrypt the message and read it. No one listening in can decrypt the message. Although anyone can send an encrypted message to B, only B can read it. Obviously, one requirement is that no one be able to figure out the private key from the corresponding public key.

Authentication in a digital system is a process whereby the receiver of a digital message can be confident of the identity of the sender and the integrity of the message. Authentication protocols can be based on either secret-key cryptosystems or public-key systems.

Authentication systems today generally use *digital signatures*, which serve a function for digital documents similar to the role played by handwritten signatures for printed documents: The signature is an unforgeable piece of data asserting that a named person wrote or otherwise agreed to the document to which the signature is attached. The recipient, as well as a third party, can verify that the document originated from the person whose signature is attached and that the document has not been altered since it was signed. A secure digital signature system therefore consists of two parts: a method of signing a

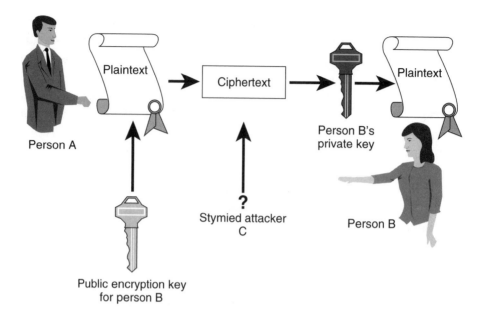

FIGURE 10-2

Use of public-key cryptography

document such that forgery is not feasible, and a method of verifying that a signature was actually generated by the claimed party. Furthermore, secure digital signatures cannot be repudiated; that is, the signer of a document cannot later disown it by claiming it was forged.

Unlike encryption, digital signatures are a fairly recent development, whose creation was inspired by the proliferation of digital communications. They generally use *message digests*, which are described later in this chapter.

Public-key cryptography provides for authentication in the following way. To sign a message, person A does a computation involving both A's private key and the message itself; the output is called the digital signature and is attached to the message, which is then sent to B. To verify the signature, B does some computation involving the message, the purported signature, and A's public key. If the results properly hold in a simple mathematical relation, the signature is verified as genuine; otherwise, it may be fraudulent or the message may be altered, and both are discarded. This process is shown in Figure 10-3 using the MD5 message digest.

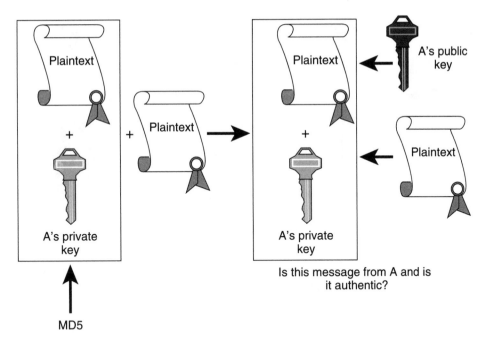

FIGURE 10-3

Using public-key cryptography and message digest to authenticate

One major disadvantage to public-key cryptography is speed; private-key encryption methods are many times faster than currently available public-key encryption algorithms. The most modern systems incorporate the best of both worlds; a public key is used to encrypt a private symmetric key for distribution, which is then used to encrypt and decrypt the data. The public-key encryption of the private symmetric key requires minimal processing power because the key is typically small; the private symmetric key, with its much smaller processing needs, is then used to encrypt the data. This process is shown in Figure 10-4.

10.3.1   Message Digests and Hash Functions

A *hash* function is a computation that takes a variable-size input and returns a fixed-size string that is a smaller representation of the original data. The smaller representation is called the *hash value*. If the hash function is one-way—that is, if it is a mathematical function that is significantly easier to perform in one direction (the forward direction) than in the opposite direction (the inverse

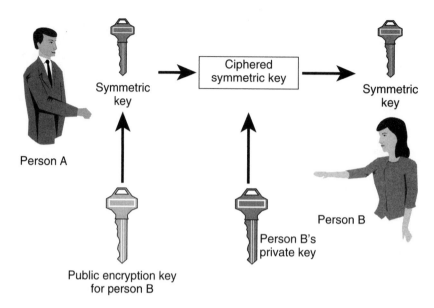

FIGURE 10-4

Distribution of a private (symmetric) key using public cryptography

direction) — the result is called a *message digest*. One might, for example, compute the function in seconds but be able to compute the inverse only in years.

Message digests (one-way hash functions) are commonly used to provide a small string of bits that can securely represent much larger entities, such as files. In this sense, they act as "digital signatures" of the larger data represented. Message digests are often used for authentication and constitute a useful tool in the bag of tricks needed in security systems. A number of message digest functions have been developed; MD2, MD4, and MD5 are specified in RFCs 1319 [10-5], 1320 [10-6] and 1321 [10-7], respectively, along with sample C-language code that can be used to implement them. MD5, the most popular, is specified in a number of security systems, including IPsec.

10.3.2   Key Management

Secure methods of key management are extremely important. In practice, most attacks on public-key systems will probably be aimed at the key management levels, rather than at the cryptographic algorithm itself.

Users must be able to securely obtain a key pair suited to their efficiency and security needs. There must be a way to look up other people's public keys and to publicize one's own key. Users must have confidence in the legitimacy of others' public keys; otherwise an intruder can either change public keys listed in a directory or impersonate another user.

Certificates are used to realize this goal. Certificates must be unforgeable, obtainable in a secure manner, and processed in such a way that an intruder cannot misuse them. The issuance of certificates must proceed in a secure way, impervious to attack. If someone's private key is lost or compromised, others must be made aware of the situation, so that they will no longer encrypt messages under the invalid public key or accept messages signed with the invalid private key. Users must be able to store their private keys so that no intruder can find them, yet keep the keys readily accessible for legitimate use. Keys need to remain valid only until a specified expiration date, which itself must be chosen properly and publicized securely. Some documents need to include verifiable signatures that endure beyond the expiration of the key used to sign them.

Anyone who wishes to sign messages or to receive encrypted messages must have a key pair. A user may possess multiple keys. For example, someone might have a key affiliated with his or her work as well as a separate key for personal use. Other entities will also have keys, including electronic components such as modems, workstations, and printers, as well as organizational entities such as corporate departments, hotel registration desks, and university registrar's offices.

Each user should generate his or her own key pair. It may be tempting to have a single site within an organization that generates keys for all members who request one. This system is a security risk, however, because it involves the transmission of private keys over a network. Catastrophic consequences may ensue if an attacker infiltrates the key-generation site. Each node on a network should be capable of local key generation, so that private keys are never transmitted and no external key source need be trusted. Of course, the local key-generation software must itself be trustworthy.

Once generated, a user must register his or her public key with some central administration, called a certifying authority (CA). The CA returns to the user a certificate attesting to the veracity of the user's public key along with other information. Most users should not obtain multiple certificates for the same key so as to simplify various key-related bookkeeping tasks.

Certificates are digital documents that validate the binding of a public key to an individual or other entity. They allow verification of the claim that a given public key does, in fact, belong to a specific individual. Certificates help prevent someone from using a phony key to impersonate someone else.

In their simplest form, certificates contain a public key and a name. As commonly used, they also contain the expiration date of the key, the name of the CA that issued the certificate, the serial number of the certificate, and perhaps other information. Most importantly, they contain the digital signature of the certificate issuer. The most widely accepted format for certificates is defined by the ITU X.509 international standard [10-8]; these certificates can be read or written by any application complying with X.509.

A certificate issued by a CA is signed with the CA's private key. A CA can comprise any trusted central administration willing to vouch for the identities of the parties to whom it issues certificates. For example, a company may issue certificates to its employees, a university to its students, and a town to its citizens. To prevent certificate forgery, the CA's public key must be trustworthy; that is, a CA must either publicize its public key or provide a certificate from a higher-level CA attesting to the validity of its own public key. The latter solution gives rise to CA hierarchies.

Certificate issuance operates as follows. Person A generates his or her own key pair and sends the public key to an appropriate CA with some proof of user identification. The CA checks the identification and takes any other steps necessary to assure itself that the request really did come from person A, and then returns a certificate attesting to the binding between person A and that public key, along with a hierarchy of certificates verifying the CA's own public key. Person A can present this certificate chain whenever desired to demonstrate the legitimacy of his or her public key.

Because the CA must check for proper identification, organizations often find it convenient to act as a CA for their own members and employees. Some commercial companies sell "smart cards" that are used by organizations seeking to be their own CAs. These smart cards are distributed to the organization's employees and are used to distribute keys to individuals in a secure manner. Employees can then access the corporate network securely with their laptop computers when they are away from the office.

Different CAs may issue certificates with varying levels of identification requirements. One CA may insist on seeing a driver's license, another may want the certificate request form to be notarized, and yet another may want the fingerprints of anyone requesting a certificate. Each CA should publish its own identification requirements and standards, so that verifiers can attach the appropriate level of confidence in the certified name-key bindings.

10.4 FIREWALLS

With the growth of the Internet, which anyone can access, organizations have a greater need to protect their private networks from intrusion from the public Internet. Individuals within a corporate network access the Internet every day to perform research on the Web, to download documents and software, to communicate via e-mail, and to carry out many other tasks. Without firewalls, every corporate network would simply be an extension to the Internet, open to anyone in the world who has Internet access.

Many companies have sprung up to provide firewall services that isolate the organization's private network from the global Internet. Firewalls are inserted between the private network and the Internet as shown in Figure 10-5. If the organization has a number of branches at different locations, each location commonly has its own firewall.

Firewalls use two basic different techniques to provide isolation. The first is packet filtering, where the firewall observes packets and filters based on protocol and ports. In this approach, internal and external nodes are visible at the IP level, but the firewall filters out certain undesirable types of packets, based on their header or even contents. Routers inherently have this capability. This technique can be limiting, however, and sophisticated security policies cannot be implemented under this scheme.

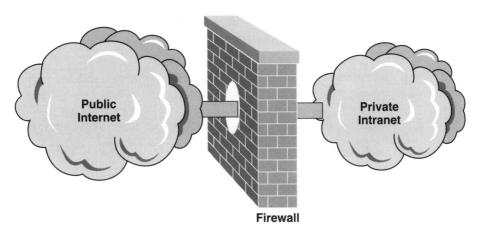

Firewall

FIGURE 10-5

Firewall inserted between the Internet and a private Intranet

As a result, firewalls have become more complex proxy devices, where the firewall acts as a "protocol end point." With this second approach, no internal node except for the firewall is directly accessible from the external Internet and no external node is directly accessible from within the Intranet. This type of firewall is also known as an *Application-layer gateway*.

Application-layer gateway firewalls are now emerging as the major enforcers of an organization's security policies. Firewalls therefore provide important mechanisms to allow multicast applications that originate outside of an organization's private network to interoperate with group members residing in the corporate network.

Another major function of firewalls is to provide audit trails of suspicious activity, allowing hacker activity to be traced. Many security personnel think this capability may even be the most important, as countermeasures can be taken upon detection of suspicious activity.

A critical issue for multicast traffic is that many firewalls currently block all non-TCP-based traffic. TCP-based traffic could have further restrictions, based on the application operating above TCP. As all multicast applications are not based on TCP, they will be blocked by these firewalls. Firewall vendors are moving to remove this restriction, however, as a number of unicast, UDP-based multimedia applications would otherwise be blocked.

Firewalls pose other problems for multicast applications, however. An organization does not want any multicast application to be able to be propagated through the private network, as it provides an easy mechanism to distribute malicious content. A recent Internet Draft [10-9] discussed some of the challenges facing firewalls in handling multicast applications. It suggests that a firewall needs to do three things to handle multicast traffic:

1. Support the chosen multicast security policy (which establishes particular multicast groups to be relayed).

2. Determine dynamically when each candidate group should be relayed.

3. Relay each candidate group's data across the firewall and remulticast it at the far end.

These requirements create some unique problems. For example, how does the firewall determine the policy about forwarding particular multicast group traffic into the private network? Even if so authorized, how does it know whether any group members on the private network have joined the group? How does it handle temporary groups?

In loosely coupled sessions, the sender does not know the identities of the group members. Thus, not only does it not know who is listening, but it also does not know whether the group membership has changed during the session. This dilemma is shown in Figure 10-6.

One large problem for the firewall proxy server is that, given certain policies about remulticasting certain streams into the private Intranet, it has no way of knowing whether the Intranet includes any group members. Group membership is conveyed to routers via IGMP messages which could be listened for by the firewall. If the private Intranet contains multiple subnets, however, then the firewall may not hear them even if it sets itself up to listen for them. Another possibility is to use the newly defined Domain-Wide Multicast Group Membership Reports [10-10]. This concept is a very new proposal, however, and has not been implemented anywhere yet. Other approaches would have the firewall send multicast "ping" probes or mandate that nodes joining a group explicitly notify the firewall of their existence — in essence, creating IGMP-like notifications to the firewall. Of course, if the firewall is also a multicast router, it will know whether downstream group members exist, but this case is not a general solution.

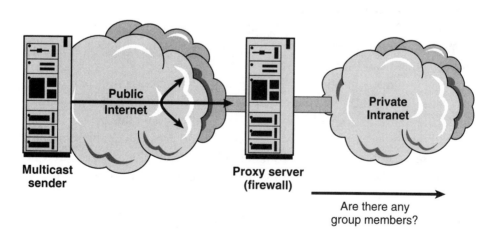

FIGURE 10-6

Firewall as multicast proxy

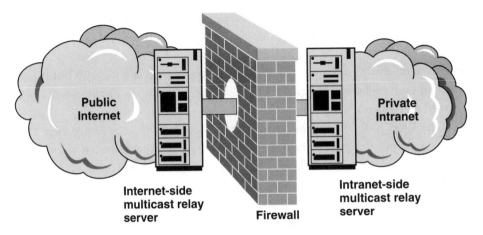

FIGURE 10-7

Tunneling multicast traffic through a firewall

If the multicast session were tightly coupled, as under the MFTP closed group model mentioned in Chapter 9, then the sender could determine the group membership and the firewall could more easily determine whether the private Intranet includes any group members.

Another approach, shown in Figure 10-7, involves two servers, one on either side of the firewall. The server on the Internet side forwards multicast packets through a tunnel that can pass through the firewall and then be remulticast by the server on the private Intranet side. Many tunneling protocols have been proposed that would serve this purpose.

As one-to-many multicast traffic in loosely coupled sessions bears some resemblance to broadcast media, the approach to privacy likewise has natural similarities. Thus data encryption is the only way to guarantee privacy, just as subscription broadcast television over satellite and cable is usually scrambled to prevent unauthorized access by nonpaying viewers. As a result, firewalls may need to get involved in multicast key-distribution tasks in the future.

10.5 VIRTUAL PRIVATE NETWORKS (VPNs)

VPNs are receiving much attention of late. A VPN is defined as a piece of the public Internet that has been sectioned off to be used by a private organization.

The reason for taking this step is cost; this approach is substantially less expensive for the organization, and the organization largely outsources its network support needs.

The most common incarnation of a VPN (although not usually called one) arises when individuals perform electronic commerce connecting to a secure Web site. A user who has purchased anything over the Web will have used a personal VPN — that is, a secure tunnel through the Internet that connects the consumer's host computer with the Web site. Individual VPNs of this sort have mostly been implemented using Secure Sockets Layer (SSL) [10-11], which was developed by Netscape Communications. SSL has since evolved into the Transport Layer Security (TLS) protocol [10-12]. As noted earlier, however, secure Web transactions involving individuals are not usually referred to as VPNs.

For VPNs for organizations, two important issues arise: security and quality of service. Because the Internet is a set of public networks, security is essential when creating an organizational VPN. Products are now available that provide means to create tunnels to isolate private IP addresses from the general Internet and then make those tunnels secure by encryption using IPsec (described in Section 10.6). What is not resolved satisfactorily yet is the need for a guaranteed service level that an ISP can offer to the organization.

Most of the organizational VPNs implemented to date deal only with dial-up access for employees who travel. The employees can make local calls to their VPN service provider, with the call being secured and tunneled back through the service provider's part of the Internet to the corporate Intranet. The "road warriors" can then collect their e-mail without having to make long-distance telephone calls to the home office.

The quality-of-service problem is being intensely attacked by Internet researchers and infrastructure suppliers, and VPNs connecting distributed organizations' facilities are likely to occur in the future. When that time comes, security will be needed for multicast traffic as well as unicast traffic. The vehicle that the IETF expects to provide that security is Ipsec [10-13].

Additionally, many large carriers such as AT&T, MCI, and Sprint now offer IP services that, although they are tied to the Internet, have their own backbone. They use these private backbones to provide private network services at the IP layer while simultaneously blocking general Internet traffic from their networks. This offering is a natural extension to their frame relay or other Link-layer service offerings, except that the service is at the Network layer rather than the Link-layer. This type of service will employ IPsec security services in many cases.

10.6 IPsec

IPsec is a set of proposed Internet standards for providing security services at the IP layer that can then serve all layers above IP. It is designed to provide interoperable, high-quality, cryptographically based security for IPv4 and IPv6. The set of security services offered includes access control, connectionless integrity, data origin authentication, protection against replays (a form of partial sequence integrity), confidentiality (encryption), and limited traffic-flow confidentiality.

These objectives are met through the use of two traffic security protocols, the Authentication Header (AH) and the Encapsulating Security Payload (ESP), and through the use of cryptographic key management procedures and protocols. The choice of IPsec protocols employed, and the ways in which they are employed, will be determined by the security and system requirements of users, applications, and sites or organizations.

When these mechanisms are correctly implemented and deployed, they should not adversely affect users, hosts, and other Internet components that do not employ these security mechanisms to protect their traffic. These mechanisms also are designed to be algorithm-independent. This modularity permits selection of different sets of algorithms without affecting other parts of the implementation. For example, different user communities may select different sets of algorithms.

A standard set of default algorithms is specified to facilitate interoperability in the global Internet. The use of these algorithms, in conjunction with IPsec traffic protection and key management protocols, is intended to permit system and application developers to deploy high-quality, Internet-layer, cryptographic security technology.

The AH provides connectionless integrity, data origin authentication, and an optional anti-replay service. The ESP protocol provides confidentiality (encryption) and limited traffic-flow confidentiality. It also may provide connectionless integrity, data origin authentication, and anti-replay service.

These two protocols may be applied alone or together to provide a set of security services. Both can operate in one of two modes of operation: *transport* mode and *tunnel* mode. In transport mode, the protocols provide protection primarily for protocols above the IP layer; in tunnel mode, they are applied to tunneled IP packets.

The basic IPsec architecture supports both the manual and automatic distribution of keys. Although it specifies the ISAKMP/Oakley [10-14, 10-15] public-key distribution approach for automatic distribution of keys, other automated key distribution techniques may be used, such as Simple Key management for IP (SKIP) [10-16].

IPsec specifications are relatively new and are just now solidifying for use with unicast traffic. Extension of IPsec to provide multicast support is planned but not yet implemented.

Firewall vendors are starting to support IPsec for VPN services, albeit usually with manual key distribution. More vendors will support this feature in future.

10.7 THE GROUP KEY MANAGEMENT PROBLEM

The largest security problem faced by multicast applications is that of key management and distribution. This problem plagues even normal unicast traffic, as there is a need to set up CAs or use a CA service to authenticate the binding of keys to individuals or sites. In the case of multicast, keys are bound to groups, whose membership can be large and varying. A basic rule in security is that the more people who know a secret, the less secret is the "secret." Thus security is more difficult to accomplish in multicast environments.

Membership variability can create excessive traffic in distributing keys by limiting scalability. As new members join a secure group, they need to be authenticated as being authorized to join the group and then need to receive the appropriate keys. As members leave a group, the entire group needs to be "rekeyed" — that is, members need a new group key to prevent a security breach caused by the egress of a member with valid key information. This situation necessitates that group membership be known, which is not the case in loosely coupled sessions.

A number of proposals [10-16, 10-17] have been made to solve the group key management and distribution problem. None has been implemented or commercialized as yet, however, and some suggestions do not seem to be general solutions that fit with the IPsec architecture.

The aforementioned SKIP protocol, which is specifically allowed in the IPsec architecture, has specified multicast extensions that support both semi-permanent and temporary multicast sessions. Although this protocol was developed by a company (Sun Microsystems) rather than researchers, it is not available in products yet and may need more refinement given the lack of commercial products supporting unicast.

10.8 CONCLUSIONS

Security solutions for multicast applications are essentially nonexistent. Many applications will not need security per se, but rather will require a means to punch through an organization's firewall without jeopardizing the security of the corporate Intranet. This problem will be easier to solve than the general multicast security problem.

In fact, many Information Systems personnel in large organizations will attest that, for the typical organization that is not a magnet for potential hackers (that is, an organization that is not the Defense Department or a security agency), most security breaches occur from within the organization rather than from outside. The attack often comes from a disgruntled employee who has been fired or is otherwise estranged from the organization. Often, these former employees may retain passwords or other means to access the organization. Thus the security breach is really caused by poor procedures.

That truth does not mean that the need for security is minimal. Many applications require encryption of content, especially since many — if not most — multicast applications are set up as loosely coupled sessions, where the sender does not know who is listening. If the content has value or is made available on a subscription basis, it will need to be made private so as to be available only to authorized recipients. All authorized recipients may not, in fact, receive the content at any given time. This model is very similar to the model used by broadcast subscription television; the television signal is scrambled, and only viewers with the proper set-top box can unscramble the signal. Although a determined hacker can descramble this signal, the loss of revenue is very small. Multicast content over the public Internet is likely to follow a similar model.

Some applications will need a high level of security, and users needing this assurance are likely to be willing to pay for it. For example, any financial data is likely to be highly confidential.

Multicast applications will need to start supporting some level of security and traverse firewalls if they are to become widely used over public networks in the future. The problems are very solvable, and solutions will become available in products as more multicast applications arrive and more public networks support multicast.

REFERENCES

[10-1] ISO/IEC 7498, Security Architecture, part 2, 1994.

[10-2] Gurley JW. Data Broadcast: The New Frontier. Above the Crowd, December 22, 1997.

[10-3] Smith R. Internet Cryptography. Reading, MA: Addison Wesley Longman Publishing Co., 1997.

[10-4] Diffie W, Hellman M. New Directions in Cryptography. IEEE Transactions on Information Theory, 1976; 22:644–654.

[10-5] Kaliski B. The MD2 Message-Digest Algorithm. RFC 1319, April 1992.

[10-6] Rivest R. The MD4 Message-Digest Algorithm. RFC 1320, April 1992.

[10-7] Rivest R. The MD5 Message-Digest Algorithm. RFC 1321, April 1992.

[10-8] ITU-T Recommendation X.509, November 1993.

[10-9] Finlayson R. IP Multicast and Firewalls. Internet Draft, Work in Progress, draft-finlayson-mcast-firewall-00.txt, March 5, 1998.

[10-10] Fenner W. Domain-Wide Multicast Group Membership Reports. Internet Draft, Work in Progress, draft-ietf-idmr-membership-reports-00.txt, November 12, 1997.

[10-11] Freier AO, Karlton P, Kocher PC. The SSL Protocol Version 3.0. Internet Draft, Work in Progress, draft-freier-ssl-version3-02.txt, November 18, 1996. This draft has expired but can be found at http://home.netscape.com/eng/ssl3/draft302.txt.

[10-12] Dierks T, Allen C. The TLS Protocol Version 1.0. Internet Draft, Work in Progress, draft-ietf-tls-protocol-05.txt, November 12, 1997.

[10-13] Kent S, Atkinson R. Security Architecture for the Internet Protocol. Internet Draft, Work in Progress, draft-ietf-ipsec-arch-sec-02.txt, November 1997.

[10-14] Maughan D, Schertler M, Schneider M, Turner J. Internet Security Association and Key Management Protocol (ISAKMP). Internet Draft, Work in Progress, March 1998.

[10-15] Orman HK. The Oakley Key Determination Protocol. Internet Draft, Work in Progress, draft-ietf-ipsec-oakley-02.txt, July 1997.

[10-16] Information on the SKIP protocol may be found at the SKIP Web page at http://skip.incog.com/.

[10-17] Harney H, Muckenhirn C. Group Key Management Protocol (GKMP) Architecture. RFC 2094, July 1997.

[10-18] The multicast extensions to the SKIP protocol may be found at http://skip.incog.com/spec/EIPM.html.

11

BARRIERS TO
DEPLOYMENT

In previous chapters, we saw how multicast applications can bring great benefit to users and organizations and offer new business opportunities to service providers and product vendors. We also saw that IP multicast has been around in some form for quite a long time — dating back to the late 1980s for some of the technology and to 1992 for first deployment of the Mbone, the experimental multicast network used as a test bed by Internet researchers. In Internet time, this period is analogous to many millennia in Earth time.

Given that multicast offers so many benefits and that the technology has been known for quite some time, why has it not been deployed to a greater extent in real networks?

11.1 RELUCTANCE TO CHANGE TODAY'S NETWORKS

One of the major reasons for the reluctance to adopt multicast is simply a resistance to change, especially when it means introducing a technology that is not well known by the population of technical personnel that will need to support that network. "If it's not broken, don't fix it" is the motto of network operators. This basic premise holds for both private and public networks, though the issues holding up deployment are somewhat different in these two cases.

One important issue in general is the lack of test tools for troubleshooting network problems with multicast. A multicast distribution tree in a land-line routed network can be very large and complex with many nodes, as shown in Figure 3-11. If any node experiences a problem, all downstream nodes are affected, and network operators need to be able to quickly identify malfunctioning nodes to correct the problem in a timely fashion. A utility called "mtrace" [11-1] is supported by both routers and some UNIX workstations and can be used to trace multicast paths. This tool can be used for troubleshooting, although it is not packaged with other network test tools and is not easy to use. This lack of test tools represents an opportunity for network test equipment vendors. Until products employing mtrace become commercially available, however, this need is a practical barrier to deployment, particularly in land-line routed networks.

A more basic utility used very often in IP networks is often called "ping" [11-2]. The Internet Control Message Protocol (ICMP) echo message, ping is commonly used to determine "reachability" — that is, whether a particular host can be reached by a user on another host.

Multicast ping is a natural extension to the ping utility in cases in which the destination address is a Class D multicast address rather than a Class A, B, or C unicast address that identifies an individual host. Multicast ping, illustrated in Figure 11-1, can determine the reachability of all members who have joined a particular group and provides another basic multicast troubleshooting tool. This utility operates correctly on some, but not all, popular operating systems. With luck, these deficiencies will be corrected in the near future.

Both mtrace and multicast ping can be viewed as extensions to the more common unicast troubleshooting tools, "trace" and "ping." Multicast utilities need to be viewed as simply extensions of familiar features to gain immediate acceptance by network support personnel. They must also require only minimal training to win over this audience.

It would also be desirable to have "agents" in the network that can inform network management systems about changes in group membership, forwarding tree changes, or, most importantly, high resource utilization by multicast transmissions.

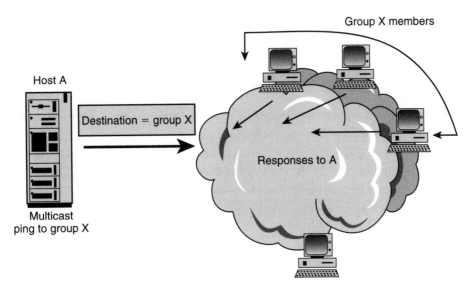

FIGURE 11-1

Multicast "ping" (ICMP echo) to determine reachability

Network operators managing all network types, whether private or public, will want a rigorous admission control mechanism based on established policies for multicast transmissions. These policies would be implemented at both the core and edges of the multicast tree. Additionally, the network administrators will want to set limits on the amount of bandwidth allowed for multicast sessions.

A major issue associated with multimedia streaming applications is quality of service (QoS). To gain high-quality multimedia viewing, high-bandwidth streams of more than 1 Mbps are needed and a QoS has to be provided for each stream. The questions about RSVP (discussed in Chapter 7) raise some doubts about the viability of multimedia applications in the minds of those potentially implementing multicast services in their networks. The implementation of QoS in these networks, while desirable, creates another technical barrier that must be overcome, and one that most network operators believe will pose a greater challenge than implementation of multicast.

Many of these issues were discussed at an Internet2 working group meeting [11-3] held in August 1997. This meeting included a discussion of the needs for implementation of multicast in the future Internet2 network connecting the major universities in the United States.

11.1.1   Private Network Barriers

Private networks have some unique issues that represent barriers to multicast. The most significant is that most organizations are simply overwhelmed with the task of keeping their own private networks operational. Often technical personnel are present only at the central headquarters or at a few large branches, and it would not be a trivial project to send these personnel to the field to turn on multicast in routers everywhere. Some analysts suggest that it will take a few well-publicized WAN "meltdowns," where the network is so overloaded as to bring it to its knees, to spur on the upgrade to multicast. Essentially, when the organization faces a costly upgrade in WAN bandwidth due to traffic overload, the addition of multicast services in its network can offer a very cost-effective solution if action must be taken to avert a crisis.

The network technicians in such organizations are also not very familiar with multicast. This new technology would require training on their part — which means time that most do not have.

Information Systems departments in organizations must deal with a number of other, more pressing issues that may lead to disaster if not fixed, such as the Year 2000 bug. Many organizations are just now migrating their networks from some other protocol, such as IBM's SNA or Novell's IPX/SPX, to IP and that move is consuming the bulk of the organization's resources.

Many large organizations are now contemplating outsourcing their network needs to service providers because they are having trouble retaining scarce technical people, or because they may have multiple network solutions based on the whims of each department or subsidiary in that organization that need to be consolidated. The most recent prominent example of this trend toward outsourcing involves Citicorp, which signed a $750 million contract with AT&T in early 1998 to totally outsource its network needs.

Outsourcing of multicast applications is especially applicable to organizations that do not have as many knowledgeable networking personnel as a service provider. Many organizations also have the impression that if they turn on multicast, many users of the private network may actually end up using more bandwidth with high bandwidth multimedia applications.

These barriers are all typical of a new technology, where early adopters become the first to deploy the technology and then the benefits become more widely known, prompting others to follow suit. The IPMI commissioned a report in 1997 [11-4] that listed the "top ten" IP multicast barriers:

- Limited application software integrating IP multicast
- Overall network effects of new content not understood by network planners
- Corporate network architects and network service planners who perceive that their networks are operating at capacity and that adding new multimedia content will push existing networks and applications beyond that capacity
- Remote sites connected at 56 Kbps, which will limit the functionality of applications targeting users at those sites
- Security concerns
- Limited administrative tools for IP multicast networks
- Conferencing, collaboration, and distance learning applications, which may create a new paradigm that end users resist
- Limited ISP implementations that restrict consumer and business application expansion potential
- Multiple multimedia content distribution standards coupled with interoperability concerns among IP multicast products
- "Push" technology vendors have created confusion

Some of these barriers are just perceptions, some equate multimedia to multicast but ignore reliable multicast applications, and some are real issues.

11.1.2   Public Network Barriers

Public network operators face somewhat different barriers than those in charge of private networks. The technical personnel force for these networks is larger and better able to cope with the addition of new technology, as it is their business.

There are actually two types of public networks, each having its own barriers to the deployment of multicast. In the first type, the service provider offers a private network service to an organization for its own internal use via outsourcing. This approach has been called a virtual private network (VPN) when a piece of the Internet is carved out for a private network. More popular, however, are IP services where the network is shared by multiple private organizations but is not the general Internet. This type of network is also sometimes referred to as a VPN.

The second type of public network is the Internet itself, where an ISP might provide multicast services in its segment of the Internet.

11.1.2.1   Virtual Private Networks (VPNs)

As noted earlier, "Virtual Private Network" (VPN) is used loosely and may refer to different network types [11-5]. Figure 11-2 shows a family tree of networks that are commonly identified as VPNs.

The most important of these VPNs are IP services offered by service providers that do not share general Internet traffic, although they have ties to the Internet. These networks are just being put in place today, and thus service providers have an opportunity to turn on multicast in the routers as they are initially deployed, reducing the burden of sending technical people to the field specifically to perform this task.

These networks are probably the ones with the least barriers to turning on multicast; they are new and can be configured to support multicast from the start. They represent an easy opportunity to add multicast services for organizations that decide to outsource their networking needs by specifying multicast support to their service provider as part of their negotiations for the service. They are, however, likely to need firewall support for multicast applications at the entrance to each facility along with security. Solving this problem is just a matter of implementation, however. Multicast traffic can be "punched" through

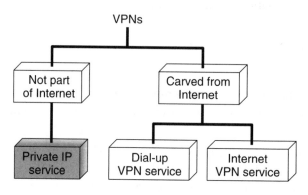

FIGURE 11-2

VPN family tree

(the shaded area indicates the most important VPN Category for multicast)

the firewalls with tunnels, as shown previously in Figure 10-7. This approach eliminates the problem that arises when the firewall does not know whether any group members are present at a particular facility.

11.1.2.2 The Internet

The Internet, and more specifically ISPs, face much more formidable barriers to deployment. Some of these obstacles are technical in nature; others are business-oriented.

ISPs are now struggling to keep up with the exponential growth in traffic in the Internet while at the same time attempting to make money. Thus any new service will be scrutinized carefully before deployment to determine how to extract more money from the service rather than to simply deploy it as an upgrade to current network services. ISPs also wish to provide support for multimedia multicast services, and the cloud over RSVP means they have no standard means to provide a QoS to support these streams.

Another unresolved business issue encompasses peering of multicast traffic. Peering between ISPs is relatively straightforward for unicast traffic; many operate on the precept that "if you carry my traffic, I will carry yours." This approach is a simple one when the session includes only two participants. It is less straightforward when group members can be located anywhere and can number in the thousands (or even higher), and many ISPs can potentially be traversed with a single session.

There are also technical issues to be resolved, some of which were discussed previously. Besides the lack of test tools and the concern about destabilizing the network, more global issues have not yet been resolved by the Internet engineering community.

The most glaring is the lack of an interdomain multicast routing protocol, as discussed in Chapter 4. Such a protocol was proposed in December 1997, but its details are still being worked on. It would provide the tools to enforce peering policies between ISPs. Today, however, both the policies and the tools to enforce them are nonexistent.

Closely associated with interdomain multicast routing is multicast address allocation in the global Internet. A new IETF working group has been proposed, Multicast Address ALLOCation (MALLOC), to formulate standards that would provide an automatic means to allocate multicast addresses to ISPs, which would then allocate them to applications (as described in Chapter 4). This working group first officially convened in spring, 1998. The concepts in MALLOC were first presented at the December 1997 IETF meeting in a "Birds of a Feather" (BOF) informational session.

Fears of multicast "abuse" have also arisen. As previously mentioned, there are some fears that new kinds of hacking could potentially expose more users using multicast.

For services that need to be made secure or authenticated, we have seen that the standards for security have not yet been extended to multicast. If the demand grows, however, vendors will begin implementing their own proprietary extensions, just as they did with unicast security.

Another potential barrier is the lack of an official standard for reliable multicast. The standards activities regarding reliable multicast currently reside in the IRTF, which is studying these techniques. Internet researchers believe that a reliable multicast protocol must behave in similar fashion as TCP—that is, it must have congestion control. The prospect for a standard in this area is years away, even though many reliable multicast protocols have been deployed in private networks and the Mbone. Even without flow control, ISPs could treat reliable multicast without flow control much like a multimedia stream, as long as they retained tight control of the rate and admission policy. It is possible that the concept of reliable multicast use may eventually become totally different than the model of TCP use today, where the desktop host usually initiates the TCP session.

Even facing these barriers, however, a number of ISPs have begun to offer experimental multicast services. Most of these services have been built as an overlay to the ISPs' current pieces of the Internet and are offered as special services to businesses rather than as general Internet services. UUNet was the first to offer and advertise such a service, and it provides a snapshot as to what we might expect to see from other ISPs in the future. The company offers an overlay multicast service and provides a multicast "pipe" at a particular rate for that user. The charge for the service is based on the relevant rate.

Other ISPs with experimental service include MCI, GTE-BBN, and Telecom Finland.

11.2 CONCLUSIONS

For all of the benefits of multicast services, barriers to deployment exist, particularly in the public Internet. Here, both business and technical issues remain to be overcome. As a result, general Internet multicast services are likely to be a number of years away.

The new IP services that service providers are beginning to offer to large organizations are the ones with the least barrier to deployment. The more knowledgeable organizations will likely demand that multicast services be included in their network outsourced service.

Operators of private networks will likely add multicast only as they perform major upgrades dictated by saturation of their networks with traffic. In such cases, multicast can help avoid major new expense associated with increasing the WAN's capacity.

Thus the likely general deployment of multicast in networks will occur in the following order:

1. Public IP networks used for outsourcing by private organizations
2. Private IP networks
3. The general Internet

REFERENCES

[11-1] Fenner W, Casner S. A Traceroute Facility for IP Multicast. Internet Draft, Work in Progress, draft-ietf-idmr-traceroute-ipm-00.txt, March 1995.

[11-2] Postel J. Internet Control Message Protocol. RFC 792, September 1981.

[11-3] Bradner S, ed. Internet Protocol Multicast Problem Statement. Internet Draft, Work in Progress, draft-bradner-multicast-problem-00.txt, September 1997.

[11-4] Stardust Technologies, Inc. 1997 IP Multicast Usage Report. IP Multicast Initiative (IPMI), July 1997.

[11-5] A very comprehensive article on VPNs can be found at http://www.mba1998. hbs.edu/sdalton/Overview/VPN Overview/htm.

12

MUSINGS AND PROGNOSTICATIONS — WHAT DOES THE FUTURE HOLD?

I n the last chapter in this book, we will reflect on the current state of multicast networking and applications and attempt to predict what will happen in the future. Predicting the future is always a problematical exercise, especially in a field that is changing as rapidly as networking and network-based applications. For example, the Web exploded out of nowhere in the early 1990s, fueled by the development of HTML, HTTP, and browsers by a physicist at CERN who hoped to facilitate communications in a large research laboratory.

Discontinuities in technology like the Web are not always the norm, but can nevertheless completely change the technology landscape. The author does not claim to be able to predict these kinds of events when even such industry stalwarts as Bill Gates were surprised by their emergence!

We can, however, look at current trends and see whether any thread ties some of them together that could affect multicast networking and its associated applications. These trends can be classified as short-term and long-term, with the short term being defined as from now until the year 2000. The long term will be defined as events that will occur in the first decade of the twenty-first century — namely, 2000 to 2010, with an emphasis on the early part of the decade. Most of the trends discussed here are short-term.

12.1 SHORT-TERM TRENDS

12.1.1 Relative Costs of Storage and Bandwidth

Storage costs are plummeting, following a curve faster than Moore's law for semiconductors. This law states that the number of transistors in an integrated circuit doubles every 18 months (this law has roughly held since 1970). PCs costing between $1,000 and $2,000 two years ago were shipped with 500 Mbytes of hard drive memory and 8 Mbytes of RAM. Today's PCs costing less than $1,000 commonly ship with more than 2 Gbytes of hard drive memory and 16 Mbytes of RAM. PCs costing more than $1,000 usually have 8-Gbyte hard drives. This change is a more than tenfold increase for the same price in approximately two years.

Figure 12-1 shows the trend for desktop PC storage capacity [12-1]. At this rate, by 2000, the average desktop PC will have 10 Gbytes of storage. These exponential growth curves do not show any flattening for the foreseeable future.

Even though today's PC software is notoriously bloated, it cannot keep up with this dramatic availability of storage. Other forms of storage are also greatly expanding for the same price, including flash memory, writable CD-ROM, digital video disk (DVD) cartridges, and others. The most significant storage form, however, remains the magnetic hard disk. Also, PCMCIA-based flash cards (the standard size to fit inside portable PCs) are now available from multiple vendors at 1 Gbyte sizes.

If this hard drive memory is not used for software, it will be used for other purposes, most likely multimedia content. Uncompressed CD-quality stereo sound consumes memory at a rate of 10 Mbits/minute, which can be compressed with modern techniques to 1 Mbit/minute. Thus a 10 Gybte hard drive can hold 10,000 minutes of high-quality stereo music, or more than 175

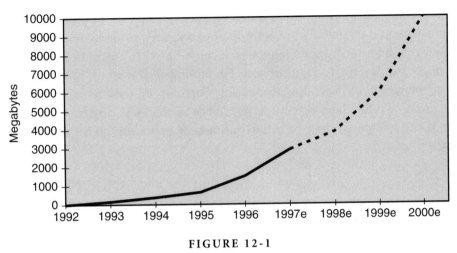

FIGURE 12-1

Desktop hard drive storage increases. *(Source: Paine Webber Research.)*

full-length albums. Television-quality MPEG2 operates at a rate of about 4 Mbits/second; thus, a 1.5-hour movie or television program would occupy 21.6 Gbytes of storage, an amount that will be commonly and inexpensively available in the near future. Even today, data warehouses are on the market from a number of vendors at reasonable prices that provide as much as 1 terabyte of storage, as mentioned in Chapter 5.

The bandwidth trend in LANs is clearly headed up, with today's 100 Mbps Ethernet now costing the same amount as yesterday's 10 Mbps Ethernet, and Ethernet switching products replacing shared LANs to provide orders of magnitude more bandwidth available on the campus. In contrast, WAN bandwidth increases do not show the same trend. As mentioned in Chapter 5, the backbone bandwidth used to tie the major U.S. universities together has increased in price with time. Consequently, Internet2 has concluded that throwing bandwidth at its network to improve performance and add new network-based applications is just not a viable option for the future. For all the talk of higher-speed network services, the overwhelming connection speed for businesses is still 56 Kbps and to the home is dial modem.

The advent of fiber has significantly increased the bandwidth of WAN backbones, but the "last mile" to the facility has remained an expensive bottleneck, as have high-speed connections into a backbone. A number of promising technologies could potentially break this bottleneck, such as cable modems for cable access and xDSL technology, which can be used to upgrade local copper pairs to support high-speed services. For a number of reasons, however, these technologies have been slow to develop. Some of the reasons for this lag are technical, while others reflect the reluctance of the local carriers (in the case of xDSL) to subvert their lucrative business of providing high-speed lines at high prices.

12.1.2 The Conversion of the Broadcast Industry from Analog to Digital

The broadcast industry is rapidly migrating from analog to digital technology. This conversion has already happened with broadcast television over satellite, and cable television will follow suit in the next couple of years. Digital HDTV television sets will become available for sale at the end of 1998.

The digital broadcast "carriers" — in particular, satellite, which is already broadcasting digital content — will offer IP data services, including multicast IP, as an adjunct to their mainstream entertainment business. A number of digital satellite equipment providers are planning to statistically multiplex data with digital MPEG video streams, in effect using "free" bandwidth to carry data. This "free" bandwidth amounts to many megabits per second of bandwidth that can be used to provide new services.

12.1.3 Diminishing Costs for Remote Equipment for Wireless Transmission

The price of remote satellite terminals is also plummeting, a trend fueled by the demands for inexpensive satellite receivers to receive television content in competition with cable television systems. The size of satellite dishes is also shrinking significantly, as the industry moves to higher-frequency (lower-wavelength) transmission systems at the Ka and Ku bands.

One satellite equipment manufacturer has publicly stated its intention to offer a full remote data terminal supporting IP and multicast IP for about $500 by 2000. This is a one-way system, which would support data rates as high as 2 Mbps [12-2], and would require a terrestrial back channel.

Cards for PCs that can pick off IP data from the vertical blanking interval (VBI) of analog broadcast television signals are becoming available at prices of only hundreds of dollars. The same trend applies to PC cards that can receive streams from digital satellite systems and deliver IP-based data into a PC.

12.1.4 The Continuing Explosion of the Internet

The growth of the Internet does not show any signs of slowing. The latest figures indicate that the number of users on the Internet is doubling every 100 days [12-3].

Along with the growth in usage, electronic commerce is finally starting to become commonplace on the Internet, with upstarts like Amazon.com paving the way for more established companies to enter the fray.

12.1.5 Organizations Are Becoming More Distributed

In this networking age, organizations are becoming increasingly distributed. Many mergers and acquisitions have occurred, creating many centers within the organization. More employees are spending part of their work time at home, connected via dial modem or some other method to the organization.

Organizations are also becoming more global, as the economy itself becomes more global in nature.

12.1.6 Outsourcing of WAN Network Services

The economic boom occurring in the 1990s has made it more difficult for organizations to find and retain talented network personnel to plan, implement, and manage their corporate networks, which are essential elements of all companies' business today. The result is an increasing trend to outsource the network needs of the corporation to a carrier. Citicorp's outsourcing of its network support to AT&T was just the start of a more far-reaching trend that has been picked up by other large organizations.

Carriers such as AT&T, WorldCom, Sprint, and MCI will provide IP network services to these organizations, much as carriers offered the frame relay services that boomed in the late 1980s and early 1990s (and are still growing at a healthy clip).

12.2 LONG-TERM TRENDS

12.2.1 Huge Projects to Add High-Speed Wireless Data Infrastructures

Although none of the projects has come to fruition yet, multiple billions of dollars are being invested in efforts to add global wireless data infrastructures based on low-Earth-orbiting (LEO) satellites, medium-Earth-orbiting (MEO) satellites, combinations of LEO and MEO satellites with conventional geostationary (GEO) satellites, blimps that hover in the stratosphere over cities, and wireless local loops.

The LEO and MEO satellite projects, in particular, are very ambitious. Teledesic, funded by Bill Gates and Craig McCaw among others, is spending an estimated $9 billion to launch a 288-satellite LEO system that will not become operational until about 2002. Celestri, led by Motorola, had planned to spend about $12.9 billion on its system. At the time this book was going to press in late May 1998 it was announced that Celestri and Teledesic were joining forces, providing added assurance of deployment of the new Teledesic system, which promises high-speed rates in excess of 1 Mbps. This new system will be available throughout the world, with scheduled service availability sometime after 2000.

The stratospheric blimp project is even more novel. This European initiative will not offer service until after 2000.

These wireless projects promise very-high-speed data services that can penetrate virtually anywhere (with the exception of the blimps, which provide city coverage).

Wireless local loops are starting to be deployed today as a way to gain access to subscribers where local loops are not available. They are also being implemented in developed countries as these nations deregulate, breaking the local carriers' stranglehold on local access.

12.2.2 Continued Internet Growth Fueled by Voice

Sometime during the first decade of the next century, Internet growth rates for data will slow, as penetration by businesses, government, educational institutions, and educated households becomes high. This decline is relative, however; hypergrowth data transmission will simply diminish to very high growth. Other traffic sources on the Internet will institute another wave of traffic growth, as fax and voice traffic explodes. The result will be continued hypergrowth.

12.3 WHAT ARE THE IMPLICATIONS FOR MULTICAST?

What threads can we tie together in these trends to discern multicast's future? From the trend of lower storage costs without commensurate reductions in WAN bandwidth, the first prediction for the future can be derived:

> *Replication of content to the edges of networks will become pervasive and will use reliable multicast, often with multicast overlay networks specifically set up for this purpose. This trend will enable more widespread use of multimedia streaming applications, as they will be closer to the consumer.*

The entertainment industry is going digital and clearly wants to participate in the Internet boom. Many have predicted a convergence of the television set and the PC. The television set is more of an entertainment vehicle, however, whereas the PC is a working tool. There will likely be some convergence, as television programming has already begun to be augmented by Web material.

> *Data will take advantage of the inexpensive transport provided by broadcast-oriented digital video to deliver multicast services. These transports may be cable, broadcast satellite, or terrestrial television. The new services transported over broadcast media, called "datacasting," could eventually become more popular than the Web.*
>
> *Pressure will continue on bandwidth demand in the Internet, fueled by new traffic such as voice. It will spur the use of multicast as a means of reducing redundant traffic.*

Richer multimedia content is desired on the Internet, Intranets, and Extranets. Distributed organizations will continue to be the norm, requiring the rapid dispersion of information throughout the organization to keep it running smoothly. Storage costs will continue to plummet, while bandwidth costs will decline only modestly. Alternative wireless networks are coming online, all of which natively support multicast. These trends will push multicast networks and applications into the mainstream with terrestrial and wireless networks.

When multicast ubiquity will occur is difficult to predict, but it is likely to happen in only a few years. Stay tuned!

REFERENCES

[12-1] Kerschner E, Geraghty M. Converging Technologies: Investing in the Information Age for the New Millenium. Paine-Webber Research Report, September 1, 1997.

[12-2] From a presentation made by Gilat, Ltd., at Telexpo '98 Conference, Sao Paulo, Brazil, April 1998. See Gilat's Web page at http://www.gilat.com.

[12-3] Zakon RH. Hobbes' Internet Timeline. http://info.isoc.org/guest/zakon/Internet/History/HIT.html.

GLOSSARY

AAP: Address Allocation Protocol. A protocol that allows multicast address allocation servers to communicate with one another in the proposed multicast address allocation architecture.

ABR: Area border router. ABRs serve as gateways between OSPF areas in OSPF-based routed networks.

ACK: Acknowledgment. Used as an indicator from a receiver to a sender to signal that a range of data was sent and received correctly.

Administratively scoped multicast address: Certain multicast addresses are limited in scope defined by a particular network region. The scoping is enforced by routers at the borders of this region.

AH: IP authentication header. It provides connectionless integrity, data origin authentication, and an optional anti-replay service. AH is a part of the IPsec set of proposed IETF standards.

Announce/Registration: The process used by MFTP to set up a Closed Group (see *Closed Group*).

Application-layer framing (ALF): An architecture in which the transport protocol is tied to the application. Retransmissions may be entities oriented to the application rather than transport data entities.

ARPA: Advanced Research Projects Agency. A U.S. government agency.

ARQ: Automatic Repeat Request. The most common architectural form of error correction in communication protocols. For example, TCP uses ARQ.

AS: Autonomous System. A network with a common routing domain governed by the same policy with one administration.

ASF: Advanced Streaming Format. An open file format for storing streaming multimedia content created by Microsoft.

ATM: Asynchronous Transfer Mode. A cell-switching technology that was originally devised by the telephone carriers to support multiple sources of traffic (such as digitized voice, video, and data) at very high speeds. Traffic is broken into 53-byte cells.

Authentication: In security systems, authentication techniques are used to ensure that the received data was actually sent by the claimed sender. Authentication systems are often used in conjunction with access control systems to verify that a user is actually the claimed party when the user attempts to access a network or other system.

AVI: Audio/Video Interleaved. A simple audio and video file format for Windows PCs created by Microsoft.

B Channel: The "bearer" channel in ISDN that carries data or voice traffic (see *ISDN*).

BGMP: Border Gateway Multicast Protocol. An interdomain multicast routing protocol proposal now being developed in the IETF.

BOF: "Birds of a Feather." A BOF is a meeting of individuals interested in a particular subject.

Bootstrap: Messages conveyed in the PIM-SM multicast routing protocol to notify PIM-SM routers about the location of Rendezvous Points.

Bridge: A MAC-layer device that segments shared LANs to reduce traffic on each segment.

BSR: Bootstrap router. In PIM-SM, bootstrap routers originate Bootstrap messages, which carry out a dynamic election of a BSR from among the candidates in a PIM domain and distribute Rendezvous Point information in steady state.

CA: Certifying Authority. In a security system, the CA returns to the user a certificate attesting to the veracity of a user's public key along with other information.

Cache: A device that stores information locally or regionally based on demand for that information, allowing content to be brought closer to the user and thereby improving performance.

CBT: Core-Based Trees. A shared tree multicast routing protocol documented in RFC 2189.

CDF: Channel Definition Format. This protocol can be used to define a "push" channel.

Class A IP address: The unicast address space in IPv4 that is partitioned with 7 bits for the network address and 24 bits for the host address. The first bit of a Class A address is 0.

Class B IP address: The unicast address space in IPv4 that is partitioned with 14 bits for the network address and 16 bits for the host address. The first two bits of a Class B address are 10.

Class C IP address: The unicast address space in IPv4 that is partitioned with 21 bits for the network address and 8 bits for the host address. The first three bits of a Class C address are 110.

Class D IP address: The address space in IPv4 that is used to identify multicast addresses. The first four bits of a Class D address are 1110.

Closed group: A group created and managed from the sender under MFTP.

Codec: Compressor/decompressor. A device that encodes and decodes video and audio streams efficiently using compression/decompression algorithms.

Connectionless: A network architecture in which the end-to-end link does not have to be specifically set up, and in which the packets making up the end-to-end session may take different paths based on routing algorithms.

Connection-oriented: A network architecture in which the end-to-end link needs to be set up as a virtual circuit at the beginning of a session and torn down at the end of the session (in the case of switched virtual circuits) or provisioned by the network provider (in the case of permanent virtual circuits). (See also *PVC* and *SVC*.)

Core: In the Core-Based Trees multicast routing protocol, the core is the node through which all traffic in a particular group traverses. Different multicast groups will have different cores.

DAMA: Demand Assignment Multiple Access. A common method for sharing back channels in VSAT systems. A common back channel is shared by a number of remote sites on a contention basis.

DARPA: Defense Advanced Research Projects Agency. The U.S. government agency that succeeded ARPA.

Data streaming: The characteristic flow of data from a particular type of data application where the data flows as a stream based on events such as in a ticker-tape or news feed.

D Channel: The "data" channel in ISDN that carries signaling traffic (see *ISDN*).

Dense mode: A class of multicast routing protocols that use flooding techniques to set up source-rooted multicast routing trees. These protocols are best suited to network environments where the members are densely concentrated in a portion of the network—hence the term "dense."

DHCP: Dynamic Host Control Protocol. A protocol used to assign IP addresses dynamically to host computers as they log on to a network.

Digital signature: An unforgeable piece of data asserting that a named person wrote or otherwise agreed to the document to which the signature is attached. The digital equivalent to a handwritten signature.

Distance vector: A class of routing protocols. In the case of multicast routing protocols, they form a subset of the dense mode class.

Distribution tree: The multicast routes set up by multicast routing protocols to distribute multicast packets to a particular group address.

DLCI: Data Link Connection Identifier. The Link-layer address used by the frame relay Link-layer protocol.

DNS: Domain Naming System; Domain Name Server. The Domain Naming System uses Domain Name Servers to notify hosts of other hosts' IP addresses when given their name. This mechanism associates names with IP addresses.

Domain: Networks are broken into domains, which may also be Autonomous Systems (see *AS*).

DR: Designated Router. The router on the border of a subnet that provides IGMP communication to the hosts on that subnet and communicates with other routers, notifying them about the presence of group members on that subnet.

DRP: (1) Distribution and Replication Protocol. A protocol submitted by Marimba to W3C that proposes transmitting only changes in material so as to reduce the amount of data sent. (2) Director Response Protocol. Cisco's proprietary protocol that finds the closest replicated Web server by interrogating routers for their metrics.

DS0: Digital Signal 0, the lowest level of telephone systems' digital signal hierarchy. One DS0 is designed to carry one digitized voice call at 56 Kbps, with 8 Kbps of control giving a total of 64 Kbps.

DVB: Digital Video Broadcast. A digital video standard originating in Europe for sending multimedia and data content. It is strongly supported by the television broadcast industry in Europe and other parts of the world.

DVMRP: Distance Vector Multicast Routing Protocol. The first multicast routing protocol, described in RFC 1075.

EGP: Exterior Gateway Protocol. The class of routing protocols used to route and enforce policy between Autonomous Systems.

Erasure correction: A technique that sends FEC parity packets for "repair" retransmissions. It can significantly reduce the amount of repair traffic when losses at multiple receivers are uncorrelated. (See also *FEC* and *repair.*)

ERP: Enterprise Resource Planning. Certain software systems used by organizations to automate their business processes.

ESP: Encapsulating Security Payload. A protocol that is part of the IPsec set of proposed IETF standards and provides confidentiality (encryption) and limited traffic-flow confidentiality.

Ethernet: The most popular form of LAN. Ethernet is standardized as IEEE 802.3.

Extranet: Term used to identify a network, based on TCP/IP and Web technology, that is private among a set of corporations or other organizations that form a community of interest.

FEC: Forward Error Correction. A technique whereby coded redundant data is sent with the user data to enable the correction of errors or missed data at the receiver without requiring retransmissions.

Firewall: A device that blocks undesirable traffic between networks. It is typically used by private networks to block certain types of traffic from the Internet from entering the private networks.

Flooding: A technique used by some routing protocols to determine routes by broadcasting packets and then pruning back unused paths.

Frame: One picture in a series of pictures that make up a video stream.

Frame relay: A common connection-oriented Link-layer protocol.

FTP: File Transfer Protocol. The protocol commonly used in TCP/IP networks to transfer files from one host to another. FTP operates over TCP and is dependent on TCP to provide error control.

G.723: An ITU standard audio codec.

G.728: Another ITU standard audio codec.

Gbyte: One thousand million bytes, where a byte is an eight bit word.

GEO: Geostationary Earth Orbit. Satellites that reside in geostationary orbit are located at a distance of 36,000 kilometers above the Earth and rotate in synchrony with the Earth thus staying in the same relative position above the Earth.

GIF: Graphics Interchange Format. A defacto graphics standard and encoding method created by CompuServe and often used on Web sites.

Group: In multicast, the set of members that receives transmissions destined for that group's multicast address.

GSM: Global System for Mobile Communication. The standard for digital cellular telephone service that originated in Europe.

H.261: An ITU standard for a multimedia codec, targeted at low-data-rate, low-quality video conferencing.

H.263: An ITU standard for a multimedia codec, targeted at high-movement multimedia and not exclusively focused on very low bit rates.

Hacker: (Slang) An individual who is proficient with computers and delights in probing different organizations' networks and computer systems. This activity may sometimes be done with malicious intent.

HALE: High-altitude, long-endurance. A system consisting of solar-powered blimps or other high-altitude aircraft that reside in the lower stratosphere and hover in fixed positions over areas with high population densities for the purpose of providing data services to those areas.

Harvest: One of the earliest network cache systems.

Hash function: A computation that takes a variable-size input data string and returns a fixed-size string that is a smaller representation of the original data.

HDTV: High-Definition Television. New digital television standards that provide much higher quality and resolution than today's television systems.

Host: The formal name for a computer or other computing device that resides on a network.

Host list pruning: A technique used in MFTP to reduce traffic flow in the MFTP Closed Group and Open Limited Group models for group set-up.

HTML: Hypertext Markup Language. The standard used to create Web content.

HTTP: Hypertext Transport Protocol. The protocol used by Web browsers to communicate with Web servers.

IANA: Internet Address Naming Authority. The organization that assigns well-known addresses and ports for protocols.

ICMP: Internet Control Message Protocol. A control protocol that is part of the TCP/IP protocol suite and that is used by routers and hosts to communicate error messages, network status, and warnings.

ICP: Internet Cache Protocol. A lightweight protocol used to find content from a mesh of caches. It has been applied to both the Harvest and Squid cache systems.

IETF: Internet Engineering Task Force. The organization that is responsible for creating Internet standards and technologies.

IGMP: Internet Group Management Protocol. A protocol that is part of the TCP/IP protocol suite and that is used by a host to inform the nearest multicast router of its presence in a group or its departure from a group.

IGP: Interior Gateway Protocol. A routing protocol used to route packets within a single Autonomous System.

IGRP: Interior Gateway Routing Protocol. Cisco's proprietary IGP routing protocol.

Interdomain routing: The routing that occurs between Autonomous Systems.

Interleaving: A technique used in FEC systems that spreads the data at the source, causing burst errors to appear as single errors at the receiver and hence be more easily corrected by the FEC code.

Internet: A collection of networks tied together to provide a global network that is commonly accessed by both businesses and individuals.

Internet Draft: An IETF document that represents work in progress. Any individual or organization may submit Internet Drafts, which have an official lifetime of six months.

Intranet: A private network that uses the TCP/IP protocol suite and other Internet technologies.

IP: Internet Protocol. The Network layer (Layer 3) of the TCP/IP protocol suite.

IPsec: IP security. The set of proposed standards for security being developed by the IETF for use on the Internet, Intranets, and Extranets.

IPv4: The current version of IP being deployed in TCP/IP networks.

IPv6: Sometimes called IPng, or IP next generation. A new version of IP with more services and more address space.

IPX/SPX: Novell's protocol suite targeted primarily at campus networks.

IPMI: IP Multicast Initiative. An organization formed by a set of companies dedicated to promoting multicast.

IRTF: Internet Research Task Force. An organization of researchers that study problems that need resolution before the IETF can develop standards. The IRTF recommends solutions to the IETF but does not create standards.

ISAKMP/Oakley: A set of standards for the automatic distribution of cryptographic keys.

ISDN: Integrated Services Digital Network. A technology that integrates voice and data over the telephone network. Often used today only for high-speed data services.

ISO: International Standards Organization. An international standards body that publishes a set of standards for data networking.

ISP: Internet Service Provider. A company that enables individuals and organizations to connect to the Internet and which provides ancillary Internet-related services.

ITU: International Telecommunications Union. An international standards body dealing with telecommunications. It subsumes the standards body formerly called the CCITT.

JPEG: Joint Photographic Experts Group. A standard for still pictures often used on Web sites.

Kbps: One thousand bits per second. A measure of data rate.

Key management: The management of cryptographic keys.

LAN: Local Area Network. A network that spans a building or other small area.

LAP B: Link Access Protocol "B," the Link layer protocol used in X.25 systems.

Layering: A technique proposed for reliable multicast protocols to provide congestion control.

LBL: Lawrence Berkeley Laboratories. A government research laboratory that has created many MBone tools.

LEO: Low Earth Orbit. Satellite systems that reside in orbit close to Earth and that orbit Earth at a rate relative to the Earth.

More than one satellite is thus needed to cover a particular area of the Earth.

Link layer: The protocol layer responsible for delivery of data over a particular link. Layer 2 in the OSI communications model.

Link state: A class of routing protocols that converge quickly but require more computing and memory resources than other techniques.

Local repair: In reliable multicast protocols, techniques whereby missing data is recovered by hosts relatively locally rather than from the original source.

Loosely coupled session: A type of multicast session with loose control, in which the sender usually does not know who receives the data.

LSA: Link State Announcement. The mechanism used by OSPF to communicate link state information to other OSPF routers.

MAAS: Multicast Address Allocation Server. In the proposed new multicast address allocation architecture, a MAAS keeps track of all other multicast addresses in use within the same allocation domain. When allocating an address, it ensures that the address is not already in use in that domain.

MAC: Medium Access Control. The sublayer of the data link layer responsible for arbitrating access to a shared medium and for filtering packets at a data link-level receiver. Most often used with LANs.

MALLOC: Multicast Address Allocation. A proposed architecture that would provide an automatic means of allocating multicast addresses to ISPs, which would then allocate those addresses to applications. Also used to describe the working group in the IETF that is developing this set of standards.

MARS: Multicast Address Resolution Server. In ATM networks, MARS acts as a registry to associate IP multicast group addresses with the ATM interfaces representing the group's members.

MASC: Multicast Address Set Claim. A protocol that is a part of the MALLOC architec-

ture. Certain nodes, which are usually routers, use MASC to claim address sets that satisfy the needs of MAASs within their allocation domain. (See also *MAAS.*)

MBone: Multicast backbone (of the Internet). An experimental multicast network that is used by researchers to perform multicast research on a real network.

Mbps: One million bits per second. A measure of data rate.

Mbyte: One million bytes, where a byte is an eight bit word.

MCF: Meta Content Framework. One of the earliest meta-data systems on the Web, having been first introduced by Apple Computer in September 1996. It is still in use by hundreds of Web sites today.

MDHCP: Multicast Dynamic Host Control Protocol. The Dynamic Host Control Protocol with proposed extensions for multicast addresses.

MEO: Medium Earth Orbit. Satellite systems that reside at a middle orbit relative to the Earth and that move around the planet at a rate relative to the Earth. More than one satellite is thus needed to cover a particular area of the Earth.

Message digest: In cryptographic systems, a hash function that is significantly easier to perform in one direction (the forward direction) than in the opposite direction (the inverse direction).

MFTP: Multicast File Transfer Protocol. A reliable multicast protocol that is commercially available in applications and toolkits from StarBurst Communications.

MiMaze: An experimental network-based game created by Inria, a French research institution.

Mirror: A replicated server.

MMUSIC: Multiparty Multimedia Session Control. A working group of the Internet Engineering Task Force that has developed most of the official protocols and architecture for group creation.

MOSPF: Multicast Open Shortest Path First. A multicast IGP routing protocol.

MPEG: Motion Picture Experts Group. A set of multimedia codecs heavily used by the broadcast television industry for digital television.

MTU: Maximum Transmission Unit. Refers to the amount of data included above the transport layer at the application layer in one packet.

Multicast: The system by which a packet is delivered to a "group" defined by a multicast address.

Multicast Applications: Applications that use the underlying multicast networking technology to deliver packets, such as one-to-many multimedia streaming, many-to-many video conferencing, or one-to-many data delivery.

Multicast Networking: The underlying technology in TCP/IP networks that allows multicast transmission of packets to occur based on hosts informing routers of their presence in multicast groups and multicast routing protocols being used for creating optimal multicast routes. Also used generically to indicate multicast technologies in other networks besides TCP/IP, such as ATM, frame relay, and DECNet.

Multimedia: A source of data that consists of many media, such as video, audio, and text.

NAK (NACK): Negative acknowledgment. Used by receivers to notify senders that data has been lost at that receiver.

Networked Multimedia Connection: A consortium promoting multimedia networking technology that was formed by Microsoft, Cisco, and Intel.

Network layer: The Communication layer (Layer 3) responsible for routing packets through a network.

NSF: National Science Foundation. A U.S. government agency that funds scientific research.

OC3: The third level of the SONET hierarchy that operates at 155 Mbps.

OSD: Open Software Description. OSD was submitted to the W3C in August 1997 by Marimba and Microsoft. It describes a new data formatting scheme that will allow any company to update software over the Internet.

OSPF: Open Shortest Path First. A unicast link state routing protocol.

PC: Personal computer.

PIM-DM: Protocol Independent Multicast—Dense Mode. A dense-mode multicast routing protocol.

PIM-SM: Protocol Independent Multicast—Sparse Mode. A shared-tree (sparse-mode) multicast routing protocol.

Ping: A term commonly used to describe the ICMP echo packet, which is used to determine whether a destination is reachable.

PGM: Pragmatic General Multicast (originally Pretty Good Multicast). A reliable multicast protocol developed by Cisco Systems.

POP: Point of Presence. The access points of a network service provider through which users access a network.

PPP: Point to Point Protocol. A Link-layer protocol commonly used for dial and other serial links.

Proxy: In many systems, a server that collects queries for another host so as to perform a particular function, such as creating a firewall.

PSTN: Public Switched Telephone Network. The common dial-up telephone network.

Public-key cryptography: In this cryptographic system, each person gets a pair of keys, called the public key and the private key. Each person's public key is published, while the private key is kept secret.

Publish/subscribe: A term first promoted by TIBCO that is another name for send and listen. "Publish" implies that based on an event (that is, when the content becomes available), data is sent (published). Receivers that are interested in the content then listen (subscribe) to it.

"Push":   The delivery of information to a subscribing consumer, who receives data without explicitly requesting it.

PVC: Permanent virtual circuit. A virtual circuit that is permanently connected in connection-oriented Link-layer protocols, such as frame relay and ATM.

QuickTime: The oldest multimedia file format, first introduced by Apple Computer in 1991.

QoS: Quality of Service.

RAM: Random Access Memory. The volatile memory used in computers for temporary storage.

RAMP: Reliable Adaptive Multicast Protocol. A reliable multicast protocol created by The Analytic Science Corporation (TASC) for collaborative applications.

Raw sockets: The interface applications use to interface directly to the IP layer (Layer 3), rather than one of the Transport-layer (Layer 4) protocols in the TCP/IP protocol suite.

RDF: Resource Description Framework. RDF was submitted to W3C in September 1997 by Netscape. It is designed to be a single mechanism for organizing, describing, and navigating information on Web sites.

Reliable multicast: A system or protocol that guarantees delivery to a multicast group.

Repair: A term used to describe the data lost due to various reasons by members of a multicast group and which needs to be resent to particular members of that group.

Replication: The act of reproducing data from one host to another.

RFC: Request for Comments. An Internet document used to gather data on standards and other information relevant to the Internet.

RIP: Routing Information Protocol. A distance-vector unicast routing protocol.

RMRG: Reliable Multicast Research Group. The group studying reliable multicast in the IRTF.

RMTP: Reliable Multicast Transport Protocol. A reliable multicast protocol originally developed at Bell Laboratories (now a part of Lucent Technologies). RMTP is offered commercially in a toolkit by GlobalCast Corporation.

RMTP II: An update to RMTP first documented in an Internet Draft in April 1998.

Roots: The equivalent to a core or RP for BGMP, a proposed interdomain multicast routing protocol.

RP: Rendezvous Point. The node in PIM-SM to which all group members join.

RPM: Reverse Path Multicasting. An algorithm used by some dense-mode routing protocols to determine the optimal multicast routing distribution trees.

RSVP: Resource Reservation Protocol. An Internet protocol used to provide QoS routing paths.

RTCP: Real-Time Control Protocol. A companion control protocol to RTP.

RTP: Real-Time Protocol. An Internet standard protocol used for multimedia unicast and multicast transport.

RTSP: Real-Time Streaming Protocol. A control protocol very similar to HTTP/1.1 that is used to establish and control either a single stream or several time-synchronized streams of continuous media such as audio and video.

SAP: Session Announcement Protocol. SAP provides for multicast announcement of sessions described in its payload using SDP.

SDP: Session Description Protocol. A protocol used to describe multicast sessions.

Selective reject: In an ARQ error control system, a feature that rejects only missing packets or packets in error. Thus packets that are received out of order do not need to be retransmitted.

Shared LAN: A LAN where the physical medium is shared by all nodes on the network.

Shared tree: A type of multicast routing protocol.

SIP: Session Invitation Protocol. A protocol developed by IETF's MMUSIC working group to invite hosts to join a session.

SKIP: Simple Key management for IP. A protocol developed by Sun Microsystems for automatically distributing keys in cryptographic systems.

Slow start: The TCP start-up algorithm.

SMDS: Switched Multimegabit Data Service. A WAN connectionless network system within which all nodes inherently can communicate to all other nodes on the network, similar to shared LANs.

SMIL: Synchronized Multimedia Integration Language. An XML-based language for writing "TV-like" multimedia presentations for the World Wide Web. The SMIL specification was issued as a proposed W3C Recommendation in April 1998.

SMTP: Simple Mail Transport Protocol. The protocol used in the Internet for the delivery of electronic mail.

SNA: Systems Network Architecture. A protocol suite developed by IBM to provide mainframe computer communications. SNA is rapidly being displaced by TCP/IP.

Sparse mode: A class of multicast routing protocols.

Squid: A network caching system that evolved from the Harvest cache system.

SRM: Scalable Reliable Multicast. A reliable multicast protocol first developed by Internet researchers to support the "wb" whiteboarding MBone tool. SRM is offered commercially in toolkit form by Globalcast Corporation.

SSL: Secure Sockets Layer. A protocol developed by Netscape Communications to provide secure Web transactions over the Internet.

Subcast: A technique in reliable multicast whereby repairs are sent only to regions experiencing the particular loss that the repair corrects.

Subject-based addressing: The ability to filter out particular subjects of interest in a data stream at the host receiver.

SVC: Switched virtual circuit. A virtual circuit that is set up dynamically in connection-oriented Link-layer protocols, such as frame relay and ATM.

Switched LAN: A LAN where each host occupies one segment and packets are switched to other hosts based on destination address.

Symmetric cryptography: A cryptographic system where the data is encrypted and decrypted with the same key.

T1: The first layer in the telephone network trunking hierarchy. The T1 data rate is 1.544 Mbps.

T3: The third layer in the telephone network trunking hierarchy. The T3 data rate is 45 Mbps.

TCP: Transmission Control Protocol. The error-correcting Transport layer (Layer 4) in the TCP/IP protocol suite.

TCP/IP: The protocol suite used in the Internet, Intranets, and Extranets.

Timing jitter: Time arrival variations. These differences need to be minimized when transmitting and receiving multimedia streams.

TLS: Transport Layer Security. The protocol that has superseded Secure Sockets Layer and is used to secure individual link transmissions to Web sites for the purpose of securing Web based electronic commerce.

TTL: Time to live. A field in IP packets used to limit scope. The TTL number is decremented at every router hop, and the packet is discarded when the number reaches zero.

Tunnel: A mechanism that enables one protocol to be transported through a network that does not support it, by encapsulation into the native protocol on that network.

UDLR: Unidirectional Link Routing. An IETF working group set up to develop protocols that enable routing protocols to cope with unidirectional links, such as satellite overlay networks.

UDP: User Datagram Protocol. A transport protocol in the TCP/IP protocol suite that provides the minimal services of error detection and port multiplexing.

URL: Universal Resource Locator. The name and address of a Web site to be accessed by a browser, from which an IP address is found via a Domain Name Server (DNS).

VBI: Vertical Blanking Interval. In analog television systems, the time required for the raster scan to go from the bottom of the screen to the top to start the next scan. This gap represents dead time, which is often used to send data along with the television signal.

VPN: Virtual Private Network. A network that is carved out of the Internet to create a private network for an organization.

VSAT: Very-Small-Aperture Terminal. Geostationary satellite systems that use very small remote terminals.

W3C: World Wide Web Consortium. A standards body that develops standards related to the Web.

WAN: Wide Area Network. A network that covers a large geographical area and may be global in scope.

Webcasting: A method of disseminating data from a Web site in which the site pushes data to subscribers without their explicit requests. Synonymous with "push."

Whiteboard: A collaborative system in which all members of a conference may draw on an electronic screen and have all members of the session observe the drawings.

X.25: An ITU standard for Link-layer packet transmission created in the 1980s. X.25 is rapidly being displaced by newer systems, particularly frame relay.

xDSL: "x" Digital Subscriber Line. A family of technologies to provide high-speed transmission on copper local loops. DSL is a modem standard for basic-rate ISDN, operating at 160 Kbps in both directions. The next in the family is HDSL, which delivers T-1 or E-1 (1.544 Mbps or 2.048 Mbps) over two twisted-pairs. For connection to the Internet, ADSL is touted as the premier offering. ADSL is asymmetrical and is capable of data transmission rates of 1.5 Mbps to 9 Mbps downstream and 15 Kbps to 640 Kbps upstream over two twisted-pair wires. ADSL trials are now occurring, and HDSL and DSL are in common use.

XML: eXtensible Markup Language. XML is an extension of the Hypertext Markup Language (HTML) now used to create Web pages. XML and HTML are both subsets of the SGML language for content creation. Microsoft and other organizations are committed to supporting XML in their future Web server products. A significant number of larger Web sites are expected to convert to XML.

INDEX